American Drama
Criticism

American
Drama Criticism

Supplement I

to the

Second Edition

COMPILED BY

FLOYD EUGENE EDDLEMAN

The Shoe String Press Inc
HAMDEN, CONNECTICUT
1984

34.50

12-11-90

First Edition 1967
Supplement I published 1970
Supplement II published 1976
Second Edition published 1979
Supplement I to the Second Edition published 1984

Printed in the United States of America

*The paper in this book meets the guidelines for performance and
durability of the Committee on Production Guidelines for Book
Longevity of the Council on Library Resources.*

Library of Congress Cataloging in Publication Data
Main entry under title:

American drama criticism.

(Drama explication series)
Bibliography: p.
Includes indexes.
1. American drama--History and criticism--Bibliography.
2. Theater--United States--Reviews--Bibliography.
I. Eddleman, Floyd Eugene. II. Eddleman, Floyd Eugene.
American drama criticism. III. Series.
Z1231.D7P3 1979 Suppl. [PS332] 016.812'009 83-25410
ISBN 0-208-01978-2

CONTENTS

For
my nieces and nephews,
whom I love dearly:

Sherri Jean Eddleman Smith
Jeffrey Clayton Eddleman
D'Ann Dellinger
Travis Wayne Eddleman
Mark Alan Eddleman

PREFACE

This First Supplement to the Second Edition of *American Drama Criticism* lists interpretations of American plays published in books, periodicals, and monographs. The abundance of research done in recent years on early American plays and on Canadian drama is reflected in this supplement. The quality of the articles was not considered; the only criterion was that critical material relating to a certain play could be located in a particular book or article.

An exhaustive search cannot be claimed, but, in addition to books and periodicals not listed in indexes, these indexes were examined: *Bulletin Signalétique*, *Dramatic Index*, *Essay and General Literature Index*, *Humanities Index*, *International Index*, *Internationale Bibliographie der Zeitschriftenliteratur*, *MLA International Bibliography*, *Popular Periodical Index*, *Reader's Guide to Periodical Literature*, and *Social Sciences and Humanities Index*.

To avoid duplication and to conserve space, the full names of authors of books and the subtitles of books are provided only in the List of Books Indexed, and the full names of critics are provided only in the Index of Critics. Subtitles of journals appear in the List of Journals Indexed.

For the first time, *American Drama Criticism* has included a General category, which appears immediately below a playwright's name. Otherwise, the arrangement is like that of the preceding editions—alphabetical by playwright, with the plays alphabetized under the playwright's name. Dates of first production, not always in New York, have been included. Interpretations from books and scholarly journals are then alphabetized by author or, if anonymous, by title. A listing of criticisms in periodicals, alphabetized by title, follows, including volume number, page or pages, and date.

Every effort has been made to prevent and to correct errors and omissions. If some mistakes have escaped detection, both the compiler and the publisher will be grateful to have them brought to their attention.

I wish to express my thanks to the members of the staff of the Texas Tech University Library who provided assistance in locating material.

Floyd Eugene Eddleman

Texas Tech University
Lubbock, Texas
September 1983

I am also most grateful to Jason Farthing, Mena, Arkansas, for his indispensable assistance in checking proofs.

F.E.E.

January 1984

GEORGE ABBOTT and PHILIP DUNNING

Broadway, 1926
  Texas Monthly, 8:160+, Mar. 1980

GEORGE ABBOTT, RICHARD RODGERS, and LORENZ HART

The Boys from Syracuse (adaptation of Shakespeare's *Comedy of Errors*), 1938
  Educational Theatre Journal, 30:124, 1978

GEORGE ADE

The College Widow, 1904
  Herron, I. H., *The Small Town in American Drama*, pp. 198-200

The County Chairman, 1903
  Herron, I. H., *The Small Town in American Drama*, pp. 196-98
  Nannes, C. H., *Politics in the American Drama*, pp. 35-37

CHARLES AIDMAN

Spoon River (dramatization of E. L. Masters's *Spoon River Anthology*), 1963
  Herron, I. H., *The Small Town in American Drama*, pp. 483-84

GEORGE L. AIKEN

Uncle Tom's Cabin (dramatization of novel by H. B. Stowe), 1852
  McDowell, J. H., " 'I'm Going There, Uncle Tom': Original Scenery, Documents, and a Promptbook Production of *Uncle Tom's Cabin*," *Theatre Studies*, 24-25:119-38, 1977-79

JOANNE AKALAITIS

Dead End Kids: A History of Nuclear Power, 1980
  After Dark, 13:68, Mar. 1981
  Nation, 231:683-84, 20 Dec. 1980

Southern Exposure, 1979
  Theatre Journal, 32:120, 1980

ZOË AKINS

General

Sutherland, C., "American Women Playwrights as Mediators of the 'Woman Problem,' " *Modern Drama*, 21:319-36, 1978

EDWARD ALBEE

General

Adler, T. P., "Art or Craft: Language in the Plays of Albee's Second Decade," pp. 45-57 in *Edward Albee*, ed. P. De La Fuente, D. E. Fritz, J. Seale, and D. Schmidt

Brede, R., "Edward Albee," *Literatur in Wissenschaft und Unterricht*, 8:30-46, 1975

Brunkhorst, M., "Albees Frühwerk im Kontext des absurden Theaters: Etappen der Deutungsgeschichte," *Literatur in Wissenschaft und Unterricht*, 12:304-18, 1980

Cohn, R., "Camp, Cruelty, Colloquialism," pp. 281-303 in *Comic Relief*, ed. S. B. Cohen

Cohn, R., *Dialogue in American Drama*, pp. 130-69

Cotrău, L., "Edward Albee şi drama confruntării," *Steaura*, 28, i:50, 1977

Duplessis, R. B., "In the Bosom of the Family: Contradiction and Resolution in Edward Albee," *Minnesota Review*, 8:133-45, 1977

Fletcher, J., " 'A Psychology Based on Antagonism': Ionesco, Pinter, Albee, and Others," pp. 175-95 in *The Two Faces of Ionesco*, ed. R. C. Lamont and M. J. Friedman

Gabbard, L. P., "Edward Albee's Triptych on Abandonment," *Twentieth Century Literature*, 28:14-33, Spring 1982

Gabbard, L. P., "Unity in the Albee Vision," pp. 18-32 in *Edward Albee*, ed. P. De La Fuente, D. E. Fritz, J. Seale, and D. Schmidt

Gardner, R. H., *The Splintered Stage*, pp. 146-53

Gottfried, M., *A Theater Divided*, pp. 264-74

Gould, J., "Edward Albee and the Current Scene," pp. 273-86 in Gould's *Modern American Playwrights*

Green, C. L., *Edward Albee*

Haas, R., "Wer hat Angst vor Edward Albee? Gedanken zum modernen amerikanischen Drama," *Das amerikanische Drama von den Anfängen bis zur Gegenwart*, 5:420-35, 1972

Hirsch, F., *Who's Afraid of Edward Albee?*

Inge, M. T., "Edward Albee's Love Story of the Age of the Absurd," *Notes on Contemporary Literature*, 8,v:4-9, 1978

Julier, L., "Faces to the Dawn: Female Characters in Albee's Plays," pp. 34-44 in *Edward Albee*, ed. P. De La Fuente, D. E. Fritz, J. Seale, and D. Schmidt

Krohn, C. S. and J. N. Wasserman, "An Interview with Edward Albee, March 18, 1981," pp. 1-27 in *Edward Albee*, ed. Wasserman

Mayberry, R., "A Theatre of Discord: Some Plays of Beckett, Albee and Pinter," *Kansas Quarterly*, 12, iv:7-16, 1980

Meserve, W. J., *An Outline History of American Drama*, p. 358

Morrison, K., "Pinter, Albee, and 'The Maiden in the Shark Pond,' " *American Imago*, 35:259-74, 1978

Otten, T., " 'Played to the Finish': Coward and Albee," *Studies in the Humanities*, 6, i:31-36, 1977

Quackenbush, L. H., "Albee y el teatro hispanoamericano del absurdo," *Texto Crítico*, 10:136-50, 1978

Razum, H., "Edward Albee und die Metaphysik," pp. 353-63 in *Theater und Drama in Amerika*, ed. E. Lohner and R. Haas

Reed, M. D. and J. L. Evans, "Edward Albee: An Updated Checklist of Scholarship,

1977-1980," pp. 121-29 in *Edward Albee*, ed. P. De La Fuente, D. E. Fritz, J. Seale, and D. Schmidt

Robinson, J. A., "O'Neill and Albee," *West Virginia University Philological Papers*, 25:38-45, 1979

Samuels, C. T., "The Theatre of Edward Albee," *Das amerikanische Drama von den Anfängen bis zur Gegenwart*, 5:385-400, 1972

Sarotte, G. M., "Homosexuality and the Theater: Edward Albee: Homosexual Playwright in Spite of Himself," pp. 134-49 in Sarotte's *Like a Brother, Like a Lover*

Scanlan, T., *Family, Drama, and American Dreams*, pp. 189-94, *passim*

Schlueter, J., *Metafictional Characters in Modern Drama*

Siniscalco, A., "On His Plays: An Interview with Edward Albee," *Dismisura*, 39-50:93-97, 1980

Vos, N., "The Process of Dying: The Plays of Edward Albee," pp. 110-19 in Vos's *The Great Pendulum of Becoming*

Wasserman, J. N., " 'The Pitfalls of Drama': The Idea of Language in the Plays of Edward Albee," pp. 29-53 in *Edward Albee*, ed. Wasserman

Wellwarth, G., *The Theatre of Protest and Paradox*, rev. ed., pp. 321-36

White, K. S., "Scientists' Dilemmas: Prophetic Metaphors in Twentieth Century Drama," pp. 533-36 in *Proceedings of the 7th Congress of the International Comparative Literature Association, I*, ed. M. V. Dimić and J. Ferraté

Woggon, B., "Avant-garde Albee," *Writer's Digest*, 60:18+, Oct. 1980

Worth, K., "Edward Albee: Playwright of Evolution," pp. 33-53 in *Essays on Contemporary American Drama*, ed. H. Bock and A. Wertheim

Wyler, S., "Zu Edward Albees Bühnenschaffen," *Das amerikanische Drama von den Anfängen bis zur Gegenwart*, 5:401-19, 1972

All Over, 1971

Harris, J. N., "Edward Albee and Maurice Materlinck: *All Over* as Symbolism," *Theatre Research International* 3:200-08, 1978

Jones, D. R., "Albee's *All Over*," pp. 87-93 in *Edward Albee*, ed. P. De La Fuente, D. E. Fritz, J. Seale, and D. Schmidt

The American Dream, 1961

Greenfield, T. A., *Work and the Work Ethic in American Drama 1920-1970*, pp. 154-55

Houghton, N., *The Exploding Stage*, pp. 189-90

Vos, N., *The Great Pendulum of Becoming*, p. 41

The Ballad of the Sad Café (dramatization of story by C. McCullers), 1963

Herron, I. H., *The Small Town in American Drama*, pp. 444-47

Drama, 133:64-65, Summer 1979

Box, 1968

Houghton, N., *The Exploding Stage*, pp. 195-96

Mayberry, R., "Dissonance in a Chinese Box: Edward Albee's *Box* and *Quotations from Chairman Mao Tse-tung*," pp. 70-85 in *Edward Albee*, ed. P. De La Fuente, D. E. Fritz, J. Seale, and D. Schmidt

Counting the Ways, 1976

Kolin, P. C., "Edward Albee's *Counting the Ways*: The Ways of Losing Heart," pp. 121-40 in *Edward Albee*, ed. J. N. Wasserman

Educational Theatre Journal, 29:407-08, 1977
Educational Theatre Journal, 29:408-09, 1977

A Delicate Balance, 1966
    Fumerton, M. P., "Verbal Prisons: The Language of Albee's *A Delicate Bal-*
       ance," *English Studies in Canada*, 7, ii:201-11, Summer 1981
    Manocchio, T. and W. Petitt, "The Albee Family," pp. 169-203 in their *Families*
       under Stress
    Perry, V. I., "Disturbing Our Sense of Well-Being: The 'Uninvited' in *A Delicate*
       Balance," pp. 55-64 in *Edward Albee*, ed. J. N. Wasserman
    Porter, M. G., "Toby's Last Stand: The Evanescence of Commitment in *A*
       Delicate Balance," *Theatre Journal*, 31:398-408, 1979
    Vos, N., *The Great Pendulum of Becoming*, pp. 34, 54-55, 87-88
    Winston, M., "Edward Albee: *A Delicate Balance,*" pp. 29-43 in *Das ameri-*
       kanische Drama der Gegenwart, ed. H. Grabes

The Lady from Dubuque, 1980
    Adler, T. P., "The Pirandello in Albee: The Problem of Knowing in *The Lady*
       from Dubuque," pp. 109-19 in *Edward Albee*, ed. J. N. Wasserman
    Roudané, M. C., "On Death, Dying, and the Manner of Living: Waste as Theme
       in Edward Albee's *The Lady from Dubuque,*" pp. 65-81 in *Edward Albee*,
       ed. J. N. Wasserman
    Schlueter, J., "Is It 'All Over' for Edward Albee? *The Lady from Dubuque,*"
       pp. 112-19 in *Edward Albee*, ed. P. De La Fuente, D. E. Fritz, J. Seale, and
       D. Schmidt
    After Dark, 12:22, Apr. 1980
    Nation, 230:221, 23 Feb. 1980
    New Republic, 182:26-27, 8 Mar. 1980
    New York, 13:74-75, 11 Feb. 1980
    New Yorker, 55:63-64, 11 Feb. 1980
    Newsweek, 95:102-03, 11 Feb. 1980
    Plays and Players, 27:36-37, Apr. 1980
    Saturday Review, 7:34-35, 15 Mar. 1980
    Time, 115:69, 11 Feb. 1980

Listening, 1977
    Educational Theatre Journal, 29:408-09, 1977

Lolita (dramatization of novel by V. Nabokov), 1981
    Cameron, B., "Who's Afraid of Vladimir Nabokov? Edward Albee's *Lolita,*"
       Theater, 12:77-80, Summer/Fall 1981
    Copeland, R., "Should Edward Albee Call It Quits?," *Saturday Review*, 8:28-
       31, Feb. 1981
    After Dark, 14:18, June 1981
    Maclean's, 94:62, 6 Apr. 1981
    Nation, 232:474-76, 18 Apr. 1981
    New Republic, 184:27-28, 11 Apr. 1981
    New York, 14:35-39, 16 Mar. 1981
    New York, 14:34, 30 Mar. 1981
    New Yorker, 57:62, 30 Mar. 1981

Newsweek, 97:85, 30 Mar. 1981
People, 15:44-46, 6 Apr. 1981
Saturday Review, 8:78-79, May 1981
Time, 117:65, 30 Mar. 1981

The Man Who Had Three Arms, 1982
Time, 119:69, 28 June 1982

Quotations from Chairman Mao Tse-tung, 1968
Houghton, N., *The Exploding Stage*, pp. 195-96
Mayberry, R., "Dissonance in a Chinese Box: Edward Albee's *Box* and *Quotations from Chairman Mao Tse-tung*," pp. 70-85 in *Edward Albee*, ed. P. De La Fuente, D. E. Fritz, J. Seale, and D. Schmidt

Seascape, 1975
Adler, T. P., "Albee's *Seascape*: Humanity at the Second Threshold," *Renascence*, 31:107-14, 1979
Bernstein, S. J., *The Strands Entwined*, pp. 111-35
Gabbard, L. P., "Albee's *Seascape*: An Adult Fairy Tale," *Modern Drama*, 21:307-17, 1978
Purdon, L. O., "The Limits of Reason: *Seascape* as Psychic Metaphor," pp. 141-53 in *Edward Albee*, ed. J. N. Wasserman
Smither, K. H., "A Dream of Dragons: Albee as Star Thrower in *Seascape*," pp. 99-110 in *Edward Albee*, ed. P. De La Fuente, D. E. Fritz, J. Seale, and D. Schmidt
Plays and Players, 27:20-21, May 1980

Tiny Alice, 1965
Anderson, M. C., "Staging the Unconcscious: Edward Albee's *Tiny Alice*," *Renascence*, 33:178-92, 1980
Casper, L., "*Tiny Alice*: The Expense of Joy in the Persistence of Mystery," pp. 83-92 in *Edward Albee*, ed. J. N. Wasserman
Houghton, N., *The Exploding Stage*, pp. 192-93

Who's Afraid of Virginia Woolf?, 1962
Gale, S. H., "Breakers of Illusion: George in Edward Albee's *Who's Afraid of Virginia Woolf?* and Richard in Harold Pinter's *The Lover*," *Vision*, 1, i:70-77, 1979
Greenfield, T. A., *Work and the Work Ethic in American Drama 1920-1970*, pp. 157-59
Hall, V., "Albee's *Who's Afraid of Virginia Woolf?*," *Explicator*, 37, ii:32, Winter 1979
Halperen, M., "What Happens in *Who's Afraid...?*," pp. 129-43 in *Modern American Drama*, ed. W. E. Taylor
Herron, I. H., *The Small Town in American Drama*, pp. 467-73
Houghton, N., *The Exploding Stage*, pp. 190-93
Leff, L. J., "Play into Film: Warner Brothers' *Who's Afraid of Virginia Woolf?*," *Theatre Journal*, 33:453-66, Dec. 1981
Quackenbush, L. H., "The Legacy of Albee's *Who's Afraid of Virginia Woolf?* in the Spanish American Absurdist Theatre," *Revista*, 9:57-71, 1979

Robbins, J. A., "Albee's *Who's Afraid of Virginia Woolf?*," *Explicator*, 37, iv:17-18, Summer 1979

Sawyer, P., "Some Observations on the Character of George in *Who's Afraid of Virginia Woolf?*," *CEA Critic*, 42, iv:15-19, 1980

Schlueter, J., "Albee's Martha and George," pp. 79-87 in Schlueter's *Metafictional Characters in Modern Drama*

Vos, N., *The Great Pendulum of Becoming*, pp. 33, 53-54, 70-71, 83, 84, 86

Watzlawick, P., *An Anthology of Human Communication*

Wilson, R., "The Dynamics of *Who's Afraid of Virginia Woolf?*," pp. 58-69 in *Edward Albee*, ed. P. De La Fuente, D. E. Fritz, J. Seale, and D. Schmidt

Educational Theatre Journal, 30:545, 1978

Drama, 143:37, Spring 1982

The Zoo Story, 1959

Anderson, M. C., "Ritual and Initiation in *The Zoo Story*," pp. 93-108 in *Edward Albee*, ed. J. N. Wasserman

Ditsky, J. M., "Albee's Parabolic Christ: *The Zoo Story*," pp. 147-56 in Ditsky's *The Onstage Christ*

Greenfield, T. A., *Work and the Work Ethic in American Drama 1920-1970*, pp. 156-57

Houghton, N., *The Exploding Stage*, pp. 186-89

Kesselring, K.-P., "Die Kontaktsuche des Menschen im modernen Drama exemplifiziert an Samuel Becketts *Fin de partie*, Harold Pinters *The Caretaker* und Edward Albees *The Zoo Story*," *Maske und Kothurn*, 25:50-57, 1977

Sato, S., "The Fourth Wall in an Age of Alienation: *The Zoo Story* and *The Connection*," pp. 161-66 in *American Literature in the 1950's* (American Literature Society of Japan 1976 Annual Report)

Vos, N., *The Great Pendulum of Becoming*, pp. 33-34, 53-54

ALLAN ALBERT

Corral, 1975

Texas Monthly, 6:218-19, Nov. 1978

JAMES ALBRIGHT

Medea at the Stardust Grill (based on Euripides's *Medea*), 1981

Los Angeles, 27:226-27, Jan. 1982

ALONSO ALEGRÍA

Crossing Niagara, 1981

Nation, 233:585, 28 Nov. 1981

New Republic, 185:24-25, 25 Nov. 1981

New York, 14:126, 16 Nov. 1981

New Yorker, 57:183, 16 Nov. 1981

RONALD ALEXANDER

Time Out for Ginger (originally titled *Season with Ginger*), 1952

Herron, I. H., *The Small Town in American Drama*, pp. 456-57

WILLIAM ALFRED

General

New Yorker, 57:26-30, 25 Jan. 1982

The Curse of an Aching Heart, 1982
  New Republic, 186:24, 24 Feb. 1982
  New York, 15:44-45, 8 Feb. 1982
  New Yorker, 57:115-16, 1 Feb. 1982
  Newsweek, 99:76, 8 Feb. 1982
  Saturday Review, 9:46-47, Mar. 1982
  Time, 119:81, 8 Feb. 1982

Hogan's Goat, 1965
  Gottfried, M., *A Theater Divided*, p. 73
  Commonweal, 109:146-47, 12 Mar. 1982

JAY PRESSON ALLEN

A Little Family Business (adaptation of play by P. Barillet and J.-P. Grédy), 1982
  Los Angeles, 27:338 + , Nov. 1982
  New Yorker, 58:61, 27 Dec. 1982
  Newsweek, 100:62, 27 Dec. 1982

WOODY ALLEN

The Floating Light Bulb, 1981
  After Dark, 14:19 + , July 1981
  America, 144:487, 13 June 1981
  Commonweal, 108:500-01, 11 Sept. 1981
  Georgia Review, 35:605, Fall 1981
  New Leader, 64:20, 1 June 1981
  New Republic, 184:26 + , 23 May 1981
  New York, 14:58 + , 11 May 1981
  New Yorker, 57:101-02, 4 May 1981
  Newsweek, 97:93, 11 May 1981
  Time, 117:83, 11 May 1981

GARLAND ANDERSON

Appearances, 1925
  Bigsby, C. W. E., *A Critical Introduction to Twentieth-Century American Drama*,
    Vol. I, p. 239

MAXWELL ANDERSON

General

Avery, L. G., ed., *Dramatist in America*
Bigsby, C. W. E., *A Critical Introduction to Twentieth-Century American Drama*,
  Vol. I, pp. 146-56

Gould, J., "Maxwell Anderson," pp. 118-34 in Gould's *Modern American Playwrights*

Klink, W., *Maxwell Anderson and S. N. Behrman*

Meserve, W. J., *An Outline History of American Drama*, pp. 250-53, 265-68, 301-03, 341-42

Nicoll, A., "The Vogue of the Historical Play," pp. 727-40 in Nicoll's *World Drama*

Smeall, J. F. S., "Additions to the Maxwell Anderson Bibliography," *North Dakota Quarterly*, 48, iii:60-63, 1980

Taylor, W. E., "Maxwell Anderson: Traditionalist in a Theatre of Change," pp. 47-57 in *Modern American Drama*, ed. Taylor

Tees, A. T., "Maxwell Anderson's Changing Attitude toward War," *North Dakota Quarterly*, 48, iii:5-11, 1980

Barefoot in Athens, 1951

    Wertheim, A., "The McCarthy Era and the American Theatre," *Theatre Journal*, 34:211-22, 1982

Both Your Houses, 1933

    Himelstein, M. Y., *Drama Was a Weapon*, pp. 129-30

    Nannes, C. H., *Politics in the American Drama*, pp. 107-09

Candle in the Wind, 1941

    Himelstein, M. Y., *Drama Was a Weapon*, pp. 150-51

Key Largo, 1939

    Mason, J. D., "Maxwell Anderson's Dramatic Theory and *Key Largo*," *North Dakota Quarterly*, 48, iii:38-52, 1980

    Smiley, S., *The Drama of Attack*, pp. 48-49

Night over Taos, 1932

    Herron, I. H., *The Small Town In American Drama*, pp. 132-34

    Orlin, L. C., "*Night over Taos*: Maxwell Anderson's Sources and Artistry," *North Dakota Quarterly*, 48,iii:12-25, 1980

Valley Forge, 1934

    Himelstein, M. Y., *Drama Was a Weapon*, p. 133

The Wingless Victory, 1936

    Herron, I. H., *The Small Town in American Drama*, pp. 423-25

Winterset, 1935

    Luckett, P. D., "*Winterset* and Some Early Eliot Poems," *North Dakota Quarterly*, 48, iii:26-37, 1980

    Nannes, C. H., *Politics in the American Drama*, pp. 94-96

    Sahu, N. S., "*Winterset*: A Tragedy by a Gifted Technician," *Commonwealth Quarterly*, 4, xiii:3-15, 1980

MAXWELL ANDERSON and HAROLD HICKERSON

Gods of the Lightning, 1928

    Nannes, C H., *Politics in the American Drama*, pp. 92-94

MAXWELL ANDERSON and KURT WEILL

Knickerbocker Holiday, 1938
  Himelstein, M. Y., *Drama Was a Weapon*, pp. 144-45
  Nannes, C. H., *Politics in the American Drama*, pp. 141-42

Lost in the Stars (musical based on A. Paton's novel *Cry, the Beloved Country*), 1949
  Smock, S. W., "*Lost in the Stars* and *Cry, the Beloved Country*: A Thematic
  Comparison," *North Dakota Quarterly*, 48, iii:53-59, 1980

ROBERT ANDERSON

General

Meserve, W. J., *An Outline History of American Drama*, pp. 351-52

All Summer Long (dramatization of D. Wetzel's novel *A Wreath and a Curse*), 1954
  Herron, I. H., *The Small Town in American Drama*, pp. 457-59

The Days Between, 1965
  Herron, I. H., *The Small Town in American Drama*, pp. 463-65

Silent Night, Lonely Night, 1959
  Herron, I. H., *The Small Town in American Drama*, pp. 462-63

Solitaire/Double Solitaire, 1971
  Bernstein, S. J., *The Strands Entwined*, pp. 87-109

Tea and Sympathy, 1953
  Herron, I. H., *The Small Town in American Drama*, pp. 459-62
  Wertheim, A., "The McCarthy Era and the American Theatre," *Theatre Journal*,
  34:211-22, 1982

SHERWOOD ANDERSON

General

Herron, I. H., *The Small Town in American Drama*, pp. 256-62

ANONYMOUS

The Paxton Boys, 1764
  Meserve, W. J., *An Emerging Entertainment*, pp. 46-47

RAY ARANHA

New Year's, 1979
  Theatre Journal, 31:413, 1979

Remington, 1980
  Time, 115:58, 31 Mar. 1980

ROBERT ARDREY

Sing Me No Lullaby, 1954
> Wertheim, A., "The McCarthy Era and the American Theatre," *Theatre Journal*, 34:211-22, 1982

Thunder Rock, 1939
> Himelstein, M. Y., *Drama Was a Weapon*, pp. 177-78
> Smiley, S., *The Drama of Attack*, pp. 48, 96-100

GEORGE AXELROD

The Seven Year Itch, 1952
> Gottfried, M., *A Theater Divided*, pp. 215-16, *passim*

THOMAS BABE

Fathers and Sons, 1978
> *After Dark*, 11:29, Feb. 1979
> *After Dark*, 13:59, June 1980
> *Drama*, 131:25-26, Winter 1979
> *Los Angeles*, 25:274 +, May 1980
> *New York*, 11:146, 4 Dec. 1978

A Prayer for My Daughter, 1977
> *After Dark*, 11:114, May 1978
> *America*, 138:124, 18 Feb. 1978
> *Drama*, 130:69, Autumn 1978
> *Drama*, 131:52-53, Winter 1979
> *Harper's*, 256:84-85, May 1978
> *Nation*, 226:154, 11 Feb. 1978
> *New Leader*, 61:25-26, 13 Feb. 1978
> *New York*, 11:60, 30 Jan. 1978
> *New Yorker*, 53:45-46, 23 Jan. 1978
> *Plays and Players*, 26:23, Jan. 1979
> *Texas Monthly*, 8:194 +, Sept. 1980
> *Time*, 111:70, 30 Jan. 1978

Salt Lake City Skyline, 1980
> *New York*, 13:57-58, 4 Feb. 1980
> *New Yorker*, 55:96, 99, 4 Feb. 1980
> *Newsweek*, 95:84, 4 Feb. 1980

Taken in Marriage, 1979
> *After Dark*, 12:24, May 1979
> *Nation*, 228:285, 17 Mar. 1979
> *New Republic*, 180:25, 21 Apr. 1979
> *New York*, 12:95, 26 Mar. 1979
> *New Yorker*, 55:108, 12 Mar. 1979
> *Newsweek*, 93:103, 12 Mar. 1979
> *Time*, 113:90, 19 Mar. 1979

DON BACHARDY
SEE
CHRISTOPHER ISHERWOOD and DON BACHARDY

FRANK BACON
SEE
WINCHELL SMITH and FRANK BACON

PETER JOHN BAILEY

Passing Through, 1982
  Los Angeles, 27:277, Apr. 1982

DON BAKER and DUDLEY COCKE

Red Fox/Second Hangin', 1978
  New Yorker, 54:90, 20 Mar. 1978

EDWARD ALLAN BAKER

What's So Beautiful About a Sunset Over Prairie Avenue? (also called *Prairie Avenue*),
  1980
  Los Angeles, 26:254+, Apr. 1981
  New Yorker, 56:101-02+, 14 Apr. 1980

PAUL BAKER and EUGENE McKINNEY

Of Time and the River (dramatization of novel by T. Wolfe), 1959
  Herron, I. H., *The Small Town in American Drama*, pp. 396-98

JOHN BALDERSTON and HAMILTON DEANE

Dracula (dramatization of novel by B. Stoker), 1927
  Miner, M. D., "Grotesque Drama in the '70s," *Kansas Quarterly*, 12, iv:99-
  109, 1980
  After Dark, 10:62-67, Mar. 1978
  Crawdaddy, pp. 26-33, June 1978
  Hudson Review, 31:151-52, Spring 1978
  New West, 3:122+, 6 Nov. 1978
  Plays and Players, 26:28, Nov. 1978

JAMES BALDWIN

General

Cohn, R., *Dialogue in American Drama*, pp. 188-92
Gould, J., "Edward Albee and the Current Scene," pp. 287-88 in Gould's *Modern
  American Playwrights*
Molette, C. W., "James Baldwin as a Playwright," pp. 183-88 in *James Baldwin*,
  ed. T. B. O'Daniel

Phillips, L., "The Novelist as Playwright: Baldwin, McCullers, and Bellow," pp. 145-62 in *Modern American Drama*, ed. W. E. Taylor
Turner, D. T., "James Baldwin in the Dilemma of the Black Dramatist," pp. 189-94 in *James Baldwin*, ed. T. B. O'Daniel

Blues for Mister Charlie, 1964
　　Gottfried, M., *A Theater Divided*, pp. 63-64
　　Freese, P., "James Baldwin: *Blues for Mister Charlie*," pp. 328-52 in *Theater und Drama in Amerika*, ed. E. Lohner and R. Haas
　　Schwank, K., "James Baldwin: *Blues for Mister Charlie*," pp. 169-84 in *Das amerikanische Drama der Gegenwart*, ed. H. Grabes
　　Weixlmann, J., "Staged Segregation: Baldwin's *Blues for Mister Charlie* and O'Neill's *All God's Chillun Got Wings*," *Black American Literature Forum*, 11:35-36, 1977

DOUGLAS BALENTINE
SEE
JOHNNY SIMONS and DOUGLAS BALENTINE

IMAMU AMIRI BARAKA
SEE
LEROI JONES

MARK BARKAN
SEE
DAVID VANDO and MARK BARKAN

JAMES NELSON BARKER

General

Herron, I. H., *The Small Town in American Drama*, pp. 9-12
Meserve, W. J., *An Emerging Entertainment*, pp. 177-84, 259-63, *passim*
Meserve, W. J., *An Outline History of American Drama*, pp. 64-66, 76-77, 83-84
Vaughn, J. A., *Early American Dramatists*, pp. 63-69

Superstition; or, The Fanatic Father, 1824
　　Herron, I. H., *The Small Town in American Drama*, pp. 10-12

CHARLES BARNARD and NEIL BURGESS

The County Fair, 1889
　　Recklies, D. F., "Treadmills, Panoramas, and Horses in Neil Burgess's *The County Fair*," *Theatre Studies*, 24-25:9-18, 1977-1979

DJUNA BARNES

General

Cohn, R., *Dialogue in American Drama*, pp. 207-11

The Antiphon, 1961
　　Abel, L., *Metatheatre*, pp. 116-22

Gerstenberger, D., "Three Verse Playwrights and the American Fifties," pp. 117-28 in *Modern American Drama*, ed. W. E. Taylor

BOB BARRY

Murder Among Friends, 1976
Plays and Players, 25:22-23, Apr. 1978

PHILIP BARRY

General

Bigsby, C. W. E., *A Critical Introduction to Twentieth-Century American Drama*, Vol. I, pp. 131-33
Broussard, L., *American Drama*, pp. 56-58
Embler, W., "Comedy of Manners 1927-1939," pp. 59-70 in *Modern American Drama*, ed. W. E. Taylor
Gould, J., "Philip Barry," pp. 78-98 in Gould's *Modern American Playwrights*
Meserve, W. J., *An Outline History of American Drama*, pp. 291-94, 303-06, 343

Holiday, 1928
Greenfield, T. A., *Work and the Work Ethic in American Drama 1920-1970*, pp. 64-65
Sanello, F., "The Lowdown on High Society: 'Holiday,' Los Angeles," *After Dark*, 13:31-34, Dec. 1980
Los Angeles, 25:294 + , Nov. 1980

Hotel Universe, 1930
Kleb, W., "*Hotel Universe*: Playwriting and the San Francisco Mime Troupe," *Theater*, 9,ii:15-20, 1978

Liberty Jones, 1941
Himelstein, M. Y., *Drama Was a Weapon*, p. 150

The Philadelphia Story, 1939
Stasio, M., "The Lowdown on High Society: 'The Philadelphia Story,' New York," *After Dark*, 13:28-31, Dec. 1980
After Dark, 13:28-29, Jan. 1981
America, 143:391, 13 Dec. 1980
Drama, 140:32-33, 1981
Educational Theatre Journal, 30:273-74, 1978
Nation, 231:620, 6 Dec. 1980
New Leader, 63:22-23, 1 Dec. 1980
New Republic, 183:25-26, 27 Dec. 1980
New West, 5:SC-25, 2 June 1980
New York, 13:68, 1 Dec. 1980
New Yorker, 56:134-35, 24 Nov. 1980
Newsweek, 96:83, 1 Dec. 1980
Theatre Journal, 33:260-62, 1981
Time, 116:98, 1 Dec. 1980

PAUL R. BASSETT

Inside the White Room, 1978
  Texas Monthly, 6:136, 138, July 1978

MRS. SIDNEY F. BATEMAN

Self, 1856-57
  Meserve, W. J., *An Outline History of American Drama*, p. 88

KURT BEATTIE

Oregon Gothic, 1980
  Texas Monthly, 8:194, Sept. 1980

S. N. BEHRMAN

General

Embler, W., "Comedy of Manners 1927-1939," pp. 59-70 in *Modern American Drama*, ed. W. E. Taylor
Hoy, C., "Clearings in the Jungle of Life: The Comedies of S. N. Behrman," *New York Literary Forum*, 1:199-227, 1978
Klink, W., *Maxwell Anderson and S. N. Behrman*
Klink, W., *S. N. Behrman*
Meserve, W. J., *An Outline History of American Drama*, pp. 268-69, 290-91, 342-43

Biography, 1932
  New York, 13:88-89, 31 Mar. 1980
  New Yorker, 56:93, 31 Mar. 1980

Jane (dramatization of story by W. S. Maugham), 1952
  Drama, 138:69, Oct. 1980

No Time for Comedy, 1939
  Nannes, C. H., *Politics in the American Drama*, p. 166

Rain from Heaven, 1934
  Himelstein, M. Y., *Drama Was a Weapon*, pp. 133-34
  Nannes, C. H., *Politics in the American Drama*, pp. 166-68

ALBERT BEIN

Let Freedom Ring (dramatization of *To Make My Bread*, a novel by G. Lumpkin), 1935
  Herron, I. H., *The Small Town in American Drama*, p. 230
  Himelstein, M. Y., *Drama Was a Weapon*, p. 198

DAVID BELASCO

General

Herron, I. H., *The Small Town in American Drama*, pp. 130-32, 146-47
Meserve, W. J., *An Outline History of American Drama*, pp. 133, 177-79, 183-84, *passim*
Styan, J. L., "Realism in America: Belasco to 'The Method,' " pp. 109-22 in Styan's *Modern Drama in Theory and Practice*
Vaughn, J. A., *Early American Dramatists*, pp. 153-68

NEAL BELL

Two Small Bodies, 1982
    Los Angeles, 27:255-56, Oct. 1982

SAUL BELLOW

General

Cohn, R., *Dialogue in American Drama*, pp. 192-97

The Last Analysis, 1964
    Phillips, L., "The Novelist as Playwright: Baldwin, McCullers, and Bellow," pp. 145-62 in *Modern American Drama*, ed. W. E. Taylor

JERRY BELSON and GARRY MARSHALL

The Roast, 1980
    New Republic, 182:24, 7 June 1980
    New Yorker, 56:105-06, 19 May 1980

BEN BENGAL

Plant in the Sun, 1937
    Himelstein, M. Y., *Drama Was a Weapon*, pp. 46-47

STEVE BEN ISRAEL

the how you gonna stay open in the 80's cookbook, 1979
    Theatre Journal, 32:269, 1980

ERIC BENTLEY

Are You Now or Have You Ever Been?, 1975
    After Dark, 11:94-95, Dec. 1978
    America, 139:411, 2 Dec. 1978
    Drama, 127:58, Winter 1977-1978
    Nation, 227:484, 4 Nov. 1978
    New York, 11:123-24, 20 Nov. 1978
    Plays and Players, 25:32, Oct. 1977
    Saturday Review, 6:48, 6 Jan. 1979

JUDE BENTON

Windmills, 1982
  Texas Monthly, 10:150, July 1982

ALAN BERGMAN
SEE
JEROME KASS, ALAN BERGMAN, MARILYN BERGMAN,
and BILLY GOLDENBERG

MARILYN BERGMAN
SEE
JEROME KASS, ALAN BERGMAN, MARILYN BERGMAN,
and BILLY GOLDENBERG

RALPH BERKEY
SEE
HENRY DENKER and RALPH BERKEY

LEONARD BERNSTEIN
SEE
ARTHUR LAURENTS, LEONARD BERNSTEIN, and STEPHEN SONDHEIM
AND
HUGH WHEELER, LEONARD BERNSTEIN, RICHARD WILBUR,
JOHN LATOUCHE, and STEPHEN SONDHEIM

DAVID BERRY

G. R. Point, 1977
  After Dark, 12:88, June 1979
  America, 140:416, 19 May 1979
  Georgia Review, 33:577-78, Fall 1979
  Nation, 228:548-49, 12 May 1979
  New Yorker, 55:95, 30 Apr. 1979
  Newsweek, 93:97-98, 30 Apr. 1979

The Whales of August, 1982
  New Yorker, 57:110, 15 Feb. 1982

ARTHUR BINDER
SEE
IRENE Le HERISSIER and ARTHUR BINDER

SALLIE BINGHAM

Milk of Paradise, 1980
  Nation, 230:412, 5 Apr. 1980

ROBERT MONTGOMERY BIRD

General

Meserve, W. J., *An Emerging Entertainment*, pp. 297-301

Meserve, W. J., *An Outline History of American Drama*, pp. 56-59
Vaughan, J. A., *Early American Dramatists*, pp. 89-99

STEWART BIRD and PETER ROBILOTTA

The Wobblies, 1976
    Dubofsky, M., ''Film as History: History as Drama—Some Comments on the
    The Wobblies, a Play by Steward Bird and Peter Robilotta, and *The Wobblies*,
    a Film by Steward Bird and Deborah Shaffer,'' *Labor History*, 22:136-40,
    Winter, 1981

GEORGE BIRIMISA

Pogey Bait, 1977
    After Dark, 10:23-24, Feb. 1978

A Rainbow in the Night, 1978
    New West, 3:SC-40+ , 27 Mar. 1978

JOHN BISHOP

Cabin 12, 1978
    After Dark, 10:80, Apr. 1978
    New Yorker, 54:89, 20 Mar. 1978

Confluence, 1982
    New York, 15:56, 25 Jan. 1982

The Great Grandson of Jedediah Kohler, 1982
    New Republic, 186:25-28, 12 May 1982
    New Yorker, 58:165, 5 Apr. 1982

Winter Signs, 1979
    After Dark, 12:93, June 1979
    New Yorker, 55:55, 26 Mar. 1979

LEWIS BLACK

Crossing the Crab Nebula, 1982
    New York, 15:60+ , 22 Mar. 1982
    New Yorker, 58:128-29, 22 Mar. 1982

MICHAEL BLANKFORT

The Sailors of Cattaro (adaptation of play by F. Wolf), 1934
    Himelstein, M. Y., *Drama Was a Weapon*, pp. 61-62

SEE ALSO
MICHAEL GOLD and MICHAEL BLANKFORT

LEE BLESSING

Oldtimers Game, 1982
  Time, 119:78, 12 Apr. 1982

MARC BLITZSTEIN

The Cradle Will Rock, 1937
  Herron, I. H., *The Small Town in American Drama*, pp. 230-31
  Himelstein, M. Y., *Drama Was a Weapon*, pp. 113-18
  Smiley, S., *The Drama of Attack*, pp. 133-35
  Vacha, J. E., "The Case of the Runaway Opera: The Federal Theatre and Marc
    Blitzstein's *The Cradle Will Rock*," pp. 133-52 in *New York History*, ed. W.
    Tripp
  Catholic World, 146:598-99, Feb. 1938
  Current History, 48:53, Apr. 1938
  Literary Digest, 125:34-35, 1 Jan. 1938
  Magazine of Art, 32:356-57 + , June 1939
  Nation, 146:107, 22 Jan. 1938
  New Republic, 95:280, 13 July 1938
  Scribner's Magazine, 103:70-71, Mar. 1938
  Theatre Arts Monthly, 22:98-99, Feb. 1938
  Time, 29:46 + , 28 June 1937

DAVID BLOMQUIST

Weekends Like Other People, 1982
  New Republic, 186:25-26, 21 Apr. 1982
  New York, 15:60, 22 Mar. 1982
  New Yorker, 58:128, 22 Mar. 1982

SAM BOBRICK and RON CLARK

Wally's Café, 1981
  Mademoiselle, 87:130-31 + , Nov. 1981
  New Yorker, 57:86, 22 June 1981

SEE ALSO
RON CLARK and SAM BOBRICK

JERRY BOCK
SEE
JOSEPH STEIN, JERRY BOCK, and SHELDON HARNICK

MORISON BOCK

Mister Wonderful, 1981
  After Dark, 13:69, Mar. 1981

GEORGE HENRY BOKER

General

Gallagher, K. G., "The Tragedies of George Henry Boker: The Measure of American Romantic Drama," *ESQ*, 20:187-215, 1974
Meserve, W. J., *An Outline History of American Drama*, pp. 59-61
Vaughn, J. A., *Early American Dramatists*, pp. 99-111

Francesca da Rimini, 1853
    Evans, O. H., "Shakespearean Prototypes and the Failure of Boker's *Francesca da Rimini*," *Educational Theatre Journal*, 30:211-19, 1978
    Sherr, P. C., "George Henry Boker's *Francesca da Rimina*: A Justification for the Literary Historian," *Pennsylvania History*, 34:361-71, 1967
    Voelker, P., "George Henry Boker's *Francesca da Rimini*: An Interpretation and Evaluation," *Educational Theatre Journal*, 24:383-95, 1972
    Woods, A., "Producing Boker's *Francesca da Rimini*," *Educational Theatre Journal*, 24:396-401, 1972
    Zanger, J., "Boker's *Francesca da Rimini*: The Brothers' Tragedy," *Educational Theatre Journal*, 25:410-19, 1973

WILLIAM BOLCOM
SEE
ROBERT KALFIN, STEVE BROWN, JOHN McKINNEY, and WILLIAM BOLCOM
AND
ARNOLD WEINSTEIN and WILLIAM BOLCOM

JOSEPH BOLOGNA
SEE
RENÉE TAYLOR and JOSEPH BOLOGNA

CAROL BOLT

Escape Entertainment, 1981
    Maclean's, 94:60, 23 Feb. 1981

JONATHAN BOLT

Threads, 1981
    New York, 14:70, 9 Nov. 1981
    New Yorker, 57:154, 9 Nov. 1981

CLARE BOOTHE

General

Mersand, J., *The American Drama Since 1930*, pp. 47-59

Margin for Error, 1939
    Nannes, C. H., *Politics in the American Drama*, pp. 135-37
    Smiley, S., *The Drama of Attack*, pp. 188-92, *passim*

ALEXANDER BORODIN
SEE
LUTHER DAVIS, ROBERT WRIGHT, GEORGE FORREST,
and ALEXANDER BORODIN
AND
CHARLES LEDERER, LUTHER DAVIS, ROBERT WRIGHT,
GEORGE FORREST, and ALEXANDER BORODIN

JOHN BORUFF and WALTER HART

Washington Jitters, 1938
> Nannes, C. H., *Politics in the American Drama*, pp. 113-15

DION BOUCICAULT

General

Booth, M. R., "Irish Landscape in the Victorian Theatre," pp. 159-72 in *Place, Personality and the Irish Writer*, ed. A. Carpenter
Fawkes, R., *Dion Boucicault*
Krause, D., "Manners and Morals in Irish Comedy: The Playboys and the Paycock of Boucicault," pp. 181-95 in Krause's *The Profane Book of Irish Comedy*
LaCasse, D., "Edwin Booth on Dion Boucicault, Playwriting, and Play Production— A Previously Unpublished Letter," *Theatre Survey*, 21:181-84, Nov. 1980
Meserve, W. J., *An Outline History of American Drama*, pp. 175-76
Vaughn, J. A., *Early American Dramatists*, pp. 112-31

The Octoroon, 1859
> Galassi, F. S., "Slavery and Melodrama: Boucicault's *The Octoroon*," *Markham Review*, 6:77-80, 1977
> Meserve, W. J., *An Outline History of American Drama*, pp. 75-76
> Richardson, G. A., "Boucicault's *The Octoroon* and American Law," *Theatre Journal*, 34:155-64, 1982

Old Heads and Young Hearts, 1844
> *Drama*, 138:68-69, Oct. 1980

The Streets of New York (also called *The Streets of London*, etc.; adaptation of *Les Pauvres de Paris* by E. Brisbarre and E. Nus), 1857
> Meserve, W. J., *An Outline History of American Drama*, pp. 100-02
> *After Dark*, 13:62, Sept. 1980
> *Drama*, 137:63, July 1980
> *Plays and Players*, 27:29-30, June 1980
> *Theatre Journal*, 33:119-20, 1981

ALAN BOWNE

Forty-Deuce, 1981
> *After Dark*, 14:72, June 1981

HUGH HENRY BRACKENRIDGE

General

Meserve, W. J., *An Emerging Entertainment*, pp. 81-83
Meserve, W. J., *An Outline History of American Drama*, pp. 17-18
Winton, C., "The Theater and Drama," pp. 95-96 in *American Literature, 1764-1789*, ed. E. Emerson

RAY BRADBURY

Farenheit 451 (dramatization of his novel), 1979
    Los Angeles, 24:259 + , Sept. 1979

MARK BRAMBLE
SEE
MICHAEL STEWART, MARK BRAMBLE, and JERRY HERMAN
AND
MICHAEL STEWART, MARK BRAMBLE, DOUG KATSAROS, and RICHARD ENGQUIST

CHARLES BRECK

General

Meserve, W. J., *An Emerging Entertainment*, pp. 215-16

GEORGE BREWER, JR.

Tide Rising, 1937
    Greenfield, T. A., *Work and the Work Ethic in American Drama 1920-1970*, pp. 79-81
    Himelstein, M. Y., *Drama Was a Weapon*, pp. 201-02

JAMES F. BRICE

A Country Clown; or, Dandyism Improved, 1829
    Herron, I. H., *The Small Town in American Drama*, pp. 69-70

JAY BROAD

White Pelicans, 1976
    Nation, 227:558, 18 Nov. 1978
    New Republic, 179:26-27, 18 Nov. 1978
    New Yorker, 54:131-32, 30 Oct. 1978

GEORGE H. BROADHURST

The Man of the Hour, 1906
    Nannes, C. H., *Politics in the American Drama*, pp. 47-51

CONRAD BROMBERG

Two Brothers, 1978
    After Dark, 11:112+, May 1978

ALICE BROWN

Children of Earth, 1915
    Herron, I. H., *The Small Town in American Drama*, pp. 239-40

HARVEY BROWN

A Sound of Hunting, 1945
    Greenfield, T. A., *Work and the Work Ethic in American Drama 1920-1970*,
    pp. 98-99

KENNETH BROWN

The Brig, 1963
    Dukore, B. F., "Off-Broadway and the New Realism," pp. 163-74 in *Modern
    American Drama*, ed. W. E. Taylor
    Jacquot, J. and G. Cotta-Ramusino, "The Living Theatre: Julian Beck [et] Judith
    Malina: Le Living Theatre à New York et la découverte d'Artaud: *The Brig,
    Frankenstein, Antigone*, [et] *Paradise Now*," pp. 171-269 in *Les Vois de la
    création théâtrale*, ed. Jacquot

LENNOX BROWN

The Twilight Dinner, 1978
    Encore, 7:31-32, 22 May 1978
    New Yorker, 54:67-68, 1 May 1978

STEVE BROWN
SEE
ROBERT KALFIN, STEVE BROWN, JOHN McKINNEY,
and WILLIAM BOLCOM

WILLIAM WELLS BROWN

General

Heller, M., "The Names of Slaves and Masters: Real and Fictional," *Literary Onomastics Studies*, 6:130-48, 1979

WINYARD BROWN

The Holly and the Ivy, 1982
    New York, 15:80+, 29 Nov., 1982

ED BULLINS

General

Andrews, W. D. E., "Theater of Black Reality: The Blues Drama of Ed Bullins," *Southwest Review*, 65:178-90, 1980

Bruck, P., "Ed Bullins: The Quest and Failure of an Ethnic Community Theatre," pp. 123-40 in *Essays on Contemporary American Drama*, ed. H. Bock and A. Wertheim

Cohn, R., "Camp, Cruelty, Colloquialism," pp. 281-303 in *Comic Relief*, ed. S. B. Cohen

Miller, J.-M. A., "Images of Black Women in Plays by Black Playwrights," *College Language Association Journal*, 20:494-507, 1977

Scharine, R. G., "Ed Bullins Was Steve Benson (But Who Is He Now?)," *Black American Literature Forum*, 13:103-09, 1979

Sollors, W., "Ed Bullins," pp. 201-22 in *Das amerikanische Drama der Gegenwart*, ed. H. Grabes

True, W., "Ed Bullins, Anton Chekhov, and the 'Drama of Mood,' " *College Language Association Journal*, 20:521-32, 1977

Clara's Ole Man, 1965
Hurd, M., "The Cat in the Rain in Bullins' 'Clara's Ole Man,' " *Notes on Contemporary Literature*, 11, iii:2, May 1981
New Yorker, 57:154-55, 9 Nov. 1981

The Taking of Miss Janie, 1975
Bernstein, S. J., *The Strands Entwined*, pp. 61-86

ED BULLINS and NEIL HARRIS

Man-Wo-Man (two one-acts: *Michael* by Bullins and *Passion Without Reason* by Harris), 1978
New Yorker, 54:91-93, 22 May 1978

VICTOR BUMBALO

Niagara Falls, 1981
After Dark, 14:17, Oct. 1981

HECTOR BUNYAN

Prodigals in a Promised Land, 1981
Maclean's, 94:62, 30 Mar. 1981

GRANVILLE WYCHE BURGESS

The Freak, 1982
New York, 15:64-65, 7 June 1982

NEIL BURGESS
SEE
CHARLES BARNARD and NEIL BURGESS

JOHN DALY BURK

General

Meserve, W. J., *An Emerging Entertainment*, pp. 119-25
Vaughn, J. A., *Early American Dramatists*, pp. 54-58

PATRICK BURKE
SEE
ANDREI SERBAN and PATRICK BURKE

ABE BURROWS, JO SWERLING, and FRANK LOESSER

Guys and Dolls (musical based on stories by D. Runyan), 1950
    After Dark, 13:63, Aug. 1980
    Atlantic, 245:40-47 +, Jan. 1980
    Drama, 145:11 +, Autumn 1982
    Los Angeles, 25:226 +, June 1980
    New West, 5:SC-25, 2 June 1980
    Plays and Players, 344:2-4, May 1982
    Plays and Players, 351:36-37, Dec. 1982

JOHN BYRUM

Inserts, 1982
    New York, 15:64, 27 Sept. 1982

GEORGE HENRY CALVERT

Arnold and André, 1840 (revised 1864)
    Shillingsburg, M. J., "The West Point Treason in American Drama, 1798-1891,"
        Educational Theatre Journal, 30:73:89, 1978

BARTLEY THOMAS CAMPBELL

General

Herron, I. H., *The Small Town in American Drama*, pp. 129-30

VINCENT CANBY

End of the War, 1978
    Nation, 227:485, 4 Nov. 1978
    New Yorker, 54:132-33, 30 Oct. 1978

TRUMAN CAPOTE

The Grass Harp (dramatization of his novel), 1952

Herron, I. H., *The Small Town in American Drama*, pp. 447-49
Kesting, M., "Truman Capote: *Die Grasharfe*," pp. 321-27 in *Theater und Drama in Amerika*, ed. E. Lohner and R. Haas

LEWIS JOHN CARLINO

General

Gottfried, M., *A Theater Divided*, pp. 278-79

LAURENCE CARR

Victoria's Closet, 1978
 After Dark, 11:80, Feb. 1979

MARY CLARKE CARR

General

Meserve, W. J., *An Emerging Entertainment*, pp. 242-43

The Fair Americans, 1789
 Herron, I. H., *The Small Town in American Drama*, pp. 52-53, 89

STEVE CARTER

Dame Lorraine, 1981
 Chicago, 30:70+, May 1981

Eden, 1976
 After Dark, 13:67, Feb. 1981

Nevis Mountain Dew, 1978
 Paul, J. S., "The Power of Proximity: *Nevis Mountain Dew* and *Buried Child* in the Second City," *Cresset*, 43, vi:12-14, Apr. 1980
 New Republic, 180:25, 21 Apr. 1979
 New York, 12:88-89, 25 Dec. 1978
 New Yorker, 54:51-52, Dec. 1978

JOHN CASSAVETES

East/West Game, 1980
 After Dark, 13:68, Jan. 1981

JOSEPH CHAIKIN

General

Pegnato, L. J., "Breathing in a Different Zone: Joseph Chaikin," *The Drama Review*, 25:7-18, Fall 1981 (interview)

Tourists and Refugees No. 2, 1980
 Nation, 232:770, 20 June 1981

JOSEPH CHAIKIN and STEVEN KENT

Texts (adaptation of *Texts for Nothing* and *How It Is* by S. Beckett), 1981
    Nation, 232:412, 4 Apr. 1981
    New Yorker, 57:124, 126, 23 Mar. 1981

JOSEPH CHAIKIN and SAM SHEPARD

Savage/Love, 1979
    Auerbach, D., *Sam Shepard, Arthur Kopit, and the Off Broadway Theater*, pp.
    62-65
    After Dark, 13:63, Aug. 1980

Tongues, 1979
    Auerbach, D., *Sam Shepard, Arthur Kopit, and the Off Broadway Theater*, pp.
    62-65
    Kleb, W., "Shepard and Chaikin Speaking in *Tongues*," *Theatre*, 10, i:66-69,
    1978
    After Dark, 13:63, Aug. 1980
    Georgia Review, 34:497-508, Fall 1980
    New Yorker, 55:102, 17 Dec. 1979

SEE ALSO
JEAN-CLAUDE VAN ITALLIE and JOSEPH CHAIKIN

JANE CHAMBERS

My Blue Heaven, 1981
    After Dark, 14:17, Oct. 1981
    New York, 13:43, 4 Aug. 1980

MARTIE CHARLES

Black Cycle, 1971
    Curb, R. K., " 'Goin' through Changes': Mother-Daughter Confrontations in
    Three Recent Plays by Young Black Women," *Kentucky Folklore Record*,
    25:96-102, 1979

MARTIN CHARNIN
SEE
THOMAS MEEHAN, RICHARD RODGERS, MARTIN CHARNIN,
and RAYMOND JESSEL

PADDY CHAYEFSKY

General

Black, D., "Paddy Chayefsky, RIP," *National Review*, 33:1005, 4 Sept. 1981
Gardner, R. H., *The Splintered Stage*, p. 101

Kotama, M. and M. Sata, "Secular Humanism," pp. 183-90 in *American Literature in the 1950's* (American Literature Society of Japan 1976 Annual Report)

Meserve, W. J., *An Outline History of American Drama*, p. 349

ALICE CHILDRESS

General

Childress, A., "Knowing the Human Condition," pp. 8-10 in *Black American Literature and Humanism*, ed. R. B. Miller

Miller, J.-M. A., "Images of Black Women in Plays by Black Playwrights," *College Language Association Journal*, 20:494-507, 1977

Wedding Band, 1966
> Curb, R., "An Unfashionable Tragedy of American Racism: Alice Childress's *Wedding Band*," *MELUS*, 7, iv:57-68, 1980

Wine in the Wilderness, 1969
> Brown, J., *"Wine in the Wilderness,"* pp. 56-70 in Brown's *Feminist Drama*

FRANK CHIN

General

Kim, E. H., "Frank Chin: The Chinatown Cowboy and His Backtalk," *Midwest Quarterly*, 20:78-91, 1978

Wand, D. H.-F., "The Chinese-American Literary Scene: A Galaxy of Poets and a Lone Playwright," *Proceedings of the Comparative Literature Symposium* (Lubbock, Tex.), 9:121-46, 1978

EDWARD CHODOROV

Decision, 1944
> Nannes, C. H., *Politics in the American Drama*, pp. 137-39

JEROME CHODOROV and NORMAN PANAMA

A Talent for Murder, 1981
> *After Dark*, 14:12, Dec. 1981
> *New Leader*, 64:20, 2 Nov. 1981
> *New York*, 14:86, 12 Oct. 1981
> *New Yorker*, 57:148, 12 Oct. 1981
> *Time*, 118:86, 14 Sept. 1981
> *Time*, 118:96, 12 Oct. 1981

SEE ALSO
JOSEPH FIELDS and JEROME CHODOROV

PING CHONG

Fear and Loathing, 1975
> *Theatre Journal*, 34:270, 1982

Humboldt's Current, 1978
    After Dark, 11:80-81, June 1978

RON CLARK and SAM BOBRICK

Murder at the Howard Johnson's, 1979
    New Yorker, 55:92, 28 May 1979
    Saturday Review, 6:43, 21 July 1979

SEE ALSO
SAM BOBRICK and RON CLARK

JIM CLAYBURGH
SEE
SPALDING GRAY, ELIZABETH LeCOMPTE, LIBBY HOWES,

JIM CLAYBURGH, and RON VAWTER

EDWARD CLINTON

Benefit of a Doubt, 1976
    Educational Theatre Journal, 30:420-21, 1978

GEORGE COATES

The Way of How, 1981
    Theatre Journal, 34:256, 1982

D. L. COBURN

Bluewater Cottage, 1979
    After Dark, 12:18, Dec. 1979
    New West, 4:SC-38, 22 Oct. 1979

The Gin Game, 1977
    Drama, 134:63, 72-73, Autumn 1979
    Hudson Review, 31:151, Spring 1978
    Los Angeles, 24:236+, Feb. 1979
    Mandate, 3:9, Jan. 1978
    New West, 4:80+, 29 Jan. 1979
    Plays and Players, 25:39+, June 1978
    Plays and Players, 26:25, Sept. 1979
    Texas Monthly, 6:134, June 1978
    Texas Monthly, 10:150, July 1982

DUDLEY COCKE
SEE
DON BAKER and DUDLEY COCKE

LARRY COHEN

Trick, 1979

New York, 12:70, 19 Feb. 1979
New Yorker, 54:45, 12 Feb. 1979

GUY DE COINTET

New Life, 1981
   Art in America, 69:139, May 1981

Tell Me, 1979
   Deák, F., "*Tell Me*: A Play by Guy de Cointet," *The Drama Review*, 23, iii:11-20, 1979

TOM COLE

Medal of Honor Rag, 1976
   After Dark, 12:64, Aug. 1979
   Drama, 127:75-76, Winter 1977-1978

CY COLEMAN
SEE
BETTY COMDEN, ADOLPH GREEN, and CY COLEMAN

LONNIE COLEMAN

Jolly's Progress, 1959
   New Yorker, 35:82, 19 Dec. 1959
   Time, 74:77, 14 Dec. 1959

BETTY COMDEN and ADOLPH GREEN

A Doll's Life (a musical sequel to Ibsen's *A Doll's House*), 1982
   After Dark, 14:63-65, Sept. 1982
   America, 147:235, 23 Oct. 1982
   Nation, 235:378-80, 16 Oct. 1982
   New York, 15:91-92, 4 Oct. 1982
   New Yorker, 58:122, 4 Oct. 1982
   Plays and Players, 350:34, Nov. 1982
   Theatre Crafts, 16:22-23 + , Nov./Dec. 1982

BETTY COMDEN, ADOLPH GREEN, and CY COLEMAN

On the Twentieth Century (musical version of *Twentieth Century*, play by B. Hecht and C. MacArthur, adapted from play by C. B. Milholland), 1978
   After Dark, 10:78-79, Apr. 1978
   America, 138:191, 11 Mar. 1978
   Nation, 226:282-83, 11 Mar. 1978
   New Leader, 61:27-28, 27 Mar. 1978
   New Republic, 178:24-25, 18 Mar. 1978
   New York, 11:90-91, 6 Mar. 1978
   New Yorker, 54:67, 6 Mar. 1978

New Yorker, 54:30-33, 27 Mar. 1978
Newsweek, 91:79+, 6 Mar. 1978
Saturday Review, 5:50-51, 15 Apr. 1978
Time, 111:75, 6 Mar. 1978

TOM CONE

Stargazing, 1978
  New York, 11:124, 20 Nov. 1978

E. P. CONKLE

Crick Bottom Plays, 1928
  Herron, I. H., *The Small Town in American Drama*, pp. 164-65

In the Shadow of a Rock, 1936
  Herron, I. H., *The Small Town in American Drama*, pp. 165-66

MARC CONNELLY

The Green Pastures (dramatization of tales by R. Bradford), 1930
  Daniel, W. C., "*Green Pastures*: American Religiosity in the Theatre," *Journal of American Culture*, 5:51-58, Spring 1982
  Herron, I. H., *The Small Town in American Drama*, pp. 339-42
  Negro History Bulletin, 42:42-43, Apr. 1979

SEE ALSO
GEORGE S. KAUFMAN and MARC CONNELLY

H. J. CONWAY

The Battle of Stillwater; or, The Maniac, 1840
  Herron, I. H., *The Small Town in American Drama*, pp. 54-56

Uncle Tom's Cabin (dramatization of H. B. Stowe's novel), 1852
  Theatre Journal, 34:149-54, 1982

MICHAEL COOK

The Gayden Chronicles, 1978
  After Dark, 13:59, June 1980
  Maclean's, 95:61, 31 May 1982

SUSAN COOPER
SEE
HUME CRONYN and SUSAN COOPER

ROBERT COOVER

General

McCafferey, L., "Robert Coover on His Own and Other Fictions: An Interview," *Genre*, 14, i:45-63, Spring 1981

JOHN CORIG

All the Same, 1982
  Drama-Logue, 13, xxxvii:5, 16-22 Sept. 1982

Windfall's Donuts, 1982
  Drama-Logue, 13, xxxvii:5, 16-22 Sept. 1982

BARTLETT CORMACK

The Racket, 1927
  Nannes, C. H., *Politics in the American Drama*, pp. 81-84

CAROL CORWEN

The Doctor and the Devils (adaptation of screenplay by D. Thomas and D. Taylor),
  1981
  Theatre Journal, 34:120, 1982

JOHN BRUCE COWAN

Canuck, pub. 1931
  After Dark, 13:62, Dec. 1980

JOHN CRAIG

Ain't Lookin', 1980
  After Dark, 13:62, Sept. 1980

ELISABETH GREENE CRANE

Berquin, 1897
  Telle, E. V., "The Memory of L. de Berquin in the United States of America,"
    Revue de Littérature Comparée, 217, i:105-09, Jan.-Mar. 1981

JERRY CRAWFORD

The Auction Tomorrow, 1979
  After Dark, 11:85, Apr. 1979

MICHAEL CRISTOFER
(pseud. of Michael Procassion)

Black Angel, 1978
  New West, 3:SC-21, 19 June 1978
  New York, 16:63, 10 Jan. 1983
  New Yorker, 58:51, 3 Jan. 1983

Ice, 1976
  Educational Theatre Journal, 29:264, 1977

New York, 12:130-31, 12 Nov. 1979

The Lady and the Clarinet, 1980
  Los Angeles, 25:260, Oct. 1980
  New West, 5:89, 22 Sept. 1980

The Shadow Box, 1975
  Duclow, D. F., "Dying on Broadway: Contemporary Drama and Mortality,"
    Soundings, 64, ii:197-216, Summer 1981
  Christian Century, 97:468-70, 23 Apr. 1980
  Hudson Review, 31:147-48, Spring 1978
  Plays and Players, 26:19 + , Apr. 1979
  Texas Monthly, 6:142-43, May 1978

HUME CRONYN and SUSAN COOPER

Foxfire (developed from the magazine of this title), 1982
  America, 148:50, 22 Jan. 1983
  Nation, 235:600 + , 4 Dec. 1982
  New Leader, 65:21-22, 27 Dec. 1982
  New Republic, 188 Sp. Issue:26, (3 Jan. 1983)
  New York, 15:77, 22 Nov. 1982
  New Yorker, 58:176, 22 Nov. 1982
  Newsweek, 100:123, 22 Nov. 1982
  Time, 120:105, 22 Nov. 1982

RACHEL CROTHERS

General

Gottlieb, L. C., *Rachel Crothers*
Sutherland, C., "American Women Playwrights as Mediators of the 'Woman Problem,' " *Modern Drama*, 21:319-36, 1978

He and She (originally titled *The Herfords*), 1911
  Meserve, W. J., *An Outline History of American Drama*, pp. 198-99
  After Dark, 13:62, Aug. 1980
  Blue Book, 15:470-73, July 1912
  Dramatic Mirror, 83:310, 21 Feb. 1920
  Dramatist, 11:994-95, Apr. 1920
  Green Book, 7:1070-77, May 1912
  New England Magazine, 45:616, Feb. 1912
  New York, 13:88, 16 June 1980
  New Yorker, 56:112, 114, 9 June 1980
  Review, 2:262 + , 13 Mar. 1920
  Theatre Magazine, 31:269-70, Apr. 1920

RUSSEL CROUSE
SEE
HOWARD LINDSAY and RUSSEL CROUSE

MART CROWLEY

The Boys in the Band, 1968
Vos, N., *The Great Pendulum of Becoming*, pp. 71-72

RICHARD CUMMING
SEE
ADRIAN HALL and RICHARD CUMMING

E. E. CUMMINGS

Him, 1928
Cohn, R., *Dialogue in American Drama*, pp. 237-43
Zukofsky, L., *"Him,"* pp. 84-85 in Zukofsky's *Prepositions* (review originally
pub. 1927)

LEIGH CURRAN

The Lunch Girls, 1977
After Dark, 10:84-85, Mar. 1978
Educational Theatre Journal, 30:419, 1978
Ms, 6:26, June 1978
National Review, 30:167-68, 3 Feb. 1978

GEORGE WASHINGTON PARKE CUSTIS

Pocahontas; or, The Settlers of Virginia, 1830
Meserve, W. J., *An Outline History of American Drama*, p. 177

AUGUSTIN DALY

General

Cipolla, G., "Thomas Augustine [sic] Daly: An Early Voice of the Italian Immi-
grants," *Italian Americana*, 6:45-59, 1980
Meserve, W. J., *An Outline History of American Drama*, pp. 130-31, 136-37, 149,
176-77
Vaughn, J. A., *Early American Dramatists*, pp. 132-43

Horizon, 1871
Herron, I. H., *The Small Town in American Drama*, pp. 135-38

A Legend of Norwood; or, Village Life in New England (dramatization of novel by
H. W. Beecher), 1867
Herron, I. H., *The Small Town in American Drama*, pp. 76-77

Under the Gaslight, 1867

Greenfield, T. A., *Work and the Work Ethic in American Drama 1920-1970*, pp. 30-31

JOE DARION
SEE
DALE WASSERMAN, MITCH LEIGH, and JOE DARION

BILL C. DAVIS

Mass Appeal, 1978
    After Dark, 11:84, Sept. 1978
    After Dark, 13:28-29, 68, Aug. 1980
    After Dark, 13:62, Aug. 1980
    After Dark, 14:18, Mar. 1982
    America, 145:417-18, 26 Dec. 1981
    America, 146:35, 16 Jan. 1982
    Commonweal, 109:50-51, 29 Jan. 1982
    Nation, 230:731, 14 June 1980
    Nation, 234:155-56, 6 Feb. 1982
    New Leader, 64:20, 30 Nov. 1981
    New York, 13:49-50, 2 June 1980
    New York, 14:85-86, 23 Nov. 1981
    New Yorker, 56:110, 19 May 1980
    New Yorker, 57:69, 23 Nov. 1981
    Newsweek, 95:106, 9 June 1980
    Newsweek, 98:123, 23 Nov. 1981
    Plays and Players, 350:28-29, Nov. 1982
    Saturday Review, 9:55, Jan. 1982
    Time, 115:84, 26 May 1980
    Time, 119:77, 12 Apr. 1982
    U S Catholic, 47:41, Jan. 1982

DONALD DAVIS
SEE
OWEN DAVIS and DONALD DAVIS

LUTHER DAVIS, ROBERT WRIGHT, GEORGE DAVIS,
and ALEXANDER BORODIN

Timbuktu! (an all-Black musical based on *Kismet*, which see), 1978
    Encore, 7:26-27, 3 Apr. 1978
    Los Angeles, 24:203, Jan. 1979
    New York, 11:89-90, 20 Mar. 1978
    New Yorker, 54:56+, 13 Mar. 1978
    Newsweek, 91:95, 13 Mar. 1978
    Time, 111:75, 13 Mar. 1978

SEE ALSO
CHARLES LEDERER, LUTHER DAVIS, ROBERT WRIGHT,
GEORGE FORREST, and ALEXANDER BORODIN

OSSIE DAVIS

General

Dodson, O., "Who Has Seen the Wind? Part III," *Black American Literature Forum*,
14:54-59, 1980

OWEN DAVIS

General

Meserve, W. J., *An Outline History of American Drama*, pp. 179, 234-35

The Detour, 1921
Herron, I. H., *The Small Town in American Drama*, pp. 247-48

The Great Gatsby (dramatization of novel by F. S. Fitzgerald), 1926
Morsberger, R. E., "Trimalchio in West Egg: The Great Gatsby Onstage,"
Prospects, 5:489-506, 1980

Icebound, 1923
Herron, I. H., *The Small Town in American Drama*, pp. 248-50

Jezebel, 1933
Catholic World, 138:604-05, Feb. 1934
Commonweal, 19:273, 5 Jan. 1934
Nation, 138:28, 3 Jan. 1934
New Republic, 77:226, 3 Jan. 1934
Newsweek, 2:30, 30 Dec. 1933
Theatre Arts Monthly, 18:95-97, Feb. 1934

OWEN DAVIS and DONALD DAVIS

Ethan Frome (dramatization of novel by E. Wharton), 1936
Herron, I. H., *The Small Town in American Drama*, pp. 250-54

MICHAEL E. DAWDY, CANDACE LAUGHLIN, and BARRY OPPER

Inching through the Everglades, 1978
Educational Theatre Journal, 30:551-52, 1978
Theatre Journal, 33:118, 1981

KATHERINE DAYTON
SEE
GEORGE S. KAUFMAN and KATHERINE DAYTON

CHARLES TURNER DAZEY

General

Herron, I. H., *The Small Town in American Drama*, pp. 192-93

PHILLIP HAYES DEAN

Paul Robeson, 1978
    After Dark, 10:81-82, Mar. 1978
    Commonweal, 105:178-79, 17 Mar. 1978
    Encore, 7:29, 6 Mar. 1978
    First World, 2:32-33 + , Spring 1978
    Horizon, 21:35-37, May 1978
    Nation, 226:154-55, 11 Feb. 1978
    New York, 11:76, 6 Feb. 1978
    New Yorker, 53:71-72, 30 Jan. 1978
    Newsweek, 91:66, 30 Jan. 1978
    Plays and Players, 25:19, Sept. 1978
    Theatre News, 12, iii:17, 19, Dec. 1979
    Time, 111:68, 30 Jan. 1978

HAMILTON DEANE
SEE
JOHN BALDERSTON and HAMILTON DEANE

JAMES deJONGH

Do Lord Remember Me, 1978
    After Dark, 15:12-13, Dec. 1982/Jan. 1983
    New Yorker, 58:160, 8 Nov. 1982
    Time, 121:87, 14 Feb. 1983

ALONZO DELANO

The Frontier Settlement; or, Scenes in the Far West, 1846
    Herron, I. H., *The Small Town in American Drama*, pp. 116-18

A Live Woman in the Mines; or, Pike County Ahead!, 1857
    Herron, I. H., *The Small Town in American Drama*, pp. 118-20

DREW DENBAUM

Secrets (based on two short stories by B. Gill), 1978
    After Dark, 11:97, Dec. 1978

HENRY DENKER

Horowitz and Mrs. Washington, 1980
    New Yorker, 56:105-06, 14 Apr. 1980
    Time, 115:112, 14 Apr. 1980

HENRY DENKER and RALPH BERKEY

Time Limit!, 1956
    Wertheim, A., "The McCarthy Era and the American Theatre," *Theatre Journal*,
    34:211-22, 1982

ALEXIS DeVEAUX

A Season to Unravel, 1979
  New Yorker, 54:100, 5 Feb. 1979

ELIZABETH DIGGS

Dumping Ground, 1981
  New York, 14:71+, 9 Nov. 1981

E. L. DOCTOROW

Drinks Before Dinner, 1978
  After Dark, 11:27-28, Feb. 1979
  Nation, 227:685-86, 16 Dec. 1978
  New York, 11:117, 11 Dec. 1978
  New Yorker, 54:85-86, 4 Dec. 1978
  Newsweek, 92:131, 4 Dec. 1978
  Plays and Players, 26:42, Jan. 1979
  Texas Monthly, 8:177, June 1980
  Time, 112:108, 4 Dec. 1978

OWEN DODSON

General

Hatch, J. V., "The Alchemy of Owen Dodson," *Black American Literature Forum*,
  14:51-52, 1980
Hatch, J. V., D. A. M. Ward, and J. Weixlmann, "The Rungs of a Powerful Long
  Ladder: An Owen Dodson Bibliography," *Black American Literature Forum*,
  14:60-68, 1980

JOHN DOS PASSOS

General

Cohn, R., *Dialogue in American Drama*, pp. 179-82

ARTHUR CONAN DOYLE
SEE
WILLIAM GILLETTE and ARTHUR CONAN DOYLE

THEODORE DREISER

General

Keyssar, H., "Theodore Dreiser's Dramas: American Folk Drama and Its Limits,"
  Theatre Journal, 33:365-76, 1981

The Girl in the Coffin, 1917
  Herron, I. H., *The Small Town in American Drama*, pp. 228-30

The Hand of the Potter, 1921

Cohn, R., *Dialogue in American Drama*, pp. 172-76

Herron, I. H., *The Small Town in American Drama*, pp. 227-28

ROSALYN DREXLER

General

Dasgupta, G., "Rosalyn Drexler," pp. 209-18 in Dasgupta and B. G. Marranca's *American Playwrights*

The Bed Was Full, 1972
Brown, J., "*The Bed Was Full*," pp. 22-36 in Brown's *Feminist Drama*

Home Movies, 1964
Gottfried, M., *A Theater Divided*, pp. 208-09

The Writer's Opera, 1979
After Dark, 12:26, May 1979

JOHN DRIVER and JEFFREY HADDOW

Chekhov in Yalta, 1981
Los Angeles, 26:247 + , July 1981
Theatre Journal, 34:266, 1982

Scrambled Feet, 1981
Los Angeles, 26:274, Sept. 1981

A. M. DRUMMOND and ROBERT E. GARD

The Cardiff Giant, 1939
Herron, I. H., *The Small Town in American Drama*, pp. 427-28

JED DUANE

The Glorious Pool (dramatization of novel by T. Smith), 1979
Los Angeles, 24:172 + , Aug. 1979
New West, 4:69, 30 July 1979

WILLIAM DUBOIS

Haiti (based on story by Jean-Christophe), 1932
Bigsby, C. W. E., *A Critical Approach to Twentieth-Century American Drama*, Vol. I, pp. 247, 248
Nation, 146:309, 12 Mar. 1938
New Republic, 94:194, 23 Mar. 1938
One Act Play Magazine, 1:1025-26, Mar. 1938
Theatre Arts Monthly, 22:371, May 1938
Time, 31:34, 14 Mar. 1938

TOM DULACK

Solomon's Child, 1982
    New York, 15:53, 19 Apr. 1982
    Time, 119:85, 19 Apr. 1982

WILLIAM DUNLAP

General

Leary, L. G., "The Education of William Dunlap," pp. 208-28 in Leary's *Soundings*
Martin, J., "William Dunlap: The Documentary Vision," pp. 170-93 in *Theater und Drama in Amerika*, ed. E. Lohner and R. Haas
Meserve, W. J., *An Emerging Entertainment*, pp. 102-15
Meserve, W. J., *An Outline History of American Drama*, pp. 23-30
Vaughn, J. A., *Early American Dramatists*, pp. 38-52

André, 1798
    Shillingsburg, M. J., "The West Point Treason in American Drama, 1798-1891," *Educational Theatre Journal*, 30:73-89, Mar. 1978

The Glory of Columbia—Her Yeomanry! (a revision of *André*, which see), 1803

A Trip to Niagara; or, Travellers in America, 1828
    Herron, I. H., *The Small Town in American Drama*, pp. 56-58

PHILIP DUNNING
SEE
GEORGE ABBOTT and PHILIP DUNNING

TOM DUPREE
SEE
JOHN MAXWELL and TOM DUPREE

CHRISTOPHER DURANG

General

Brustein, R., "The Crack in the Chimney: Reflections on Contemporary American Playwriting," *Theater*, 9, ii:21-29, 1978

The Actor's Nightmare, 1981
    New Yorker, 57:66, 2 Nov. 1981
    Time, 118:119, 9 Nov. 1981

Beyond Therapy, 1981
    After Dark, 13:66, Mar. 1981
    New York, 14:40, 19 Jan. 1981
    New York, 15:62, 7 June 1982
    New Yorker, 56:91, 19 Jan. 1981
    New Yorker, 58:112, 7 June 1982

Newsweek, 99:63, 7 June 1982
Time, 119:70, 7 June 1982

A History of the American Film, 1976
    After Dark, 11:78, June 1978
    After Dark, 13:67, May 1980
    Educational Theatre Journal, 29:415-16, 1977
    Horizon, 21:25-31, Mar. 1978
    Nation, 226:443, 15 Apr. 1978
    New Republic, 178:25, 22 Apr. 1978
    New York, 11:100, 17 Apr. 1978
    New Yorker, 54:91-92, 10 Apr. 1978
    Newsweek, 91:63, 10 Apr. 1978
    Saturday Review, 5:42, 27 May 1978

Das Lusitania Songspiel, 1976
    New Yorker, 55:96, 21 Jan. 1980

The Nature and Purpose of the Universe, 1971
    After Dark, 12:26, May 1971

Sister Mary Ignatius Explains It All for You, 1979
    After Dark, 14:26, Jan./Feb. 1982
    America, 145:417-18, 26 Dec. 1981
    Commonweal, 109:50-51, 29 Jan. 1982
    Los Angeles, 27:340+, Nov. 1982
    Nation, 233:649-50, 12 Dec. 1981
    New Republic, 185:24-25, 9 Dec. 1981
    New York, 15:40-43, 15 Mar. 1982
    New Yorker, 55:72-73, 24 Dec. 1979
    New Yorker, 57:66, 2 Nov. 1981
    Newsweek, 98:101, 9 Nov. 1981
    Time, 118:119, 9 Nov. 1981
    Time, 119:77, 12 Apr. 1982
    U S Catholic, 47:40, Jan. 1982

CHRISTOPHER DURANG and ALBERT INNAURATO

The Idiots Karamazov, 1974
    Texas Monthly, 7:168+, May 1979

RICHARD EBERHART

General

Cohn, R., *Dialogue in American Drama*, pp. 270-76

Visionary Farms, 1955
    Eberhart, R., "Tragedy as Limitation: Comedy as Control and Resolution,"
        Tulane Drama Review, 6:3-14, June 1962
    Gerstenberger, D., "Three Verse Playwrights and the American Fifties," pp.
        117-28 in *Modern American Drama*, ed. W. E. Taylor

GUS EDWARDS

Black Body Blues, 1978
 Encore, 7:30, 6 Mar. 1978
 New York, 11:74-75, 13 Feb. 1978
 New Yorker, 53:66, 6 Feb. 1978

The Offering, 1977
 After Dark, 10:26, Feb. 1978
 Encore, 7:35, 16 Jan. 1978
 New Leader, 61:29, 2 Jan. 1978

Old Phantoms, 1979
 New Yorker, 55:100, 19 Feb. 1979

Weep Not for Me, 1981
 Nation, 232:283-84, 7 Mar. 1981
 New Yorker, 56:59-60, 16 Feb. 1981

DEBORAH EISENBERG

Pastorale, 1982
 New Republic, 186:25, 19 May 1982
 New York, 15:83-84, 26 Apr. 1982
 New Yorker, 58:151, 19 Apr. 1982
 Newsweek, 99:102, 19 Apr. 1982

MARK EISMAN

Sightlines, 1979
 New Yorker, 55:86, 14 May 1979

LONNE ELDER III

Ceremonies in Dark Old Men, 1965 (revised 1969)
 Greenfield, T. A., *Work and the Work Ethic in American Drama 1920-1970*,
  pp. 137-41
 Fontenot, C. J., "Mythic Patterns in *River Niger* and *Ceremonies in Dark Old*
  Men," *MELUS*, 7, i:41-49, 1980

BILL ELVERMAN

Particular Friendships, 1981
 New York, 14:87-88, 12 Oct. 1981

JOHN EMERSON
SEE
ANITA LOOS and JOHN EMERSON

GILBERT EMERY
(pseud. of Emery Pottle)

The Hero, 1921
 Herron, I. H., *The Small Town in American Drama*, pp. 262-63

THOMAS DUNN ENGLISH

The Mormons; or, Life at Salt Lake City, 1858
    Herron, I. H., *The Small Town in American Drama*, pp. 120-22

RICHARD ENGQUIST
SEE
MICHAEL STEWART, MARK BRAMBLE, DOUG KATSAROS,
and RICHARD ENGQUIST

DAVID EVERETT

General

Meserve, W. J., *An Emerging Entertainment*, pp. 156-57

TOM EYEN

General

Marranca, B. G., "Tom Eyen," pp. 227-38 in Marranca and G. Dasgupta's *American Playwrights*
Wilson, L., "Meet Tom Eyen, Tom Eyen," *Horizon*, 22:43, July 1979

The Neon Woman, 1978
    After Dark, 10:79, Apr. 1978

The White Whore (originally titled *The White Whore and the Bit Player*), 1964
    After Dark, 14:30-31, June 1981

Who Killed My Bald Sister Sophie?, 1968
    Texas Monthly, 8:196, Sept. 1980

Why Hanna's Skirt Won't Stay Down, 1965
    Texas Monthly, 8:196, Sept. 1980

TOM EYEN and HENRY KRIEGER

Dreamgirls, 1981
    After Dark, 14:13-14, Mar. 1982
    America, 146:73, 30 Jan. 1982
    Dance Magazine, 56:107, Mar. 1982
    Ebony, 37:90-92 + , May 1982
    Essence, 13:15 + , May 1982
    Ms, 11:89-90 + , July/Aug. 1982
    New Leader, 65:21, 8 Feb. 1982
    New Republic, 186:25-27, 27 Jan. 1982
    New York, 14:43-45, 14 Dec. 1981
    New York, 15:52, 11 Jan. 1982
    New Yorker, 57:53, 4 Jan. 1982
    Newsweek, 99:65 + , 4 Jan. 1982
    People, 19:18-21, 10 Jan. 1983

Plays and Players, 343:35-36, Apr. 1982
Saturday Review, 8:38+, Dec. 1981
Saturday Review, 9:50, Feb. 1982
Theatre Crafts, 6:2-3+, May 1982
Time, 119:76, 4 Jan. 1982

JAMES FARRELL

In the Recovery Lounge, 1978
After Dark, 11:87, Mar. 1979
New Yorker, 54:52, 18 Dec. 1978

WILLIAM FAULKNER
SEE
RUTH FORD and WILLIAM FAULKNER

JULES FEIFFER

Grownups, 1981
After Dark, 14:14, Mar. 1982
Horizon, 24:52-55, Nov. 1981
New Leader, 65:21-22, 8 Feb. 1982
Nation, 234:123-24, 30 Jan. 1982
New York, 14:46-47, 20 July 1981
New York, 14:81, 21 Dec. 1981
New Yorker, 57:98, 21 Dec. 1981
Newsweek, 97:83, 29 June 1981
Newsweek, 98:77, 21 Dec. 1981
Saturday Review, 9:50-51, Feb. 1982
Time, 118:80, 21 Dec. 1981

Knock, Knock, 1976
Educational Theatre Journal, 30:123, 1978

EDNA FERBER

General

Gilbert, J. G., *Ferber*

SEE ALSO
GEORGE S. KAUFMAN and EDNA FERBER

LAWRENCE FERLINGHETTI

General

Cohn, R., *Dialogue in America Drama*, pp. 307-10
Skau, M., "Toward a Third Stream Theatre: Lawrence Ferlinghetti's Plays," *Modern Drama*, 22:29-38, 1979

ERNEST FERLITA

The Obelisk, 1982
  America, 147:inside cover, 10-17 July 1982

BARBARA FIELD

Marriage (adaptation of play by N. Gogol), 1978
  Plays and Players, 31:411-12, Oct. 1979
  Theatre Journal, 31:411-12, 1979
  Time, 112:126, 13 Nov. 1978

JOSEPH FIELDS and JEROME CHODOROV

The Ponder Heart (dramatization of novel by E. Welty), 1956
  Cornell, B. G., "Ambiguous Necessity: A Study of *The Ponder Heart*," pp.
    208-19 in *Eudora Welty*, ed. P. W. Prenshaw
  Herron, I. H., *The Small Town in American Drama*, pp. 451-53

HARVEY FIERSTEIN

The International Stud (see also *Torch Song Trilogy*), 1978
  After Dark, 11:81, June 1978
  After Dark, 11:81 + , Aug. 1978

Fugue in a Nursery (see also *Torch Song Trilogy*), 1980
  After Dark, 12:20, Mar. 1980

Torch Song Trilogy (three plays: *The International Stud, Fugue in a Nursery*, and
  Widows and Children First!, all of which see), 1981
    After Dark, 14:26-27, Jan./Feb. 1982
    After Dark, 14:13-14, Sept. 1982
    America, 146:320, 24 Apr. 1982
    New York, 14:110-11, 14 Dec. 1981
    New Yorker, 57:116, 1 Feb. 1982
    Newsweek, 99:63, 15 Mar. 1982
    Plays and Players, 344:30, May 1982
    Saturday Review, 9:46-47, Mar. 1982
    Time, 119:70, 22 Feb. 1982

Widows and Children First! (see also *Torch Song Trilogy*), 1979
  After Dark, 12:19, Feb. 1980

ROBERT FINCH

General

Herron, I. H., *The Small Town in American Drama*, pp. 161-64

STUART FINKELSTEIN
SEE
KENNETH FORD and STUART FINKELSTEIN

WILLIAM FINN

March of the Falsettos, 1981
    After Dark, 14:73, June 1981
    After Dark, 14:26-27, Jan./Feb. 1982
    New York, 14:59-60, 27 Apr. 1981
    New York, 14:31-33, 8 June 1981
    New Yorker, 57:144-45, 18 May 1981
    Time, 118:72, 3 Aug. 1981

CLYDE FITCH

General

Bettisworth, D. L., "The Last Plays of Clyde Fitch: Some New Evidence," *Educational Theatre Journal*, 29:569-70, 1977
Meserve, W. J., *An Outline History of American Drama*, pp. 155-59, 189

The City, 1909
    Greenfield, T. A., *Work and the Work Ethic in American Drama 1920-1970*, pp. 31-33
    Nannes, C. H., *Politics in the American Drama*, pp. 55-57

CLYDE FITCH and WILLIS STEELL

Wolfville: A Drama of the South West (dramatization of stories and sketches by A. H. Lewis), 1905
    Herron, I. H., *The Small Town in American Drama*, pp. 157-59

CLYDE FITCH and EDITH WHARTON

The House of Mirth (dramatization of Wharton's novel), 1906
    Loney, G., ed., *The House of Mirth*

SHELLEY FITZE

Daughters of Heaven, 1982
    Texas Monthly, 10:150, July 1982

F. SCOTT FITZGERALD

The Vegetable; or, From President to Postman, 1929
    Cohn, R., *Dialogue in American Drama*, pp. 182-83
    Bookman, 56:57-58, Sept. 1923
    Dramatist, 14:1183-84, Oct. 1923
    Life (New York), 93:24, 3 May 1929

LANNY FLAHERTY

Showdown at the Adobe Motel, 1981
Newsweek, 97:79, 23 Feb. 1981

ROBERT L. FLYNN

As I Lay Dying (dramatization of novel by W. Faulkner; later revised as *Journey to Jefferson*), 1960
Herron, I. H., *The Small Town in American Drama*, pp. 386-88

HORTON FOOTE

The Chase, 1952
Commonweal, 56:116, 9 May 1952
Nation, 174:437, 3 May 1952
New Yorker, 28:67, 26 Apr. 1952
Newsweek, 39:57, 28 Apr. 1952
Saturday Review, 35:30, 3 May 1952
Theatre Arts, 36:76, June 1952
Time, 59:59, 28 Apr. 1952

Traveling Lady, 1954
America, 92:194, 13 Nov. 1954
Catholic World, 180:225-26, Dec. 1954
Commonweal, 61:250, 3 Dec. 1954
Nation, 179:428, 13 Nov. 1954
New Yorker, 30:84, 6 Nov. 1954
Newsweek, 44:60, 8 Nov. 1954
Saturday Review, 37:26, 13 Nov. 1954
Theatre Arts, 39:14, 21+, Jan. 1955
Time, 64:56, 8 Nov. 1954

The Trip to Bountiful, 1953
America, 90:278, 5 Dec. 1953
Catholic World, 178:308, Jan. 1954
Commonweal, 59:257, 11 Dec. 1953
Nation, 177:433, 21 Nov. 1953
New Republic, 129:21, 30 Nov. 1953
New Yorker, 29:73-74+, 14 Nov. 1953
Newsweek, 42:61, 16 Nov. 1953
Saturday Review, 36:48+, 21 Nov. 1953
Saturday Review, 36:46, 12 Dec. 1953
Theatre Arts, 38:23, Jan. 1954
Time, 62:90+, 16 Nov. 1953

KENNETH FORD and STUART FINKELSTEIN

The Snow Queen (dramatization of story by H. C. Andersen), 1979
Texas Monthly, 7:152, July 1979

RUTH FORD and WILLIAM FAULKNER

Requiem for a Nun (dramatization of Faulkner's novel), 1957
Herron, I. H., *The Small Town in American Drama*, pp. 381-83
Time, 120:71, 16 Aug. 1982

RICHARD FOREMAN

General

Anfiero, R., "Intervista con Richard Foreman: 'Non apprezzo gli attori profession-isti," *Ridotto*, 12:7-8, 1979
Davy, K., *Richard Foreman and the Ontological-Hysteric Theatre*
Davy, K., "Richard Foreman's Ontological-Hysteric Theatre: The Influence of Gertrude Stein," *Twentieth Century Literature*, 24:108-26, 1978
Davy, K., ed., *Richard Foreman*
Foreman, R., "How I Write My (Self:Plays)," *The Drama Review*, 21,iv:5-24, 1977
Greenblatt, K. L., "La Cruauté et le théâtre: Comparaison entre les théâtres de Richard Foreman et Antonin Artaud," *Romanica*, 15:19-31, 1978-79
Kauffmann, S., "Ontological-Hysteric Theater," pp. 35-39 in Kauffmann's *Persons of the Drama*
Kirby, M., "Richard Foreman's Ontological-Hysteric Theatre," pp. 155-80 in *The New Theatre*, ed. Kirby
Leverett, J., "Old Forms Enter the New American Theater: Shepard, Foreman, Kirby, and Ludlam," pp. 107-22 in *Melodrama*, guest ed. D. C. Gerould
Leverett, J., "Richard Foreman and Some Uses of Cinema," *Theater*, 9, ii:10-14, 1978
Mango, L., "Richard Foreman nel giardino dei bersagli," *Il Ponte*, 37,iii-iv:349-55, 31 Mar.-30 Apr. 1981

Book of Splendors: Part II (Book of Levers) Action at a Distance: A Chamber Piece, 1977
Theatre Journal, 34:257-58, 1982

Boulevard de Paris (I've Got the Shakes), 1977
New Republic, 178:38-39, 25 Feb. 1978

Don Juan (adaptation of Molière's play), 1981
After Dark, 14:15-16, Nov. 1981
Newsweek, 97:81+, 29 June 1981
Theatre Journal, 33:531-32, 1981
Time, 118:74, 27 July 1981

Particle Theory, 1973
Falk, F. A., "Physics and the Theatre: Richard Foreman's *Particle Theory*," *Educational Theatre Journal*, 29:395-404, 1977

Penguin Touquet, 1980
Harris, D. A., "Richard Foreman's *Penguin Touquet*," *The Drama Review*, 25:105-08, Mar. 1981

MARÍA IRENE FORNÉS

General

Abramson, D., M. I. Fornés, C. Schneemann, F. Falk, B. Marranca, and R. C. Lamont, "Women in the Theatre," *Centerpoint*, 3,xi(3-4):31-37, Fall-Spring 1980

Fornés, M. I., " 'I write these messages that come,' " *The Drama Review*, 21, iv:25-40, 1977

Marranca, B. G., "María Irene Fornés," pp. 53-63 in Marranca and G. Dasgupta's *American Playwrights*

Eyes of the Harem, 1979
> *New Yorker*, 55:131, 7 May 1979

Fefu and Her Friends, 1977
> *After Dark*, 10:83-84, Mar. 1978
> *Harper's*, 256:83, May 1978
> *Ms*, 6:28+, June 1978
> *Nation*, 226:154, 11 Feb. 1978
> *New Republic*, 178:38, 25 Feb. 1978
> *New Yorker*, 53:46, 23 Jan. 1978
> *Theatre Journal*, 32:266-67, 1980

GEORGE FORREST

SEE
LUTHER DAVIS, ROBERT WRIGHT, GEORGE FORREST, and ALEXANDER BORODIN
AND
CHARLES LEDERER, LUTHER DAVIS, ROBERT WRIGHT, GEORGE FOREST, and ALEXANDER BORODIN

THOMAS FORREST

The Disappointment; or, The Force of Credulity, 1767
> Meserve, W. J., *An Emerging Entertainment*, pp. 51-53
> Meserve, W. J., *An Outline History of American Drama*, p. 11

PAUL FOSTER

General

Marranca, B. G., "Paul Foster," pp. 113-20 in Marranca and G. Dasgupta's *American Playwrights*

Elizabeth I, 1972
> *After Dark*, 12:20, 23+, Sept. 1979
> *Texas Monthly*, 8:161, Mar. 1980
> *Theatre Journal*, 32, iv:528, Dec. 1980

MARTIN FOX

The Office Murders, 1979

New York, 12:114, 1 Oct. 1979
New Yorker, 55:114, 3 Dec. 1979

TERRY CURTIS FOX

Cops, 1978
Patrick, R., "Gay Analysis," *The Drama Review*, 22, iii:67-72, 1978
Schechner, R., "The Performance Group's Production of *Cops*," *The Drama Review*, 22, iii:55-66, 1978
After Dark, 11:84 + , June 1978
New West, 4:154, 19 Nov. 1979

Justice, 1979
After Dark, 12:20, Feb. 1980

AARON FRANKEL
SEE
ROBERT PENN WARREN and AARON FRANKEL

J. E. FRANKLIN

General

Miller, J.-M. A., "Images of Black Women in Plays by Black Playwrights," *College Language Association Journal*, 20:494-507, 1977

Black Girl, 1971
Curb, R. K., " 'Goin' through Changes': Mother-Daughter Confrontations in Three Recent Plays by Young Black Women," *Kentucky Folklore Record*, 25:96-102, 1979

MARY E. WILKINS FREEMAN

Giles Corey, Yeoman, 1893
Herron, I. H., *The Small Town in American Drama*, pp. 20-24

DAVID FRENCH

Jitters, 1979
After Dark, 12:19, Feb. 1980
Maclean's 92:54, 5 Mar. 1979

Of the Fields, Lately, 1973
New York, 13:58-59, 9 June 1980
New Yorker, 56:112, 9 June 1980

One Crack Out, 1975
New Yorker, 53:72, 30 Jan. 1978

Riddle of the World, 1981
Maclean's, 94:61, 30 Nov. 1981

FLORIDA FRIEBUS
SEE
EVA Le GALLIENNE and FLORIDA FRIEBUS

EMANUEL FRIED

Drop Hammer, 1980
  After Dark, 12:21, Mar. 1980
  New West, 5:SC-27, 28 Jan. 1980

EVE FRIEDMAN

SEE
ISAAC BASHEVIS SINGER and EVE FRIEDMAN

KETTI FRINGS

Look Homeward, Angel (dramatization of novel by T. Wolfe), 1957
  Herron, I. H., *The Small Town in American Drama*, pp. 391-96

KETTI FRINGS, GARY GELD, and PETER UDELL

Angel (musical version of Frings's dramatization of T. Wolfe's novel *Look Homeward, Angel*), 1978
  After Dark, 11:114, May 1978
  New Yorker, 54:91, 22 May 1978

ROBERT FROST

General

Cohn, R., *Dialogue in American Drama*, pp. 229-30

ELINORE FUCHS

Year One of the Empire, 1980
  Conlin, K., "The Lady Doth Protest: Women Fuse Politics, Protest, and Play-writing," *Theatre Southwest*, 6, iii:13-17, Oct. 1980

CHARLES FULLER

A Soldier's Play, 1981
  America, 146:343, 1 May 1982
  Hudson Review, 35:439-46, Autumn 1982
  Los Angeles, 27:254 +, Oct. 1982
  Nation, 234:90, 23 Jan. 1982
  New Leader, 65:21-22, 12-26 July 1982
  New York, 14:159, 7 Dec. 1981
  New Yorker, 57:110, 113, 7 Dec. 1981
  Newsweek, 98:77, 21 Dec. 1981
  People, 17:85-86, 20 June 1982

Plays and Players, 344:31, May 1982
Time, 119:87, 18 Jan. 1982

Zooman and the Sign, 1980
   Commonweal, 108:178-79, 27 Mar. 1981
   Georgia Review, 35:600-01, Fall 1981
   New Yorker, 56:55-56, 22 Dec. 1980

GEORGE FURTH

The Supporting Cast, 1981
   After Dark, 14:10+, Nov. 1981
   Los Angeles, 27:277, Apr. 1982
   New York, 14:68, 24 Aug. 1981
   New Yorker, 57:79, 17 Aug. 1981
   Time, 118:76, 17 Aug. 1981

GEORGE FURTH and STEPHEN SONDHEIM

Company (musical version of some short plays by Furth), 1970
   Berkowitz, G., "The Metaphor of Paradox in Sondheim's *Company*," *West
      Virginia University Philological Papers*, 25:94-100, 1979
   Los Angeles, 26:312+, May 1981

Merrily We Roll Along (musical version of play by M. Hart and G. S. Kaufman),
   1981
   Sacheli, R., "Sondheim's 'Merrily' Rolls from Broadway to Campus," *Theatre
      News*, 14:5-6, Summer 1982
   After Dark, 14:18+, Mar. 1982
   New York, 14:87-88, 30 Nov. 1981
   New Yorker, 57:110, 7 Dec. 1981
   Newsweek, 98:109, 30 Nov. 1981
   Time, 118:90, 30 Nov. 1981

FRANK GAGLIANO

General

Gagliano, F., "The American Theatre Today: From the Eyes of a Practicing Playwright" (Part One: "The Market"), *Theatre News*, 14,i:1, 4, 6, 8, Jan. 1982;
   (Part Two: "Playwriting Today"), *Theatre News*, 14, ii:1, 10, 12, Feb. 1982

ZONA GALE

General

Herron, I. H., *The Small Town in American Drama*, pp. 202-05
Sutherland, C., "American Women Playwrights as Mediators of the 'Woman Problem,' " *Modern Drama*, 21:319-36, 1978

Faint Perfume, 1932
   Herron, I. H., *The Small Town in American Drama*, pp. 244-45

Miss Lulu Bett, 1920
 Herron, I. H., *The Small Town in American Drama*, pp. 241-43

Mister Pitt (dramatization of her novel *Birth*), 1924
 Herron, I. H., *The Small Town in American Drama*, pp. 243-44

SAM GALLU

Give 'Em Hell Harry, 1975
 Bordinat, P., "The One-Person Play: A Form of Contemporary Dramatic Biography," *Midwest Quarterly*, 21:231-41, 1980

LARRY GAMELL, JR.

After the Gun Goes Off, 1982
 Drama-Logue, 13, xxxvi:8, 9-15 Sept. 1982

ROBERT E. GARD
SEE
A. M. DRUMMOND and ROBERT E. GARD

HERB GARDNER

The Goodbye People, 1968
 Los Angeles, 24:234+, Feb. 1979
 New West, 4:81, 29 Jan. 1979
 New Yorker, 55:84, 14 May 1979

A Thousand Clowns, 1962
 Greenfield, T. A., *Work and the Work Ethic in American Drama 1920-1970*, p.
 146

ELAN GARONZIK

Scenes and Revelations, 1981
 New Yorker, 57:51, 6 July 1981

BARBARA GARSON

MacBird!, 1966
 Conlin, K., "The Lady Doth Protest: Women Fuse Politics, Protest, and Play-
 writing," *Theatre Southwest*, 6, iii:13-17, Oct. 1980
 Platz, N. H., "Barbara Garson: *MacBird!*," pp. 106-19 in *Das amerikanische
 Drama der Gegenwart*, ed. H. Grabes

JOHN GAY

Diversions and Delights, 1978
 After Dark, 11:78+, June 1978
 Educational Theatre Journal, 30:264, 1978

Esquire, 89:58-60, 25 Apr. 1978
New York, 11:73, 1 May 1978
New Yorker, 54:93-94, 24 Apr. 1978
Newsweek, 91:108+, 24 Apr. 1978
Time, 111:81, 24 Apr. 1978

VIRGIL GEDDES

General

Herron, I. H., *The Small Town in American Drama*, pp. 168-70

HANAY GEIOGAMAH

General

Huntsman, J., "Introduction" to Geiogamah's *New Native American Drama*

Body Indian, 1972
    Theatre Arts, 13, iv:15, Apr. 1981

Foghorn, 1973
    Theatre Arts, 13, iv:15, Apr. 1981

49, 1975
    Theatre Arts, 13, iv:15, Apr. 1981

LARRY GELBART

The Sly Fox (adaptation of B. Jonson's *Volpone*), 1976
    Los Angeles, 23:214+, Aug. 1978
    New West, 3:87, 14 Aug. 1978

JACK GELBER

General

Bermel, A., "Jack Gelber Talks about Surviving in the Theater," *Theater*, 9, ii:46-58, 1978
Marranca, B. G., "Jack Gelber," pp. 135-42 in Marranca and G. Dasgupta's *American Playwrights*
Meserve, W. J., *An Outline History of American Drama*, pp. 357-58
Wellwarth, G., *The Theater of Protest and Paradox*, rev. ed., pp. 349-51

The Apple, 1961
    Kostelanetz, R., *The Theatre of Mixed Means*, pp. 169-71

The Connection, 1959
    Dukore, B. F., "Off Broadway and the New Realism," pp. 163-74 in *Modern American Drama*, ed. W. E. Taylor
    Innes, C., "The Salesman on the Stage: A Study in the Social Influence of Drama," *English Studies in Canada*, 3:336-50, 1977
    Sato, S., "The Fourth Wall in an Age of Alienation: *The Zoo Story* and *The*

Connection," pp. 161-66 in *American Literature in the 1950's* (American Literature Society of Japan 1976 Annual Report)
Schubert, K., "Jack Gelber: *The Connection,"* pp. 91-105 in *Das amerikanische Drama der Gegenwart,* ed. H. Grabes
Vos, N., *The Great Pendulum of Becoming,* pp. 61-64
New Yorker, 56:174-75, 10 Nov. 1980

GARY GELD
SEE
KETTI FRINGS, GARY GELD, and PETER UDELL

GEORGE GERSHWIN
SEE
DOROTHY HEYWARD, DUBOSE HEYWARD, GEORGE GERSHWIN, and IRA GERSHWIN
AND
GEORGE S. KAUFMAN, MORRIE RYSKIND, GEORGE GERSHWIN, and IRA GERSHWIN

IRA GERSHWIN
SEE
DOROTHY HEYWARD, DUBOSE HEYWARD, GEORGE GERSHWIN, and IRA GERSHWIN
AND
MOSS HART, KURT WEILL, and IRA GERSHWIN,
AND
GEORGE S. KAUFMAN, MORRIE RYSKIND, GEORGE GERSHWIN, and IRA GERSHWIN

VICTOR GIALANELLA

Frankenstein (dramatization of M. W. Shelley's novel), 1981
  After Dark, 13:28, Mar. 1981
  New Yorker, 56:90, 19 Jan. 1981
  Saturday Review, 6:51, 9 June 1979
  Theatre Crafts, 15:30-34 + , June/July 1981

ANTHONY GIARDINA

Scenes from La Vie de Bohème, 1982
  New Yorker, 58:74, 31 May 1982

WILLIAM GIBSON

General

Clark, T., "Portrait of a Playwright: After the Miracle," *Yankee,* 46:66-69, 114, 117-20, 123, May 1982

Golda, 1977
  After Dark, 10:80-81, Jan. 1978

Hudson Review, 31:150-51, Spring 1978

Monday after the Miracle, 1982
  Christian Century, 99:864 + , 18-25 Aug. 1982
  New York, 16:91-92, 27 Dec. 1982/3 Jan. 1983
  New Yorker, 58:58 + , 27 Dec. 1982
  Newsweek, 100:62, 27 Dec. 1982
  Theatre Journal, 34, iv: 542-43, Dec. 1982
  Time, 119:79, 14 June 1982

WILLIAM GILLETTE

Secret Service, 1895
  Meserve, W. J., *An Outline History of American Drama*, pp. 139-40

WILLIAM GILLETTE and ARTHUR CONAN DOYLE

Sherlock Holmes (dramatization of story by Doyle), 1899
  LaBorde, Jr., C. B., "Sherlock Holmes on the Stage: William Gillette," *Baker Street Journal*, 26:170-78, 1976
  Lauterbach, E. "The Straitjacket of Success: Further Notes on Gillette's 'Sherlock Holmes,' " *Baker Street Journal*, 30:198-200, 1980
  Schuttler, G. W., "William Gillette and *Sherlock Holmes*," *Journal of Popular Culture*, 15:31-41, Spring 1982

FRANK GILROY

The Housekeeper (see also *Last Licks*), 1982
  Plays and Players, 343:32-33, Apr. 1982

Last Licks (prod. in England as *The Housekeeper*), 1979
  After Dark, 12:18, Feb. 1980
  New Yorker, 55:108, 3 Dec. 1979

The Subject Was Roses, 1964
  Gottfried, M., *A Theater Divided*, pp. 263-64

Who'll Save the Plowboy?, 1962
  After Dark, 10:79, Mar. 1978

ALLEN GINSBERG

Kaddish, 1972
  Breslin, J., "Allen Ginsburg: The Origins of 'Howl' and 'Kaddish,' " *Iowa Review*, 8, ii:82-108, 1977

PAUL GIOVANNI

The Crucifer of Blood (based on characters created by A. C. Doyle), 1978
  After Dark, 11:96, Dec. 1978

After Dark, 12:27, Apr. 1980
America, 139:314, 4 Nov. 1978
Encore, 7:36, 6 Nov. 1978
Los Angeles, 26:216+, Jan. 1981
New Leader, 61:22, 23 Oct. 1978
New Republic, 79:32, 16 Dec. 1978
New York, 11:131, 16 Oct. 1978
New Yorker, 54:126, 9 Oct. 1978
Newsweek, 92:121, 9 Oct. 1978
Saturday Review, 5:45, Dec. 1978
Time, 112:130, 16 Oct. 1978

ARTHUR GIRON

Edith Stein, 1979
    After Dark, 12:20, Feb. 1980

Innocent Pleasures, 1978
    After Dark, 11:83-84, June 1978

SUSAN GLASPELL

General

Bach, G., "Susan Glaspell (1876-1948): A Bibliography of Dramatic Criticism,"
    Great Lakes Review, 3, ii:1-34, 1977
Bach, G., "Susan Glaspell: Provincetown Playwright," *Great Lakes Review*, 4, ii:31-
    43, 1978
Bach, G., *Susan Glaspell und die Provincetown Players*
Bigsby, C. W. E., *A Critical Introduction to Twentieth-Century American Drama*,
    Vol. I, pp. 25-35
Gould, J., "Susan Glaspell and the Provincetown Players," pp. 26-49 in Gould's
    Modern American Playwrights
Meserve, W. J., *An Outline History of American Drama*, pp. 235-36
Noe, M., "Region as Metaphor in the Plays of Susan Glaspell," *Western Illinois
    Regional Studies*, 4, i:77-85, Spring 1981
Noe, M., " 'A Romantic and Miraculous City' Shapes Three Midwestern Writers,"
    Western Illinois Regional Studies, 1:176-98, 1978
Noe, M., "Susan Glaspell's Analysis of the Midwestern Character," *Books at Iowa*,
    27:3-14, 1977
Sutherland, C., "American Women Playwrights as Mediators of the 'Woman Prob-
    lem,' " *Modern Drama*, 21:319-36, 1978

Alison's House, 1920
    Herron, I. H., *The Small Town in American Drama*, pp. 239-40

Trifles, 1916
    Abramson, D., M. I. Fornés, C. Schneemann, F. Falk, B. Marranca, and R. C.
    Lamont, "Women in the Theatre," *Centerpoint*, 3, xi (3-4):31-37, Fall-Spring
    1980

The Verge, 1921

Waterman, A., "Susan Glaspell's *The Verge*: An Experiment in Feminism," *Great Lakes Review*, 6, i:17-23, 1979

JOANNA M. GLASS

Artichoke, 1979
  Los Angeles, 27:347+, Dec. 1982
  Nation, 228:284-85, 17 Mar. 1979
  New York, 12:95-96, 26 Mar. 1979
  New Yorker, 55:92, 94, 5 Mar. 1979
  Texas Monthly, 7:160, Apr. 1979

To Grandmother's House We Go, 1980
  After Dark, 13:81, May 1981
  New Leader, 64:19-20, 9 Feb. 1981
  New York, 14:43, 2 Feb. 1981
  New Yorker, 56:61, 26 Jan. 1981
  Texas Monthly, 8:212, 214, Dec. 1980

BENJAMIN GLAZER
SEE
OSCAR HAMMERSTEIN II, BENJAMIN GLAZER, and RICHARD RODGERS
AND
ERNEST HEMINGWAY and BENJAMIN GLAZER

THOMAS GODFREY

The Prince of Parthia, 1767
  Meserve, W. J., *An Emerging Entertainment*, pp. 47-51
  Meserve, W. J., *An Outline History of American Drama*, pp. 9-10
  Shuffelton, F., "The Voice of History: Thomas Godfrey's *Prince of Parthia* and Revolutionary America," *Early American Literature*, 13:12-23, 1978
  Vaughn, J. A., *Early American Dramatists*, pp. 12-18
  Winton, C., "The Theater and Drama," pp. 90-91 in *American Literature, 1764-1789*, ed. E. Emerson

MICHAEL GOLD

(pseud. of Itzok Isaac Granich;
also known as Irwin Granich)

General

Bigsby, C. W. E., *A Critical Introduction to Twentieth-Century American Drama*, Vol. I, pp. 189-97
Klein, M., "Itzok Granich and Michael Gold," pp. 231-48 in Klein's *Foreigners*

MICHAEL GOLD and MICHAEL BLANKFORT

Battle Hymn, 1936
  Himelstein, M. Y., *Drama Was a Weapon*, pp. 93-96

DICK GOLDBERG

Family Business, 1978
    After Dark, 11:79, June 1978
    After Dark, 13:66-67, Feb. 1981
    New Yorker, 54:96, 24 Apr. 1978

ROSE LEIMAN GOLDEMBERG

Letters Home (dramatization of S. Plath's letters to her mother), 1979
    New York, 12:88, 5 Nov. 1979
    New Yorker, 55:81, 5 Nov. 1979

I. J. GOLDEN

Precedent, 1931
    Smiley, S., *The Drama of Attack*, pp. 51, 152-54

BILLY GOLDENBERG
SEE
JEROME KASS, ALAN BERGMAN,
MARILYN BERGMAN, and BILLY GOLDENBERG

GEORGE GONNEAU and NORMAN ROSE

Monsieur Amilcar (adaptation of play by Y. Jamiaque), 1980
    After Dark, 12:24, Apr. 1980
    New York, 13:86-87, 18 Feb. 1980
    New Yorker, 55:104+ , 18 Feb. 1980

PAUL GOODMAN

General

Cohn, R., *Dialogue in American Drama*, pp. 265-70

Jonah, 1966
    Gottfried, M., *A Theater Divided*, pp. 73-74
    Commonweal, 86:699, 18 Mar. 1966
    New Yorker, 42:71-72, 26 Feb. 1966

FRANCES GOODRICH and ALBERT HACKETT

The Diary of Anne Frank (dramatization of A. Frank's *Diary*), 1955
    After Dark, 11:83-84, Mar. 1979
    America, 140:36, 20 Jan. 1979
    New Yorker, 54:88-89, 15 Jan. 1979
    Saturday Review, 6:48, 3 Mar. 1979
    Time, 113:70, 8 Jan. 1979

CHARLES GORDON
SEE
OYAMO

STUART GORDON and BURY ST. EDMUND
(Bury St. Edmund: pseud. of Lenny Kleinfeld)

Warp!, 1972
   After Dark, 13:63, Sept. 1980
   Chicago, 29:96+, July 1980

CHARLES GORDONE

General

Del Vecchio, T., "Irma Tucker and the Pulitzer Prize Playwright," *Phantasm*, 20:n.p.,
   1979

DEAN GOSS

God Bless Mommy, Daddy & Blue Cross, 1979
   Texas Monthly, 7:156, July 1979

ED GRACZYK

Come Back to the 5 & Dime, Jimmy Dean, Jimmy Dean, 1982
   New York, 15:26-29+, 1 Feb. 1982
   New York, 15:74-75, 1 Mar. 1982
   New Yorker, 58:94, 1 Mar. 1982
   Newsweek, 99:73, 1 Mar. 1982
   Time, 119:78, 1 Mar. 1982

GRUBB GRAEBNER

Baseball Wives, 1982
   New Yorker, 58:160, 18 Oct. 1982

Loney's 66, 1980
   After Dark, 13:65, May 1980

Qué Ubo?, 1980
   After Dark, 13:65, May 1980

PERCY GRANGER

Eminent Domain, 1982
   New Leader, 65:19-20, 19 Apr. 1982
   New York, 15:72, 12 Apr. 1982
   New Yorker, 58:125, 12 Apr. 1982
   Saturday Review, 9:60-61, June 1982

Vivien, 1981

After Dark, 13:80, May 1981
New Yorker, 57:65-66, 16 Mar. 1981

ITZOK ISAAC GRANICH
SEE
MICHAEL GOLD

BEN Z. GRANT
SEE
LARRY L. KING and BEN Z. GRANT

AMLIN GRAY

How I Got That Story, 1980
   America, 146:343, 1 May 1982
   Commonweal, 109:243-44, 23 Apr. 1982
   New York, 15:82, 8 Mar. 1982
   New Yorker, 56:56, 22 Dec. 1980
   New Yorker, 58:96, 1 Mar. 1982
   Newsweek, 99:73-74, 1 Mar. 1982
   Plays and Players, 344:30-31, May 1982
   Saturday Review, 9:49-50, May 1982
   Texas Monthly, 8:177, June 1980
   Time, 116:76, 22 Dec. 1980

JOHN GRAY

General

Anderson, I., "Coming Home from Billy Bishop's War," *Maclean's*, 94:18 + , 16
   Mar. 1981

Billy Bishop Goes to War, 1978
   After Dark, 13:69, May 1980
   Maclean's, 91:70-71, 4 Dec. 1978
   New Yorker, 56:112, 9 June 1980
   Newsweek, 95:106, 9 June 1980
   Theatre Journal, 32:267-68, 1980
   Time, 116:56, 4 Aug. 1980

Rock and Roll, 1981
   Maclean's, 94:62, 30 Mar. 1981

SPALDING GRAY, ELIZABETH LeCOMPTE, LIBBY HOWES,
JIM CLAYBURGH, and RON VAWTER

Rumstick Road (see also *Three Places in Rhode Island*), 1977
   Mehta, X., "Notes from the Avant-Garde," *Theatre Journal*, 31:5-9, 1979
   After Dark, 13:57, July 1980
   New Yorker, 56:105, 14 Apr. 1980

Three Places in Rhode Island (trilogy: *Sahonnet Point*, 1975; *Rumstick Road*, 1977; *Nyatt School*, 1978), 1979
  Bierman, J., *"Three Places in Rhode Island," The Drama Review*, 23, i:13-30, 1979
  Gray, S., "About *Three Places in Rhode Island," The Drama Review*, 23, i:31-42, 1979

ADOLPH GREEN
SEE
BETTY COMDEN and ADOLPH GREEN
AND
BETTY COMDEN, ADOLPH GREEN, and CY COLEMAN

PAUL GREEN

General

Meserve, W. J., *An Outline History of American Drama*, pp. 243-45, 247-48

The Enchanted Maze, 1935
  Greenfield, T. A., *Work and the Work Ethic in American Drama 1920-1970*, pp. 73-74

The House of Connelly, 1931
  Himelstein, M. Y., *Drama Was a Weapon*, pp. 156-57

Hymn to the Rising Sun, 1936
  Himelstein, M. Y., *Drama Was a Weapon*, pp. 43-44, *passim*
  Smiley, S., *The Drama of Attack*, pp. 110-11

The Lone Star, 1977
  Texas Monthly, 7:124, 127, Aug. 1979

Roll Sweet Chariot (originally titled *In the Valley*, 1928, and later *Potter's Field*, 1931), 1934
  Herron, I. H., *The Small Town in American Drama*, pp. 219-21

Texas, 1966
  Texas Monthly, 7:124, 127, Aug. 1979

PAUL GREEN and KURT WEILL

Johnny Johnson, 1936
  Herron, I. H., *The Small Town in American Drama*, p. 221
  Himelstein, M. Y., *Drama Was a Weapon*, pp. 173-74
  Smiley, S., *The Drama of Attack*, pp. 122-23, 181

PAUL GREEN and RICHARD WRIGHT

Native Son (dramatization of Wright's novel), 1941 (revised 1968)
  Himelstein, M. Y., *Drama Was a Weapon*, pp. 120-22

Stern, F. C., *"Native Son* as Play: A Reconsideration Based on a Revival,"
  MELUS, 8, i:55-61, Spring 1981
Drama, 131:27, Winter 1979

TOM GRIFFIN

Einstein and the Polar Bear, 1981
  After Dark, 14:12-13, Jan./Feb. 1982
  New York, 14:70, 9 Nov. 1981

The Taking Away of Willie, 1980
  Texas Monthly, 8:177, June 1980

LINDA GRIFFITHS

Maggie & Pierre, 1980
  After Dark, 13:59-60, June 1980
  Maclean's, 93:64, 9 June 1980
  Maclean's, 94:20+, 19 Oct. 1981
  New York, 14:86-87, 12 Oct. 1981
  New Yorker, 57:126, 5 Oct. 1981

ALAN GROSS

Lunching, 1978
  Nation, 227:155-56, 19 Aug. 1978

The Man in 605, 1979
  After Dark, 13:68-69, May 1980
  New Yorker, 56:100, 28 Apr. 1980

SUZANNE GROSSMAN

Number Our Days, 1982
  Los Angeles, 271:235+, Mar. 1982

JOHN GUARE

General

Cohn, R., "Camp, Cruelty, Colloquialism," pp. 281-303 in *Comic Relief*, ed. S. B. Cohen
Dasgupta, G., "John Guare," pp. 41-52 in Dasgupta and B. G. Marranca's *American Playwrights*
Wetzsteon, R., "The Coming of Age of John Guare," *New York*, 15:35-39, 22 Feb. 1982

Bosoms and Neglect, 1979
  After Dark, 12:27, Apr. 1980
  Maclean's, 93:46, 4 Aug. 1980
  New York, 12:77, 21 May 1979

New Yorker, 55:83-84, 14 May 1979
Newsweek, 93:85-86, 14 May 1979
Saturday Review, 6:40, 7 July 1979
Theatre Journal, 32:259-60, 1980

Gardenia, 1982
New Republic, 186:24-25, 19 May 1982
New York, 15:75-76, 10 May 1982
New Yorker, 58:148, 10 May 1982
Newsweek, 99:89, 10 May 1982

The House of Blue Leaves, 1971
Bernstein, S. J., *The Strands Entwined*, pp. 37-59

In Fireworks Lie Secret Codes, 1979
After Dark, 13:80, May 1981
New Yorker, 57:66, 16 Mar. 1981

Landscape of the Body, 1977
After Dark, 10:84, Jan. 1978

Lydie Breeze, 1982
Nation, 234:409-10, 3 Apr. 1982
New Republic, 18:26-27, 24 Mar. 1982
New York, 15:81, 8 Mar. 1982
New Yorker, 58:96+, 8 Mar. 1982
New Yorker, 58:33-35, 15 Mar. 1982
Newsweek, 99:84, 8 Mar. 1982
Time, 119:86, 8 Mar. 1982

Rich and Famous, 1974
Educational Theatre Journal, 30:123-24, 1978
Los Angeles, 27:380+, Aug. 1982

BILL GUNN

Rhinestone, 1982
New York, 15:153, 6 Dec. 1982

A. R. GURNEY, JR.

The Dining Room, 1982
Commonweal, 109:243-44, 23 Apr. 1982
New Republic, 186:25-28, 12 May 1982
New York, 15:81-82, 8 Mar. 1982
New Yorker, 58:94, 96, 1 Mar. 1982
Newsweek, 99:64, 15 Mar. 1982
Time, 119:79, 22 Mar. 1982

The Middle Ages, 1977

After Dark, 10:80, Apr. 1978
New Yorker, 58:165, 5 Apr. 1982

The Wayside Motor Inn, 1977
After Dark, 10:83, Jan. 1978

What I Did Last Summer, 1983
New York, 16:76, 14 Feb. 1983

Who Killed Richard Cory?, 1976
After Dark, 12:18, Dec. 1979
Los Angeles, 24:316, Nov. 1979

ALBERT HACKETT
SEE
FRANCES GOODRICH and ALBERT HACKETT

JONATHAN HADARY

Pushing Thirty, 1978
New York, 11:80+, 4 Sept. 1978

JEFFREY HADDOW
SEE
JOHN DRIVER and JEFFREY HADDOW

JAMES HAGAN

Mid-West, 1935
Himelstein, M. Y., *Drama Was a Weapon*, pp. 198-99
Commonweal, 23:356, 24 Jan. 1936
Literary Digest, 121:19, 18 Jan. 1936
Nation, 142:112, 22 Jan. 1936
Theatre Arts Monthly, 20:175-76, Mar. 1936

One Sunday Afternoon, 1933
Arts and Decoration, 38:58, Apr. 1933
Catholic World, 137:78, Apr. 1933
Commonweal, 17:160, 29 Mar. 1933
Nation, 136:272, 8 Mar. 1933
New Outlook, 161:47, Apr. 1933
Players Magazine, 9:25, May-June 1933
Stage, 10:28-29, Apr. 1933
Theatre Arts Monthly, 17:262-64, Apr. 1933
Vanity Fair, 40:60, May 1933

P. LEO HAID

Major John André, 1876
Shillingsburg, M. J., "The West Point Treason in American Drama, 1798-1891,"
Educational Theatre Journal, 30:73-89, 1978

OLIVER HAILEY

Father's Day, 1970
    After Dark, 11:116, May 1978
    After Dark, 12:18, 20, Sept. 1979
    Time, 114:65, 2 July 1979

I Can't Find It Anywhere, 1979
    Theatre Journal, 31:414, 1979

I Won't Dance, 1980
    After Dark, 14:64, July 1981
    New Yorker, 57:142-43, 18 May 1981

Red Rover, Red Rover, 1977
    Los Angeles, 24:280+, Apr. 1979

Who's Happy Now?, 1967
    Educational Theatre Journal, 29:260-62, 1977

ADRIAN HALL and RICHARD CUMMING

Uncle Tom's Cabin: A History (musical based, in part, upon H. B. Stowe's novel
    and upon various theatrical productions of it), 1977
    Theatre Journal, 32:262, May 1980

BOB HALL and DAVID RICHMOND

The Passion of Dracula (dramatization of novel by B. Stoker), 1978
    After Dark, 10:62-67, Mar. 1978
    Drama, 131:46, Winter 1979
    Plays and Players, 26:28, Nov. 1978

RICHARD HALL

The Love Match, 1977
    After Dark, 10:24, Feb. 1978

TREY HALL

The Darning Tree, 1979
    Texas Monthly, 8:135, Feb. 1980

MARTIN HALPERN

Total Recall, 1979
    After Dark, 11:87, Mar. 1979

RICHARD HAMBURGER

Memory of Whiteness, 1981
    After Dark, 13:29+, Mar. 1981

WILLIAM HAMILTON

Save Grand Central, 1978
   Nation, 230:411, 5 Apr. 1980
   New Yorker, 56:82 + , 17 Mar. 1980
   Time, 115:75-76, 17 Mar. 1980

OSCAR HAMMERSTEIN II

General

Fordin, H., *Getting to Know Him*

OSCAR HAMMERSTEIN II, BENJAMIN GLAZER, and RICHARD RODGERS

Carousel (musical version of F. Molnar's *Liliom*), 1945
   Educational Theatre Journal, 30:265, May 1978

OSCAR HAMMERSTEIN II and JEROME KERN

Show Boat (musical version of E. Ferber's novel), 1927
   Kreuger, M., *Show Boat*
   Los Angeles, 27:376 + , Aug. 1982

OSCAR HAMMERSTEIN II and RICHARD RODGERS

General

Gottfried, M., *A Theater Divided*, pp. 178-81

The King and I (musical version of M. Landon's novel *Anna and the King of Siam*), 1951
   Los Angeles, 24:278 + , Apr. 1979

Oklahoma! (musical version of L. Riggs's play *Green Grow the Lilacs*), 1943
   After Dark, 11:97, Dec. 1978
   After Dark, 12:16, Mar. 1980
   Drama, 136:57, Apr. 1980
   Drama, 139:34, 1st Quarter 1981
   Los Angeles, 24:249 + , June 1979
   New York, 13:69, 31 Dec. 1979
   New Yorker, 55:70 + , 24 Dec. 1979
   Newsweek, 94:56, 24 Dec. 1979
   Plays and Players, 27:35-36, Mar. 1980
   Sunset, 168:3-4, May 1982
   Time, 114:77, 24 Dec. 1979

LORRAINE HANSBERRY

General

Baldwin, J., "Lorraine Hansberry at the Summit," *Freedomways*, 19:269-72, 1979

Bennett, Jr., L. and M. G. Burroughs, "A Lorraine Hansberry Rap," *Freedomways*, 19:226-33, 1979

Bond, J. C., "Lorraine Hansberry: To Reclaim Her Legacy," *Freedomways*, 19:183-85, 1979

Carter, S. R., "Commitment amid Complexity: Lorraine Hansberry's Life in Action," *MELUS*, 7, iii:39-53, 1980

Carter, S. R., "The John Brown Theatre: Lorraine Hansberry's Cultural Views and Dramatic Goals," *Freedomways*, 19:186-91, 1979

Donohue, J. W., "Bench Marks," *America*, 140:30-33, 20 Jan. 1979

Elder III, L., "Lorraine Hansberry: Social Consciousness and the Will," *Freedomways*, 19:213-18, 1979

Giovanni, N., "An Emotional View of Lorraine Hansberry," *Freedomways*, 19:281-84, 1979

Gresham, J. H., "Lorraine Hansberry as Prose Stylist," *Freedomways*, 19:192-204, 1979

Haley, A., "The Once and Future Vision of Lorraine Hansberry," *Freedomways*, 19:277-80, 1979

Kaiser, E. and R. Nemiroff, comps., "A Lorraine Hansberry Bibliography," *Freedomways*, 19:285-304, 1979

Killens, J. O., "Lorraine Hansberry: On Time!," *Freedomways*, 19:273-76, 1979

Mayfield, J., "Lorraine Hansberry: A Woman for All Seasons," *Freedomways*, 19:263-68, 1979

Miller, J.-M. A., "Images of Black Women in Plays by Black Playwrights," *College Language Association Journal*, 20:494-507, 1977

Miller, J.-M. A., "Lorraine Hansberry: Feminist, Realist," *Theatre Arts*, 12, vii:2, Apr. 1980

Rich, A., "The Problem with Lorraine Hansberry," *Freedomways*, 19:247-55, 1979

Riley, C., "Lorraine Hansberry: A Melody in a Different Key," *Freedomways*, 19:205-12, 1979

Royals, D. B., "The Me Lorraine Hansberry Knew," *Freedomways*, 19:261-62, 1979

Scanlan, T., *Family, Drama, and American Dreams*, pp. 195-201

Wilkerson, M. B., "Lorraine Hansberry: The Complete Feminist," *Freedomways*, 19:235-45, 1979

Wilkerson, M. B., "The Sighted Eyes and Feeling Heart of Lorraine Hansberry," pp. 91-104 in *Essays on Contemporary American Drama*, ed. H. Bock and A. Wertheim

The Drinking Gourd, 1960

Powell, B. J., "The Black Experience in Margaret Walker's *Jubilee* and Lorraine Hansberry's *The Drinking Gourd*," *College Language Association Journal*, 21:304-11, 1977

A Raisin in the Sun, 1959

Breitinger, E., "Lorraine Hansberry: *A Raisin in the Sun*," pp. 153-68 in *Das amerikanische Drama der Gegenwart*, ed. H. Grabes

Greenfield, T. A., *Work and the Work Ethic in American Drama 1920-1970*, pp. 134-37

King, Jr., W., "Lorraine Hansberry's Children: Black Artists and *A Raisin in the Sun*," *Freedomways*, 19:219-21, 1979

Ward, D. T., "Lorraine Hansberry and the Passion of Walter Lee," *Freedomways*, 19:223-25, 1979

The Sign in Sidney Brustein's Window, 1964
   Habicht, W., "Lorraine Hansberry: *The Sign in Sidney Brustein's Window*," pp.
   364-74 in *Theater und Drama in Amerika*, ed. E. Lohner and R. Haas

ISAAC HARBY

General

Meserve, W. J., *An Emerging Entertainment*, pp. 203-04, 270

SHELDON HARNICK
SEE
JOSEPH STEIN, JERRY BOCK, and SHELDON HARNICK

EDWARD HARRIGAN

General

Meserve, W. J., *An Outline History of American Drama*, pp. 134-35

MARK HARRIS

Friedman & Son, 1962
   Cohn, R., *Dialogue in American Drama*, pp. 197-98

NEIL HARRIS
SEE
ED BULLINS and NEIL HARRIS

TED HARRIS

Hollywood and Highland, 1982
   After Dark, 14:65, Sept. 1982

GABRIEL HARRISON

The Scarlet Letter (dramatization of novel by N. Hawthorne), 1876
   Herron, I. H., *The Small Town in American Drama*, pp. 27-28

PAUL CARTER HARRISON and COLERIDGE-TAYLOR PERKINSON

The Great MacDaddy, 1974
   After Dark, 12:26, Jan. 1980

LORENZ HART
SEE
GEORGE ABBOTT, RICHARD RODGERS, and LORENZ HART
AND
GEORGE S. KAUFMAN, MOSS HART, RICHARD RODGERS,
and LORENZ HART

MOSS HART and GEORGE S. KAUFMAN

General

Gould, J., "Some Clever Collaborators," pp. 154-67 in Gould's *Modern American
Playwrights*

MOSS HART AND DAVID ROSE

Winged Victory, 1943
  Greenfield, T. A., *Work and the Work Ethic in American Drama 1920-1970*, p.
  91

MOSS HART, KURT WEILL, and IRA GERSHWIN

Lady in the Dark, 1941
  Opera, 33:429-30, Apr. 1982

SEE ALSO
GEORGE S. KAUFMAN and MOSS HART
AND
GEORGE S. KAUFMAN, MOSS HART, RICHARD RODGERS
and LORENZ HART

WALTER HART
SEE
JOHN BORUFF and WALTER HART

BRET HARTE and MARK TWAIN

Ah Sin, 1877
  Herron, I. H., *The Small Town in American Drama*, p. 128

LEZLEY HAVARD

Hide and Seek, 1980
  New Yorker, 56:106, 19 May 1980

JOHN HAWKES

General

Cohn, R., *Dialogue in American Drama*, pp. 198-201

MICAH HAWKINS

The Saw-Mill; or, A Yankee Trick, 1824
  Herron, I. H., *The Small Town in American Drama*, pp. 47-48
  Meserve, W. J., *An Emerging Entertainment*, pp. 235-36

JOSEPH HAYES

Calculated Risk (adaptation of play by G. Ross and C. Singer), 1962
  Herron, I. H., *The Small Town in American Drama*, pp. 465-66

JAMES E. HEATH

Whigs and Democrats; or, Love of No Politics, 1839
  Herron, I. H., *The Small Town in American Drama*, pp. 71-73

BEN HECHT

To Quito and Back, 1937
    Himelstein, M. Y., *Drama Was a Weapon*, p. 140

BEN HECHT and CHARLES MACARTHUR

The Front Page, 1928
    Time, 118:55-56, 13 July 1981

KEVIN HEELAN

Heartland, 1981
    New Yorker, 57:62, 16 Mar. 1981

THOMAS HEGGEN and JOSHUA LOGAN

Mister Roberts (dramatization of book by Heggen), 1948
    Greenfield, T. A., *Work and the Work Ethic in American Drama 1920-1970*,
       pp. 94-95

JACK HEIFNER

Casserole, 1982
    Texas Monthly, 10:149-50, July 1982

Music-Hall Sidelights (adaptation of Colette's reminiscences of a tour with a music-
hall troupe), 1978
    New Yorker, 54:153, 6 Nov. 1978

Patio/Porch, 1978
    After Dark, 11:77, June 1978
    New York, 11:74, 1 May 1978
    Texas Monthly, 6:134, 136, June 1978

Star Treatment, 1980
    After Dark, 12:13, Mar. 1980
    After Dark, 13:62 + , May 1980
    After Dark, 13:66, May 1980
    New York, 13:66, 24 Mar. 1980

Vanities, 1976
    Educational Theatre Journal, 29:264-65, 1977
    Texas Monthly, 6:97-98, Feb. 1978

LILLIAN HELLMAN

General

Bigsby, C. W. E., *A Critical Introduction to Twentieth-Century American Drama*,
    Vol. I, pp. 274-97

Bills, S. H., *Lillian Hellman*

Braun, D., "Lillian Hellman's Continuing Moral Battle," *Massachusetts Studies in English*, 5, iv:1-6, 1978

Broe, M. L., "Bohemia Bumps into Calvin: The Deception of Passivity in Lillian Hellman's Drama," *Southern Quarterly*, 19, ii:26-41, Winter 1981

Estrin, M. W., *Lillian Hellman, Plays, Films, Memoirs*

Falk, D. V., *Lillian Hellman*

Gardner, R. H., *The Splintered Stage*, p. 102

Gould, J., "Lillian Hellman," pp. 168-85 in Gould's *Modern American Playwrights*

Howe, I., "Lillian Hellman and the McCarthy Years," pp. 206-12 in Howe's *Celebrations and Attacks*

Lederer, K., *Lillian Hellman*

Meserve, W. J., *An Outline History of American Drama*, pp. 278-80, 346

Riordan, M. M., comp., *Lillian Hellman*

Scanlan, T., *Family, Drama, and American Dreams*, pp. 181-84, 187-89

Tischler, N. M., "The South Stage Center: Hellman and Williams," pp. 323-33 in *The American South*, ed. L. D. Rubin, Jr.

Another Part of the Forest, 1946
    Herron, I. H., *The Small Town in American Drama*, pp. 265-66

The Autumn Garden, 1951
    Herron, I. H., *The Small Town in American Drama*, pp. 442-44

The Children's Hour, 1934
    Herron, I. H., *The Small Town in American Drama*, pp. 342-44
    Smiley, S., *The Drama of Attack*, pp. 108-09
    Wertheim, A., "The McCarthy Era and the American Theatre," *Theatre Journal*, 34:211-22, 1982

Days to Come, 1936
    Himelstein, M. Y., *Drama Was a Weapon*, pp. 200-01
    Nation, 227:588, 25 Nov. 1978

The Little Foxes, 1939
    Herron, I. H., *The Small Town in American Drama*, pp. 266-67
    Lederer, K., "The Foxes Were Waiting for Horace, Not Lefty: The Use of Irony in Lillian Hellman's *The Little Foxes*," *West Virginia University Philological Papers*, 26:93-104, Aug. 1980
    Smiley, S., *The Drama of Attack*, pp. 100-05, *passim*
    After Dark, 11:112, May 1978
    After Dark, 12:22, Feb. 1980
    After Dark, 14:16+, July 1981
    America, 145:35, 18-25 July 1981
    Drama, 134:80-81, Autumn 1979
    Los Angeles, 26:338+, Nov. 1981
    Nation, 232:770+, 20 June 1981
    New Leader, 64:19-20, 1 June 1981
    New York, 14:50, 18 May 1981
    New Yorker, 57:142, 18 May 1981
    Newsweek, 97:129, 18 May 1981

People, 15:149-51, 6 Apr. 1981
People, 15:32-33, 25 May 1981
Plays and Players, 344:25, May 1982
Saturday Review, 8:86-87, July 1981
Theatre Journal, 32, iii:394-95, Oct. 1980
Time, 117:76-77, 30 Mar. 1981
Time, 117:81, 18 May 1981

The Searching Wind, 1944
    Nannes, C. H., *Politics in the American Drama*, pp. 142-44

Toys in the Attic, 1960
    Gillespie, P. P., "America's Women Dramatists, 1960-1980," pp. 189-91 in
        Essays on Contemporary American Drama, ed. H. Bock and A. Wertheim

Watch on the Rhine, 1941
    Himelstein, M. Y., *Drama Was a Weapon*, pp. 213-14
    Nannes, C. H., *Politics in the American Drama*, pp. 170-71
    After Dark, 12:17, Mar. 1980
    America, 142:104, 9 Feb. 1980
    Drama, 139:27, 1981
    Drama, 139:34, 1981
    Nation, 230:93, 26 Jan. 1980
    New York, 13:71-72, 14 Jan. 1980
    New Yorker, 55:55, 14 Jan. 1980
    Theatre Journal, 32:259, 1980
    Theatre Journal, 33:119-20, 1981
    Time, 115:76, 4 Feb. 1980

ERNEST HEMINGWAY and BENJAMIN GLAZER

The Fifth Column (Glazer's adaptation of Hemingway's play), 1940
    Cohn, R., *Dialogue in American Drama*, pp. 186-88
    Himelstein, M. Y., *Drama Was a Weapon*, pp. 146-47, 220-21

A. MARCUS HEMPHILL

Inacent Black (formerly titled *Inacent Black and the Five Brothers*), 1979
    Fletcher, W. L., "Consider the Possibilities: An Overview of Black Drama in
        the 1970's," p. 154 in *Essays on Contemporary Black Drama*, ed. H. Bock
        and A. Wertheim
    After Dark, 14:64, July 1981
    New Yorker, 57:142, 18 May 1981

BETH HENLEY

General

Time, 119:80, 8 Feb. 1982

Am I Blue, 1982
    Time, 119:80, 8 Feb. 1982

New York, 15:56, 25 Jan. 1982

Crimes of the Heart, 1979
    After Dark, 13:28-29, Mar. 1981
    After Dark, 14:13, Jan./Feb. 1982
    New Leader, 64:19, 30 Nov. 1981
    New Republic, 185:25-27, 23 Dec. 1981
    New York, 14:42+, 12 Jan. 1981
    New York, 14:125-26, 16 Nov. 1981
    New Yorker, 56:81, 12 Jan. 1981
    New Yorker, 57:182-83, 16 Nov. 1981
    Newsweek, 98:123, 16 Nov. 1981
    People, 16:124-25, 21 Dec. 1981
    Saturday Review, 8:40+, Nov. 1981
    Saturday Review, 9:54, Jan. 1982
    Time, 113:73, 5 Mar. 1979
    Time, 118:82, 5 Oct. 1981
    Time, 118:122, 16 Nov. 1981
    Time, 119:80, 8 Feb. 1982

The Miss Firecracker Contest, 1982
    Theatre Journal, 34:260-61, 1982
    Time, 119:80, 8 Feb. 1982

The Wake of Jamey Foster, 1982
    After Dark, 15:10, Dec. 1982/Jan. 1983
    New Leader, 65:20, 15 Nov. 1982
    New York, 15:78, 25 Oct. 1982
    New Yorker, 58:161, 25 Oct. 1982
    Time, 119:80, 8 Feb. 1982

JERRY HERMAN
SEE
MICHAEL STEWART, MARK BRAMBLE, and JERRY HERMAN
AND
MICHAEL STEWART and JERRY HERMAN

JAMES A. HERNE

General

Cazemajou, J., "L'*américanisme* de James A. Herne," *Etudes Anglaises*, 29, iii:402-13, 1976
Meserve, W. J., *An Outline History of American Drama*, pp. 129, 143-47
Perry, J., *James A. Herne*
Vaughn, J. A., *Early American Dramatists*, pp. 168-82

Margaret Fleming, 1891
    Bigsby, C. W. E., *A Critical Introduction to Twentiety-Century American Drama*, Vol. I, pp. 2-3
    Herron, I. H., *The Small Town in American Drama*, pp. 184-86

Hewitt, B., "*Margaret Fleming* in Chickering Hall: The First Little Theatre in America?," *Theatre Journal*, 34:165-71, 1982

Sag Harbor, 1899
Herron, I. H., *The Small Town in American Drama*, pp. 80-81, 183-84

Shore Acres, 1892
Cazemajou, J., "Le 'Realisme tranquille' de James A. Hernes *Shore Acres* (1892)," pp. 119-50 in *Naturalisme américain*, ed. Cazemajou and J.-C. Barat
Herron, I. H., *The Small Town in American Drama*, pp. 78-80, 181-83

JOHN HEUER

Innocent Thoughts, Harmless Intentions, 1980
New York, 13:66, 24 Mar. 1980

DOROTHY HEYWARD and DUBOSE HEYWARD

Mamba's Daughter, 1939
Herron, I. H., *The Small Town in American Drama*, pp. 224-25

Porgy (their dramatization of his novel), 1927
Herron, I. H., *The Small Town in American Drama*, pp. 222-23
Shirley, W. D., "Reconciliation on Catfish Row: Bess, Serena, and the Short Score of *Porgy and Bess*," *Quarterly Journal of the Library of Congress*, 38, iii:145-65, Summer 1981

DOROTHY HEYWARD, DUBOSE HEYWARD, GEORGE GERSHWIN, and IRA GERSHWIN

Porgy and Bess (musical version of the Heywards' *Porgy*), 1935
Gottfried, M., *A Theater Divided*, pp. 188-89
Herron, I. H., *The Small Town in American Drama*, pp. 223-24
Shirley, W. D., "Reconciliation on Catfish Row: Bess, Serena, and the Short Score of *Porgy and Bess*," *Quarterly Journal of the Library of Congress*, 38, iii:145-65, Summer 1981

DUBOSE HEYWARD

Brass Ankle, 1931
Herron, I. H., *The Small Town in American Drama*, pp. 225-27

ALLEN HIBBERD

Angel's Crossing, 1979
Texas Monthly, 8:135, Feb. 1980

HAROLD HICKERSON
SEE
MAXWELL ANDERSON and HAROLD HICKERSON

COLIN HIGGINS

Harold and Maude (based upon his screenplay and novel), 1980
  New York, 13:85, 18 Feb. 1980
  New Yorker, 55:104, 18 Feb. 1980
  Plays and Players, 27:37-38, Apr. 1980
  Theatre Journal, 32:531-32, Dec. 1980

ABRAM HILL

General

Walker, E. P., "The American Negro Theatre," pp. 49-62 in *The Theater of Black Americans, II*, ed. E. Hill.

JAMES ABRAHAM HILLHOUSE

General

Meserve, W. J., *An Emerging Entertainment*, pp. 27-76

FRANK HITCHCOCK
SEE
FRANK HITCHCOCK MURDOCH

JANE STANTON HITCHCOCK

Grace, 1891
  New York, 14:72, 2 Nov. 1981
  New Yorker, 57:66, 2 Nov. 1981

J. R. W. HITCHCOCK and MARTHA HALL HITCHCOCK

David Harum (dramatization of novel by E. N. Westcott), 1900
  Herron, I. H., *The Small Town in American Drama*, pp. 193-95

ELIHU G. HOLLAND

The Highland Treason, 1852
  Shillingsburg, M. J., "The West Point Treason in American Drama, 1798-1891," *Educational Theatre Journal*, 30:73-89, 1978

JOHN HAYNES HOLMES and REGINALD LAWRENCE

If This Be Treason, 1935
  Himelstein, M. Y., *Drama Was a Weapon*, pp. 137-38
  Nannes, C. H., *Politics in the American Drama*, pp. 160-62
  Smiley, S., *The Drama of Attack*, pp. 123-24

ISRAEL HOROVITZ

Alfred Dies, 1976

Witham, B. B., "Images of America: Wilson, Weller and Horovitz," *Theatre Journal*, 34:223-32, 1982

The Good Parts, 1979
   America, 146:135, 20 Feb. 1982
   New York, 15:70, 18 Jan. 1982
   Plays and Players, 343:36, Apr. 1982

The Great Labor Day Classic, 1979
   Theatre Journal, 31:414, 1979

The Primary English Class, 1975
   Drama, 137:44, July 1980
   Plays and Players, 27:20-21, Mar. 1980

The Widow's Blind Date, 1978
   Los Angeles, 25:297, Nov. 1980

BRONSON HOWARD

General

Gottlieb, L. C., "The Antibusiness Theme in Late Nineteenth Century American Drama," *Quarterly Journal of Speech*, 64:415-26, 1978
Meserve, W. J., *An Outline History of American Drama*, pp. 150-53
Vaughn, J. A., *Early American Dramatists*, pp. 143-52

SIDNEY HOWARD

General

Meserve, W. J., *An Outline History of American Drama*, pp. 239-41
White, S. H., *Sidney Howard*

Dodsworth (dramatization of novel by S. Lewis), 1934
   Herron, I. H., *The Small Town in American Drama*, pp. 269, 426-27

The Ghost of Yankee Doodle, 1937
   Himelstein, M. Y., *Drama Was a Weapon*, p. 141
   Nannes, C. H., *Politics in the American Drama*, pp. 164-65

The Late Christopher Bean (adaption of *Prenez Garde à la Peinture* by R. Fauchois), 1932
   Herron, I. H., *The Small Town in American Drama*, pp. 425-26
   After Dark, 12:20, Dec. 1979
   Los Angeles, 24:391, Dec. 1979

Ned McCobb's Daughter, 1926
   Herron, I. H., *The Small Town in American Drama*, pp. 263-64

TINA HOWE

Appearances, 1982

New Yorker, 58:104, 24 May 1982

The Art of Dining, 1979
   Nation, 230:30, 5 Jan. 1980
   New York, 12:73, 24 Dec. 1979
   New Yorker, 55:100+, 17 Dec. 1979

Birth and After Birth, 1974
   Brown, J., "*Birth and After Birth*," pp. 71-85 in Brown's *Feminist Drama*

Museum, 1978
   After Dark, 11:84, June 1978
   New Yorker, 54:67-68, 6 Mar. 1978

WILLIAM DEAN HOWELLS

General

Meserve, W. J., *An Outline History of American Drama*, pp. 140-43, 153-55, 193

The Mother and the Father, 1909
   Madsen, V., "Autobiographical and Mystical Elements in Howell's *The Mother and the Father*," *Research Studies*, 49, i:46-54, Mar. 1981

LIBBY HOWES
SEE
SPALDING GRAY, ELIZABETH LeCOMPTE, LIBBY HOWES, JIM CLAYBURGH, and RON VAWTER

PERKINS HOWES

The New England Drama, 1825
   Herron, I. H., *The Small Town in American Drama*, pp. 50-52

CHARLES HOYT

A Bunch of Keys; or, The Hotel, 1882
   Herron, I. H., *The Small Town in American Drama*, pp. 187-88

A Midnight Bell, 1889
   Herron, I. H., *The Small Town in American Drama*, pp. 188-89

A Temperance Town, 1893
   Herron, I. H., *The Small Town in American Drama*, pp. 189-90
   Nannes, C. H., *Politics in the American Drama*, pp. 19-21

A Texas Steer; or, Money Makes the Mare Go, 1890
   Herron, I. H., *The Small Town in American Drama*, pp. 138-40
   Meserve, W. J., *An Outline History of American Drama*, pp. 190-91
   Nannes, C. H., *Politics in the American Drama*, pp. 61-63

HORATIO HUBBELL

Arnold, 1847
   Shillingsburg, M. J., "The West Point Treason in American Drama, 1798-1891,"
   Educational Theatre Journal, 30:73-89, 1978

LANGSTON HUGHES

General

Cohn, R., *Dialogue in American Drama*, pp. 183-86

Mulatto, 1935
   Bigsby, C. W. E., *A Critical Introduction to Twentieth-Century American Drama*,
   Vol. I, pp. 243-45
   Smiley, S., *The Drama of Attack*, pp. 163-65

DAVID HUMPHREYS

The Yankey in England, 1814
   Herron, I. H., *The Small Town in American Drama*, pp. 44-45

ROBERT HUNTER

Androborus, 1714
   Meserve, W. J., *An Emerging Entertainment*, pp. 38-42
   Meserve, W. J., *An Outline History of American Drama*, p. 4

WILLIAM HURLBUT

General

Herron, I. H., *The Small Town in American Drama*, pp. 231-32

JOHN HUSTON and HOWARD KOCH

In Time to Come, 1941
   Nannes, C. H., *Politics in the American Drama*, pp. 191-93

JOSEPH HUTTON

General

Meserve, W. J., *An Emerging Entertainment*, pp. 212-15

DAVID HENRY HWANG

The Dance and the Railroad, 1981
   After Dark, 14:16, Oct. 1981
   Commonweal, 108:688+, 4 Dec. 1981
   Nation, 233:554-55, 21 Nov. 1981
   New Republic, 185:28-29, 14 Oct. 1981
   New York, 14:68-70, 24 Aug. 1981

New Yorker, 57:52, 27 July 1981

Family Devotions, 1981
Commonweal, 108:688+, 4 Dec. 1981
Nation, 233:554-55, 21 Nov. 1981
New York, 14:71, 2 Nov. 1981
New Yorker, 57:65-66, 2 Nov. 1981

FOB, 1979
New Yorker, 56:96-97, 16 June 1980

WILLIAM INGE

General

Burgess, C. E., "An American Experience: William Inge in St. Louis, 1943-49,"
Papers on Language and Literature, 12, iv:438-68, 1976
Gardner, R. H., *The Splintered Stage*, pp. 97-100
Gottfried, M., *A Theater Divided*, pp. 257-62
Gould, J., "William Inge," pp. 264-72 in Gould's *Modern American Playwrights*
Ishizuka, K., "William Inge and Loneliness on Broadway," pp. 167-73 in *American
Literature in the 1950's* (American Literature Society of Japan 1976 Annual
Report)
McClure, A. F., *William Inge*
Meserve, W. J., *An Outline History of American Drama*, p. 348
Mitchell, M., "William Inge," *American Imago*, 35:297-310, 1978
Sarotte, G. M., "Homosexuality and the Theater: William Inge: 'Homosexual Spite'
in Action," pp. 121-33 in Sarotte's *Like a Brother, Like a Lover*
Williams, S., "Our Gay Heritage: The Closet Dramas of William Inge," *Stallion*, 2,
iv:46-48+, July 1983

Bus Stop, 1955
Herron, I. H., *The Small Town in American Drama*, pp. 432-33

Come Back, Little Sheba, 1950
Herron, I. H., *The Small Town in American Drama*, pp. 429-30

The Dark at the Top of the Stairs, 1947 (revised 1957)
Herron, I. H., *The Small Town in American Drama*, pp. 433-35
After Dark, 12:18+, Mar. 1980
Los Angeles, 26:276+, Sept. 1981

A Loss of Roses, 1959
Herron, I. H., *The Small Town in American Drama*, pp. 435-37

Picnic (originally titled *Front Porch*), 1953
Herron, I. H., *The Small Town in American Drama*, pp. 430-32

ROBERT E. INGHAM

Custer, 1980
Theatre Journal, 32, iii:395-96, Oct. 1980

ALBERT INNAURATO

General

Baker, R., "Innaurato in Traction," *After Dark*, 10:70-73, Mar. 1978

Gemini, 1976
  Harper's, 256:85-86, May 1978
  Plays and Players, 25:34-35, Oct. 1977

Passione, 1980
  After Dark, 13:62, Aug. 1980
  After Dark, 13:23, Oct. 1980
  Nation, 231:387, 18 Oct. 1980
  New York, 13:58, 9 June 1980
  New York, 13:75-76, 6 Oct. 1980
  New Yorker, 56:147, 6 Oct. 1980
  Newsweek, 96:108, 6 Oct. 1980
  Time, 115:68, 2 June 1980

The Transfiguration of Benno Blimpie, 1973
  Los Angeles, 23:219+, Mar. 1978

Ulysses in Traction, 1977
  After Dark, 10:24, Feb. 1978
  After Dark, 10:70-73, Mar. 1978
  New Leader, 61:28-29, 2 Jan. 1978

SEE ALSO
CHRISTOPHER DURANG and ALBERT INNAURATO

WILLIAM IOOR

General

Meserve, W. J., *An Emerging Entertainment*, pp. 190-92

WASHINGTON IRVING
SEE
JOHN HOWARD PAYNE and WASHINGTON IRVING

BILL IRWIN, DOUG SKINNER, and MICHAEL O'CONNOR

The Regard of Flight, 1982
  Dance Magazine, 55:68-72, June 1982
  Nation, 233:154, 21-28 Aug. 1982
  New Yorker, 58:74, 31 May 1982
  Newsweek, 100:75, 19 July 1982

CHRISTOPHER ISHERWOOD and DON BACHARDY

A Meeting by the River (dramatization of Isherwood's novel), 1972
  New Yorker, 55:97-98, 9 Apr. 1979

CORINNE JACKER

General

Jacker, C., "Better Than a Shriveled Husk: New Forms for the Theater," pp. 25-34 in *Toward the Second Decade*, ed. B. Justice and R. Pore

Later, 1979
  After Dark, 11:85, Apr. 1979

Toe Jam, 1971
  Curb, R. K., " 'Goin' through Changes': Mother-Daughter Confrontations in Three Recent Plays by Young Black Women," *Kentucky Folklore Record*, 25:96-102, 1979

MICHAEL JACOBS

Cheaters, 1978
  After Dark, 10:81, Mar. 1978
  Drama-Logue, 13, xxxvi:8, 9-15 Sept. 1982
  New Leader, 6:26, 13 Feb. 1978
  New Yorker, 53:71, 30 Jan. 1978
  Saturday Review, 5:60, 18 Mar. 1978

HENRY JAMES

The Outcry, 1917
  Tintner, A. R., "James' *King Lear: The Outcry* and the Art Drain," *AB Bookman's Weekly*, 4 Feb. 1980:798-828 (every other page)

ROBINSON JEFFERS

General

Cohn, R., *Dialogue in American Drama*, pp. 231-37

Medea (adaptation of play by Euripides), 1946
  Georgoudaki, C., "Jeffers' *Medea*: A Debt to Euripides," *Revue des Langues Vivantes*, 42:620-23, 1976
  Strudwick, S., "Paris Premiere of *Medea*: A Memoir," *Robinson Jeffers Newsletter*, 52:15-16, 1978
  Time, 119:74, 31 May 1982

The Tower Beyond Tragedy (based on the *Oresteia* of Aeschylus), 1950
  Zaller, R., "The Birth of the Hero: Robinson Jeffers' *The Tower Beyond Tragedy*," *Robinson Jeffers Newsletter*, 58:5-16, May 1981

JOSEPH JEFFERSON III

General

Kauffmann, S., "An Actor's Life," pp. 301-05 in Kauffmann's *Persons of the Drama*

Rip Van Winkle (adaptation of story by W. Irving and of other dramatic versions), 1865
    Herron, I. H., *The Small Town in American Drama*, pp. 95-103
    Johnson, S., "Joseph Jefferson's *Rip Van Winkle*," *The Drama Review*, 26:3-20, Spring 1982
    Meserve, W. J., *An Outline History of American Drama*, pp. 91-92
    Scanlon, T., *Family, Drama, and American Dreams*, pp. 50-60, *passim*

KEN JENKINS

Swop, 1981
    Time, 117:74, 6 Apr. 1981

LEN JENKINS

The Death and Life of Jesse James, 1978
    New York, 11:83, 12 June 1978

New Jerusalem, 1979
    New Yorker, 55:95, 5 Mar. 1979

RAYMOND JESSEL
SEE
THOMAS MEEHAN, RICHARD RODGERS, MARTIN CHARNIN, and RAYMOND JESSEL

TED JOHNS

The School Scandal, 1980
    After Dark, 13:60, June 1980

HALL JOHNSON

Run Little Chillun!, 1933
    Bigsby, C. W. E., *A Critical Introduction to Twentieth-Century American Drama*, Vol. I, pp. 242-43
    Fletcher, W. L., "Federal Theatre Project of the '30s Reborn in the '70s: *Run Little Chillun* Revived at Kentucky State University," *Theatre News*, 10, vii:8-10, Apr. 1978
    Literary Digest, 115:13-14, 15 Apr. 1933
    Nation, 136:328, 22 Mar. 1933
    Nation, 157:248, 25 Aug. 1943
    New Outlook, 161:46, Apr. 1933
    New Republic, 74:160, 22 Mar. 1933
    New Republic, 74:244-45, 12 Apr. 1933
    Saturday Review of Literature, 10:13-14, 29 July 1933
    Stage, 10:30-31, Apr. 1933
    Theatre Arts Monthly, 17:338, May 1933
    Time, 42:64, 23 Aug. 1964
    Vogue, 81:49, 1 May 1933

WILLIAM JOHNSON

Benedict Arnold, the Traitor, 1891
Shillingsburg, M. J., "The West Point Treason in American Drama, 1798-1891,"
Educational Theatre Journal, 30:73-89, 1978

M. G. JOHNSTON

Blood Money, 1979
Texas Monthly, 7:168, May 1979

BROTHER JONATHAN (O.S.F.)

Bella Figura, 1980
After Dark, 13:62, Aug. 1980
New York, 15:84+, 26 Apr. 1982

The Dog Ran Away, 1977
Drama, 127:50, Winter 1977-1978

JOSEPH STEVENS JONES

General

Herron, I. H., *The Small Town in American Drama*, pp. 58-61, 92-94

The People's Lawyer, 1839
Meserve, W. J., *An Outline History of America Drama*, p. 71

LEROI JONES
(or Imamu Amiri Baraka)

General

Benston, K. W., *Baraka*
Bigsby, C. W. E., "The Plays of Amiri Baraka: Vehicles of a Simple Message?,"
Theatre Quarterly, 8:25-29, Autumn 1978
Bigsby, C. W. E., "Theatre and the Coming Revolution: Interview," *Theatre Quarterly*, 8:29-35, Autumn 1978
Brown, L. W., *Amiri Baraka*
Cohn, R., *Dialogue in American Drama*, pp. 295-302
Dace, L., "Amiri Baraka (LeRoi Jones)," pp. 121-87 in *Black American Writers*, Vol. II, ed. M. T. Inge, J. M. Duke, and J. R. Bryer
Enekwe, O. O., "An Interview with Amiri Baraka," *Okike*, 17:97-108, 1980
Fabre, M., "Les Avatars d'Amiri Baraka, citoyen-dramaturge: Un Montage documentaire," *Revue Française d'Etudes Américaines*, 10:285-301, 1980
Gottfried, M., *A Theater Divided*, pp. 78-80
Harris, W. J., "An Interview with Amiri Baraka," *Greenfield Review*, 8, iii:19-31, 1980
Lacey, H. C., *To Raise, Destory, and Create*
Marranca, B. G., "LeRoi Jones (Amiri Baraka)," pp. 121-33 in Marranca and G. Dasgupta's *American Playwrights*

Miller, J.-M. A., "Images of Black Women in Plays by Black Playwrights," *College Language Association Journal*, 20:494-507, 1977

Mottram, E., "Towards the Alternative: The Prose of LeRoi Jones," pp. 97-135 in *Black Fiction*, ed. R. A. Lee

Ogunyemi, C. O., "Iconoclasts Both: Wole Soyinka and LeRoi Jones," *African Literature Today*, 9:25-38, 1978

Richards, S. L., "Negative Forces and Positive Non-Entities: Images of Women in the Dramas of Amiri Baraka," *Theatre Journal*, 34:233-40, 1982

Sarna, M. N., "Revolt and Ritual in the Plays of LeRoi Jones," *Osmania Journal of English Studies*, 11:1-10, 1974-75

Scott, A. and J. Schechter, "On Black Theater: Interview," *Theater*, 9:59-61, Spring 1978

Sollors, W., "Amiri Baraka (LeRoi Jones)," pp. 105-22 in *Essays on Contemporary American Drama*, ed. H. Bock and A. Wertheim

Boy and Tarzan Appear in a Clearing, 1981
    New Yorker, 57:160, 26 Oct. 1981

Dutchman, 1964
    Casimir, Jr., L. J., "*Dutchman*: The Price of Culture Is a Lie," pp. 298-310 in *The Binding of Proteus*, ed. M. W. McCune, T. Orbison, and P. M. Withim

    Dukore, B. F., "Off-Broadway and the New Realism," pp. 163-74 in *Modern American Drama*, ed. W. E. Taylor

    Grabes, H., "LeRoi Jones (Amiri Baraka): *Dutchman*," pp. 185-200 in *Das amerikanische Drama der Gegenwart*, ed. Grabes

    Levesque, G. A., "LeRoi Jones' *Dutchman*: Myth and Allegory," *Obsidian*, 5, iii:33-40, 1979

    Martin, T., "*Dutchman* Reconsidered," *Black American Literature Forum*, 11:62, 1977

    Nadin, M., "A Semiotic Procedural Approach to Dramatic Literature," pp. 467-506 in *Empirical Semantics*, ed. B. B. Rieger

    Werner, C., "Brer Rabbit Meets the Underground Man: Simplification of Consciousness in Baraka's *Dutchman* and *Slave Ship*," *Obsidian*, 5, i-ii:35-40, 1979

The Great Goodness of Life (A Coon Show), 1969
    Greenfield, T. A., *Work and the Work Ethic in American Drama 1920-1970*, pp. 143-44

The Slave, 1964
    Brady, O. E., "LeRoi Jones's *The Slave*: A Ritual of Purgation," *Obsidian*, 4, i:5-18, 1978

Slave Ship, 1967
    Werner, C., "Brer Rabbit Meets the Underground Man: Simplification of Consciousness in Baraka's *Dutchman* and *Slave Ship*," *Obsidian*, 5, i-ii:35-40, 1979

PRESTON JONES

General

Anthony, O., "The Long Nights of Preston Jones," *Texas Monthly*, 7:180-89, Dec. 1979

Coulson, J. P., "Preston Jones: Alive and Well and Writing in the Southwest," *Theatre Southwest*, 4, iii:15-19, Oct. 1978

Coulson, J. P., "Preston Jones—1936-1979: Bradleyville Was Home," *Theatre Southwest*, 5, iii:21, Oct. 1979

Lu Ann Hampton Laverty Oberlander, 1974
  After Dark, 11:76, June 1978
  Educational Theatre Journal, 30:274-75, 1978

The Oldest Living Graduate, 1974
  After Dark, 13:63, Aug. 1980
  Los Angeles, 25:229, June 1980
  New West, 5:103, 16 June 1980
  Texas Monthly, 8:175+, June 1980

Remember, 1979
  Texas Monthly, 7:166+, May 1979
  Theatre Journal, 32:255, 1980

TOM JONES and HARVEY SCHMIDT

General

Gottfried, M., *A Theater Divided*, pp. 205-06

The Fantasticks (based on *Les Romanesques* by E. Rostand as tr. by G. Fleming), 1960
  Weiss, P., "The Pop Beat: Twenty Fantastick Years," *Stereo Review*, 43:54, Nov. 1979
  Newsweek, 95:12, 2 June 1980

I Do! I Do! (musical version of J. de Hartog's play *The Fourposter*), 1966
  Los Angeles, 25:248, July 1980
  New West, 5:SC-26, 14 July 1980

SEE ALSO
N. RICHARD NASH, TOM JONES, and HARVEY SCHMIDT

RICHARD JORDAN

The Venus of Menschen Falls, 1978
  Los Angeles, 23:245+, Apr. 1978
  New West, 3:SC-39, 24 Apr. 1978

SAMUEL BENJAMIN HELBERT JUDAH

General

Meserve, W. J., *An Emerging Entertainment*, pp. 256-59

A Tale of Lexington (also known as *The Battle of Lexington*), 1822
   Herron, I. H., *The Small Town in American Drama*, pp. 53-54

JOSEPH JULIAN

An Act of Kindness, 1980
   New York, 13:44, 46-47, 29 Sept. 1980

DIANE KAGAN

The Corridor, 1981
   Theatre Journal, 33:545-46, 1981

LEE KALCHEIM

Breakfast with Les and Bess, 1982
   New York, 15:54, 20 Dec. 1982
   Time, 120:87, 20 Dec. 1982

Winning Isn't Everything, 1978
   After Dark, 11:80, Feb. 1979
   Time, 112:112, 11 Dec. 1978

ROBERT KALFIN, STEVE BROWN, JOHN McKINNEY, and WILLIAM BOLCOM

Hijinks! (musical adaptation of *Captain Jinks of the Horse Marines* by C. Fitch), 1980
   New Yorker, 56:62, 5 Jan. 1981

GARSON KANIN

Born Yesterday, 1946
   Nannes, C. H., *Politics in the American Drama*, pp. 115-17

JEROME KASS

Young Marrieds at Play (presented with P. Maloney's *Lost and Found* as *Handle with Care*), 1982
   Drama-Logue, 13, xxxvii:5, 16-22 Sept. 1982

JEROME KASS, ALAN BERGMAN, MARILYN BERGMAN, and BILLY GOLDENBERG

Ballroom (musical version of Kass's TV play *Queen of the Stardust Ballroom*), 1978
   America, 140:36, 20 Jan. 1979

Dance Magazine, 53:60-62, Feb. 1979
Encore, 7:32-33, 15 Jan. 1979
New Leader, 62:21, 1 Jan. 1979
New Republic, 180:25, 27 Jan. 1979
New York, 12:64-65, 8 Jan. 1979
New Yorker, 54:46-47, 1 Jan. 1979
Newsweek, 93:56, 1 Jan. 1979
Plays and Players, 26:36, Feb. 1979
Saturday Review, 6:52, 17 Feb. 1979
Time, 112:83, 25 Dec. 1978

DOUG KATSAROS
SEE
MICHAEL STEWART, MARK BRAMBLE, DOUG KATSAROS,
and RICHARD ENGQUIST

GEORGE S. KAUFMAN

General

Goldstein, M., *George S. Kaufman*
Mersand, J., *The American Drama Since 1930*, pp. 21-33
Meserve, W. J., *An Outline History of American Drama*, pp. 286-88, 343

GEORGE S. KAUFMAN and MARC CONNELLY

Merton of the Movies (dramatization of novel by H. L. Wilson), 1922
    After Dark, 12:18, 20, Dec. 1979
    Educational Theatre Journal, 29:514-16, 1977

To the Ladies!, 1922
    Herron, I. H., *The Small Town in American Drama*, pp. 437-38

GEORGE S. KAUFMAN and KATHERINE DAYTON

First Lady, 1935
    Nannes, C. H., *Politics in the American Drama*, pp. 66-69

GEORGE S. KAUFMAN and EDNA FERBER

Minick (also known as *Old Man Minick*), 1924
    Francis, M., "The James Adams Floating Theatre: Edna Ferber's Showboat,"
        Carolina Comments, 28,v:135-42, Sept. 1980
    American Mercury, 3:376-77, Nov. 1924
    Current Opinion, 77:732-39, Dec. 1924
    Independent, 113:55, 20 Dec. 1924
    Life (New York), 84:18, 16 Oct. 1924
    Motion Picture Classic, 28:48 + , Jan. 1925
    Nation, 119:423-24, 15 Oct. 1924
    Overland, 86:19, Jan. 1928
    Survey, 53:162-64, 1 Nov. 1924

Theatre Arts, 8:804+, Dec. 1924
Theatre Magazine, 40:16, Dec. 1924
Theatre Magazine, 40:18, Dec. 1924

The Royal Family, 1927
    Texas Monthly, 6:174, 176-77, Sept. 1978

GEORGE S. KAUFMAN and MOSS HART

The Man Who Came to Dinner, 1939
    Herron, I. H., *The Small Town in American Drama*, p. 438
    Drama, 132:70-71, Spring 1979
    Drama, 134:75-76, Autumn 1979
    Los Angeles, 24:202+, Jan. 1979
    New West, 4:75+, 1 Jan. 1979
    New York, 13:51, 21 July 1980
    New Yorker, 56:58, 7 July 1980
    Plays and Players, 26:25+, Sept. 1979
    Time, 116:64, 28 July 1980

Once in a Lifetime, 1930
    After Dark, 11:80+, Aug. 1978
    After Dark, 12:24+, Mar. 1980
    Drama, 135:38, Jan. 1980
    New York, 11:74, 3 July 1978
    New Yorker, 54:51, 26 June 1978
    Plays and Players, 27:22, Oct. 1979
    Time, 112:83, 17 July 1978

You Can't Take It With You, 1936
    Houghton, N., *The Exploding Stage*, pp. 169-71
    Teichmann, H., " 'You Can't Take It With You': Bantering Friendship between
    GSK and Moss Hart Was as Successful as Their Pulitzer Prize-winning Play,"
    TV Guide, 27:33+, 12 May 1979

GEORGE S. KAUFMAN, MOSS HART, RICHARD RODGERS, and LORENZ HART

I'd Rather Be Right, 1937
    Himelstein, M. Y., *Drama Was a Weapon*, pp. 204-05
    Nannes, C. H., *Politics in the American Drama*, pp. 109-13

GEORGE S. KAUFMAN and MORRIE RYSKIND

Something New, 1922
    Shyer, L., "American Absurd: Two Nonsense Plays by George S. Kaufman and
    Morrie Ryskind, and Ring Lardner," *Theater*, 9, ii:119-21, 1978 (play on pp.
    122-24)

GEORGE S. KAUFMAN, MORRIE RYSKIND, GEORGE GERSHWIN, and IRA GERSHWIN

Let 'Em Eat Cake, 1933
  Himelstein, M. Y., *Drama Was a Weapon*, pp. 190-91
  Nannes, C. H., *Politics in the American Drama*, pp. 105-07

Of Thee I Sing, 1931
  Himelstein, M. Y., *Drama Was a Weapon*, pp. 184-85
  Nannes, C. H., *Politics in the American Drama*, pp. 103-05

SEE ALSO
MOSS HART and GEORGE S. KAUFMAN

PATRICK KEARNEY

An American Tragedy (dramatization of novel by T. Dreiser), 1926
  New Republic, 48:297-98, 3 Nov. 1926

Elmer Gantry (dramatization of novel by S. Lewis), 1928
  Outlook, 149:670, 22 Aug. 1928

A Man's Man, 1925
  Arts and Decoration, 24:43, Jan. 1926

Old Man Murphy, 1931
  Bookman, 73:524, July 1931
  Catholic World, 133:462-63, July 1931
  Nation, 132:619, 3 June 1931

JAMES W. KEARNS

Days in the Dark Light, 1980
  After Dark, 12:26, Apr. 1980
  New West, 5:SC-13, 25 Feb. 1980

MARGARET KEILSTRUP

Wonderland, 1982
  New York, 15:47, 15 Mar. 1982

BILL KEITH

The Dead-End Day, 1982
  Drama-Logue, 13, xxxvi:9, 9-15 Sept. 1982

GEORGE KELLY

General

Meserve, W. J., *An Outline History of American Drama*, pp. 276-78, 341

The Show-Off, 1924
  New Yorker, 54:86, 29 May 1978

ADRIENNE KENNEDY

General

Miller, J.-M. A., "Images of Black Women in Plays by Black Playwrights," *College Language Association Journal*, 20:494-507, 1977

Funnyhouse of a Negro, 1964
  Curb, R. K., "Fragmented Selves in Adrienne Kennedy's *Funnyhouse of a Negro* and *The Owl Answers*," *Theatre Journal*, 32:180-95, 1980

The Owl Answers, 1965
  Curb, R. K., "Fragmented Selves in Adrienne Kennedy's *Funnyhouse of a Negro* and *The Owl Answers*," *Theatre Journal*, 32:180-95, 1980

CHARLES RANN KENNEDY

General

Meserve, W. J., *An Outline History of American Drama*, pp. 201-02

The Seventh Trumpet, 1941
  Nannes, C. H., *Politics in the American Drama*, pp. 146-47

STEVEN KENT
SEE
JOSEPH CHAIKIN and STEVEN KENT

JEROME KERN
SEE
OSCAR HAMMERSTEIN II and JEROME KERN

JEAN KERR

Lunch Hour, 1980
  After Dark, 13:29, 67, Jan. 1981
  New York, 13:67, 1 Dec. 1980
  New York Times Magazine, pp. 42-43 + , 9 Nov. 1980
  New Yorker, 56:134, 24 Nov. 1980
  Newsweek, 96:129 + , 24 Nov. 1980
  Time, 116:64, 24 Nov. 1980

WENDY KESSELMAN

My Sister in This House, 1981
  New York, 14:159 + , 7 Dec. 1981
  Time, 117:74, 6 Apr. 1981

LARRY KETRON

The Trading Post, 1981
  After Dark, 14:73, June 1981

ALICE MARY KILGORE and DOUG KILGORE

Katie, Inc., 1979
  Texas Monthly, 7:152, July 1979

MICHAEL KIMBERLEY

Almost an Eagle, 1982
  New Yorker, 58:61, 27 Dec. 1982
  Newsweek, 100:62, 27 Dec. 1982

GRACE KIMMINS

Just the Immediate Family, 1978
  New York, 11:70-71, 24 July 1978

LARRY L. KING and BEN Z. GRANT

The Kingfish, 1979
  Texas Monthly, 7:202 + , Oct. 1979

SIDNEY KINGSLEY

Darkness at Noon (dramatization of novel by A. Koestler), 1951
  Nannes, C. H., *Politics in the American Drama*, pp. 172-77

Dead End, 1935
  Himelstein, M. Y., *Drama Was a Weapon*, pp. 197-98
  Meserve, W. J., *An Outline History of American Drama*, pp. 269-71, 344-45

Men in White, 1933
  Greenfield, T. A., *Work and the Work Ethic in American Drama*, pp. 77-78
  Himelstein, M. Y., *Drama Was a Weapon*, pp. 161-62

Ten Million Ghosts, 1936
  Himelstein, M. Y., *Drama Was a Weapon*, p. 200

MICHAEL KIRBY

General

Carroll, N., "The Mystery Plays of Michael Kirby: Notes on the Esthetics of Structuralist Theatre," *The Drama Review*, 23, iii:103-12, 1979
Leverett, J., "Old Forms Enter the New American Theater: Shepard, Foreman, Kirby, and Ludlam," pp. 107-22 in *Melodrama*, guest ed. D. C. Gerould

JACK KIRKLAND

Tobacco Road (dramatization of novel by E. Caldwell), 1933
  Gomery, D., "Three Roads Taken: The Novel, the Play, and the Film," pp. 9-
    18 in *The Modern American Novel and the Movies*, ed. G. Perry and R. Shatzkin
  Himelstein, M. Y., *Drama Was a Weapon*, pp. 191-92

JAMES KIRKWOOD

P.S. Your Cat Is Dead! (based on his novel), 1975 (revised 1978)
  After Dark, 11:111-12, May 1978
  Drama, 133:69-70, Summer 1979
  New York, 54:112, 3 Apr. 1978
  Plays and Players, 26:33-34, July 1979

CHARLES KLEIN

The Lion and the Mouse, 1905
  Nannes, C. H., *Politics in the American Drama*, pp. 30-33

LENNY KLEINFELD
SEE
BURY ST. EDMUND

ALLAN KNEE

Second Avenue Rag, 1980
  After Dark, 13:57, July 1980
  New Yorker, 56:77, 21 Apr. 1980

EDWARD KNOBLOCK
(also spelled Knobloch and Knoblauch)

Kismet, 1911
  Book News, 32:72, Sept. 1913
  Bookman, 34:644-49, Feb. 1912
  Everybody's, 26:382, Mar. 1912
  Green Book, 7:560-62, Mar. 1912
  Hearst's Magazine, 21:2135-50, Apr. 1912
  Literary Digest, 44:20-21, 6 Jan. 1912

CHRISTOPHER KNOWLES
SEE
ROBERT WILSON AND CHRISTOPHER KNOWLES

HOWARD KOCH
SEE
JOHN HUSTON AND HOWARD KOCH

KENNETH KOCH

General

Cohn, R., *Dialogue in American Drama*, pp. 310-12

Marranca, B. G., "Kenneth Koch,"pp. 3-14 in Marranca and G. Dasgupta's *American Playwrights*

George Washington Crossing the Delaware, 1962
Gottfried, M., *A Theater Divided*, pp. 234-36
Commonweal, 76:16-17, 30 Mar. 1962

The Red Robins (dramatization of his novel), 1978
Educational Theatre Journal, 30:416-17, 1978

ARTHUR KOPIT

General

Auerbach, D., *Sam Shepard, Arthur Kopit, and the Off Broadway Theater*
Cohn, R., "Camp, Cruelty, Colloquialism," pp. 281-303 in *Comic Relief*, ed. S. B. Cohen
Dasgupta, G., "Arthur Kopit," pp. 15-25 in Dasgupta and B. G. Marranca's *American Playwrights*
Wellwarth, G., *The Theater of Protest and Paradox*, rev. ed., pp. 345-47
Wolter, J., "Arthur Kopit: Dreams and Nightmares," pp. 55-74 in *Essays on Contemporary American Drama*, ed. H. Bock and A. Wertheim

Chamber Music, 1971
Murch, A. C., "Genêt—Triana—Kopit: Ritual as 'Danse macabre,' " *Modern Drama*, 15:369-82, 1973
After Dark, 12:13, Mar. 1980

The Conquest of Everest, 1964
After Dark, 12:13, Mar. 1980

Indians, 1968
Billman, C. W., "Illusions of Grandeur: Altman, Kopit, and the Legends of the Wild West," *Literature/Film Quarterly*, 6:253-61, 1978
Denecke, U., "Mythos und Rollenkonflikt in Arthur Kopits *Indians*," pp. 375-87 in *Theater und Drama in Amerika*, ed. E. Lohner and R. Haas
O'Neill, M. C., "History as Dramatic Present: Arthur L. Kopit's *Indians*," *Theatre Journal*," 34, iv:493-504, Dec. 1982
Wilz, H.-W., "Arthur Kopit: *Indians*," pp. 44-64 in *Das amerikanische Drama der Gegenwart*, ed. H. Grabes

Oh Dad, Poor Dad, Momma's Hung You in the Closet and I'm Feelin' So Sad, 1960
Szilassy, Z., "Yankee Burlesque or Metaphysical Farce? Kopit's *Oh Dad, Poor Dad*. . .Reconsidered," *Hungarian Studies in English*, 11:143-47, 1977

Wings, 1978
After Dark, 11:85, June 1978
After Dark, 11:83-84, Apr. 1979
Commonweal, 105:594, 15 Sept. 1978
Drama, 134:73, Autumn 1979
Horizon, 22:50-55, May 1979
Hudson Review, 32:77-81, Spring 1979

Nation, 228:189, 17 Feb. 1979
New Leader, 62:19-20, 26 Feb. 1979
New York, 11:66-67, 10 July 1978
New Yorker, 54:70, 3 July 1978
New Yorker, 54:98, 5 Feb. 1979
New Yorker, 55:33-35, 9 Apr. 1979
Plays and Players, 25:39, Aug. 1978
Plays and Players, 27:23-24, Oct. 1979
Theatre Journal, 32, iii:395-96, Oct. 1980
Time, 112:86, 3 July 1978

ARTHUR KOPIT and MAURY YESTON

Nine (based upon F. Fellini's film *8½*), 1982
   America, 147:13, 26 June-3 July 1982
   Dance Magazine, 56:76, Aug. 1982
   Dance Magazine, 56:52-57, Sept. 1982
   Nation, 235:28-29, 3 July 1982
   New Republic, 186:24-26, 9 June 1982
   New York, 15:88-89, 24 May 1982
   New Yorker, 58:100+, 24 May 1982
   Newsweek, 99:74, 24 May 1982
   Plays and Players, 346:39, July 1982
   Theatre Crafts, 16:16-19+, Aug./Sept. 1982
   Time, 119:73, 24 May 1982
   Working Woman, 7:156-57, Dec. 1982

FRANÇOISE KOURILSKY and NICK KREPOS

Far from Harrisburg (adaptation of *Loin de Hagondange* by J.-P. Wenzel), 1978
   After Dark, 10:80, Apr. 1978

WILLIAM KOZLENKO

The Earth Is Ours, 1937
   Greenfield, T. A., *Work and the Work Ethic in American Drama 1920-1970*,
   pp. 67-68

NORMAN KRASNA

Lady Harry, 1978
   Plays and Players, 25:22-23, Apr. 1978

NICK KREPOS
SEE
FRANÇOISE KOURILSKY AND NICK KREPOS

HENRY KRIEGER
SEE
TOM EYEN and HENRY KRIEGER

JOHN KUNIK

Young Bucks, 1981
    After Dark, 14:20, Aug./Sept. 1981

CASEY KURTTI

Catholic School Girls, 1982
    New Yorker, 58:126, 12 Apr. 1982
    Time, 119:77, 12 Apr. 1982

DONALD KVARES

Obsessions (two short plays, one titled *Will You Please Stand Up?*), 1979
    After Dark, 12:64, Aug. 1979

LAWRENCE LA BREE

Ebenezer Venture; or, Advertising for a Wife, 1841
    Herron, I. H., *The Small Town in American Drama*, p. 64

V. R. LANG

I Too Have Lived in Arcadia, 1980
    New York, 13:58+, 10 Nov. 1980

LOUIS LANTZ
SEE
OSCAR SAUL and LOUIS LANTZ

JAMES LAPINE

Table Settings, 1980
    America, 142:192, 8 Mar. 1980
    Los Angeles, 26:316+, May 1981
    New Yorker, 55:96, 21 Jan. 1980
    Newsweek, 95:58, 28 Jan. 1980
    Time, 115:89, 28 Jan. 1980

Twelve Dreams, 1981
    New Republic, 186:26, 10 Feb. 1982
    New York, 15:53, 11 Jan. 1982
    New Yorker, 57:53, 56, 4 Jan. 1982

RING LARDNER

General

Sonnenfeld, A., "The Last of the Red-hot Dadas: Ring Lardner, American Play-wright," *Dada/Surrealism*, 8:36-44, 1978

The Gelska Cup, 1925
Shyer, L., "American Absurd: Two Nonsense Plays by George S. Kaufman and Morrie Ryskind, and Ring Lardner," *Theater*, 9, ii:119-21, 1978 (play on pp. 126-27, with Introd. by R. Lardner, Jr., p. 125)

LOUIS LA RUSSO II

Knockout, 1979
After Dark, 12:29-30, July 1979
New Yorker, 55:84, 14 May 1979
Time, 113:93, 21 May 1979

Lamppost Reunion, 1975
Drama, 125:70-71, Summer 1977

Marlon Brando Sat Right Here, 1980
After Dark, 13:57, July 1980

KIRK LA SHELLE
SEE
OWEN WISTER and KIRK LA SHELLE

JOHN LATOUCHE
SEE
HUGH WHEELER, LEONARD BERNSTEIN, RICHARD WILBUR, JOHN LATOUCHE, and STEPHEN SONDHEIM

CANDACE LAUGHLIN

Still Time, 1980
After Dark, 13:63, Aug. 1980

SEE ALSO
MICHAEL E. DAWDY, CANDACE LAUGHLIN, and BARRY OPPER

S. K. LAUREN
SEE
REGINALD LAWRENCE and S. K. LAUREN

ARTHUR LAURENTS

General

Meserve, W. J., *An Outline History of American Drama*, p. 348

Home of the Brave, 1945
  Greenfield, T. A., *Work and the Work Ethic in American Drama 1920-1970*, p. 90

Scream, 1978
  Texas Monthly, 6:204, 206, Dec. 1978

ARTHUR LAURENTS, LEONARD BERNSTEIN, and STEPHEN SONDHEIM

West Side Story (based on J. Robbins's conception of Shakespeare's *Romeo and Juliet*), 1957
  Gottfried, M., *A Theater Divided*, pp. 189-94
  After Dark, 12:36-37, June 1979
  After Dark, 12:22, Apr. 1980
  Dance Magazine, 54:26-27, May 1980
  Encore, 9:38, Apr. 1980
  New York, 13:82, 3 Mar. 1980
  New Yorker, 56:67, 3 March 1980
  Newsweek, 95:90, 25 Feb. 1980
  Opera, 30:365, Apr. 1979
  Time, 115:63, 25 Feb. 1980
  Time, 115:59-60, 3 Mar. 1980

ARTHUR LAURENTS, JULE STYNE, and STEPHEN SONDHEIM

Gypsy (based on the memoirs of G. R. Lee), 1959
  Gottfried, M., *A Theater Divided*, pp. 194-96

DAN LAURIA

Game Plan, 1978
  After Dark, 11:94, Nov. 1978

SALLIE LAURIE

Door Play, 1977
  Texas Monthly, 6:96, Jan. 1978
  Theatre Journal, 32:256, 1980

Stillsong, 1976
  Texas Monthly, 4:85, Aug. 1976

SHIRLEY LAURO

Open Admissions, 1981
  New York, 14:72, 9 Nov. 1981

EMMET LAVERY

The Gentleman from Athens, 1947
  Nannes, C. H., *Politics in the American Drama*, pp. 117-19

EDDIE LAWRENCE

Animals (three one-acts: *The Beautiful Mariposa, Louie and the Elephant,* and *Son of an Adventure*), 1981
    New York, 14:60+, 4 May 1981

JEROME LAWRENCE and ROBERT E. LEE

First Monday in October, 1975
    After Dark, 11:95+, Dec. 1978
    America, 139:314, 4 Nov. 1978
    Encore, 7:36, 6 Nov. 1978
    Nation, 227:452, 28 Oct. 1978
    New Leader, 61:21-22, 23 Oct. 1978
    New Republic, 179:26, 28 Oct. 1978
    New York, 11:131+, 16 Oct. 1978
    New Yorker, 54:86, 16 Oct. 1978
    Newsweek, 92:94, 16 Oct. 1978
    Saturday Review, 5:45, Dec. 1978
    Time, 112:130, 16 Oct. 1978

The Gang's All Here, 1959
    Nannes, C. H., *Politics in the American Drama,* pp. 200-08

Inherit the Wind, 1955
    Herron, I. H., *The Small Town in American Drama,* pp. 231-34
    Hye, A. E., "A Tennessee Morality Play: Notes on *Inherit the Wind,*" *Markham Review,* 9:17-20, 1979
    Wertheim, A., "The McCarthy Era and the American Theatre," *Theatre Journal,* 34:211-22, 1982

REGINALD LAWRENCE and S. K. LAUREN

Men Must Fight, 1932
    Nannes, C. H., *Politics in the American Novel,* pp. 162-64

SEE ALSO
JOHN HAYNES HOLMES and REGINALD LAWRENCE

JOHN HOWARD LAWSON

General

Ludington, T., "Friendship Won't Stand That: John Howard Lawson and John Dos Passos's Struggle for an Ideological Ground to Stand On," pp. 46-66 in *Literature at the Barricades,* ed. R. F. Bogardus and F. Hobson
Meserve, W. J., *An Outline History of American Drama,* pp. 258-60
Robinson, L., "John Howard Lawson's Introduction to Broadway," *Kyushu American Literature,* 20:45-51, 1979

Atmosphere (title later changed to *Souls,* which see), 1914

Robinson, L., "John Howard Lawson's *Atmosphere* (1914)," *Kyushu American Literature*, 22:55-63, May 1981

Gentlewoman, 1934
  Himelstein, M. Y., *Drama Was a Weapon*, pp. 162-64
  Smiley, S., *The Drama of Attack*, pp. 175-76

Marching Song, 1937
  Himelstein, M. Y., *Drama Was a Weapon*, pp. 70-72, *passim*
  Smiley, S., *The Drama of Attack*, pp. 125-29

Processional, 1925
  Greenfield, T. A., *Work and the Work Ethic in American Drama 1920-1970*, pp. 82-83
  Herron, I. H., *The Small Town in American Drama*, pp. 213-14
  Himelstein, M. Y., *Drama Was a Weapon*, pp. 104-05

The Pure in Heart, 1934
  Smiley, S., *The Drama of Attack*, pp. 176-77

Roger Bloomer, 1923
  Broussard, L., *American Drama*, pp. 50-55
  Herron, I. H., *The Small Town in American Drama*, pp. 254-56
  Kaes, A., "John Howard Lawson: *Roger Bloomer*," *Studien zur Deutschen Literatur*, 43:116-21, 1975

Souls (also known as *Souls: A Psychic Fantasy*; begun in 1914 under the title *Atmosphere*, which see), 1915
  Robinson, L., "John Howard Lawson's *Souls*: A Harbinger of *Strange Interlude*," *Eugene O'Neill Newsletter*, 4, iii:12-13, 1980

Success Story, 1932
  Himelstein, M. Y., *Drama Was a Weapon*, pp. 160-61
  Smiley, S., *The Drama of Attack*, pp. 177-88, *passim*

JOHN LEACOCK

The Fall of British Tyranny, 1776
  Meserve, W. J., *An Emerging Entertainment*, pp. 78-81
  Meserve, W. J., *An Outline History of American Drama*, p. 18

ELIZABETH LeCOMPTE

General

Champagne, L., "Always Starting New: Elizabeth LeCompte" (Interview), *The Drama Review*, 25:19-28, Fall 1981

SEE ALSO
SPALDING GRAY, ELIZABETH LeCOMPTE, LIBBY HOWES,
JIM CLAYBURGH, and RON VAWTER

CHARLES LEDERER, LUTHER DAVIS, ROBERT WRIGHT,
GEORGE FORREST, and ALEXANDER BORODIN

Kismet (musical based on play by E. Knoblock), 1953
    America, 90:366, 2 Jan. 1954
    Catholic World, 178:388, Feb. 1954
    Colliers, 133:78-79, 8 Jan. 1954
    Commonweal, 59:353, 8 Jan. 1954
    Life, 35:25-28, 21 Dec. 1953
    Nation, 177:555, 19 Dec. 1953
    New Yorker, 29:85-87, 12 Dec. 1953
    Newsweek, 42:61, 14 Dec. 1953
    Newsweek, 42:60, 21 Dec. 1953
    Plays and Players, 25:32-33, May 1978
    Saturday Review, 36:28-29, 26 Dec. 1953
    Saturday Review, 5:26, 29 Apr. 1978
    Theatre Arts, 38:18-19, Feb. 1954
    Theatre Crafts, 12:13-15+, May 1978
    Time, 62:94, 14 Dec. 1953

LESLIE LEE

Colored People's Time (originally titled *C.P.T.*), 1982
    New Yorker, 58:126, 12 Apr. 1982

MARYAT LEE

General

Lee, M., "Legitimate Theater Is Illegitimate," pp. 11-24 in *Toward the Second Decade*, ed. B. Justice and R. Pore

ROBERT E. LEE
SEE
JEROME LAWRENCE and ROBERT E. LEE

EVA Le GALLIENNE and FLORIDA FRIEBUS

Alice in Wonderland (based upon the work of L. Carroll), 1932
    Life, 22:97-100, 28 Apr. 1947
    Literary Digest, 114:11, 31 Dec. 1932
    Nation, 135:654, 28 Dec. 1932
    Nation, 164:495, 26 Apr. 1947
    New Outlook, 161:49, Mar. 1933
    New Republic, 116:37, 21 Apr. 1947
    New York, 16:62, 10 Jan. 1983
    New Yorker, 58:51, 3 Jan. 1983

Newsweek, 29:89, 21 Apr. 1947
Newsweek, 101:41, 3 Jan. 1983
Saturday Review of Literature, 9:351, 31 Dec. 1932
Saturday Review of Literature, 30:24-27, 17 May 1947
Stage, 10:27-30, Feb. 1933
Theatre Arts Monthly, 17:101-03, 107-08, Feb. 1933
Theatre Arts, 31:17, 22, June 1947
Time, 21:22, 13 Feb. 1933
Time, 49:69, 14 Apr. 1947
Vogue, 81:55, 72, 15 Feb. 1933

IRENE Le HERISSIER and ARTHUR BINDER

The Ravine (based upon the life and work of N. Sachs), 1979
   Theatre Journal, 32:269, 1980

MITCH LEIGH
SEE
DALE WASSERMAN, MITCH LEIGH, and JOE DARION

JIM LEONARD, JR.

The Diviners, 1980
   After Dark, 13:68, Jan. 1981
   New York, 13:75-76, 3 Nov. 1980
   New Yorker, 56:158, 27 Oct. 1980

ALAN JAY LERNER and FREDERICK LOEWE

My Fair Lady (musical version of G. B. Shaw's play *Pygmalion*), 1956
   After Dark, 14:13, Nov. 1981
   America, 145:163, 26 Sept. 1981
   Dance Magazine, 55:112, Nov. 1981
   Drama, 135:43-44, Jan. 1980
   Drama, 139:27-28, 1981
   Los Angeles, 26:214+, Jan. 1981
   Nation, 233:249+, 19 Sept. 1981
   New York, 14:56, 31 Aug. 1981
   New Yorker, 57:78, 31 Aug. 1981
   Newsweek, 98:56, 31 Aug. 1981
   Plays and Players, 27:25+, Dec. 1979
   Saturday Review, 8:66-67, Nov. 1981
   Time, 118:70, 31 Aug. 1981

MICHAEL LESSAC

Molière in Spite of Himself (adaptation of M. Bulgakov's *A Cabal of Hypocrites*),
   1978
   New Yorker, 54:90, 20 Mar. 1978

IRA LEVIN

Break a Leg, 1979
  New Yorker, 55:130, 7 May 1979

Deathtrap, 1978
  After Dark, 11:110+, May 1978
  Drama, 131:46, Winter 1979
  Drama-Logue, 13, xxxvii:5, 16-22 Sept. 1982
  Los Angeles, 24:251, June 1979
  New West, 4:SC-45, 7 May 1979
  New York, 11:72, 13 Mar. 1978
  New Yorker, 54:56, 13 Mar. 1978
  Newsweek, 91:93+, 13 Mar. 1978
  Plays and Players, 26:24, Jan. 1979
  Saturday Review, 5:26, 29 Apr. 1978
  Time, 111:75, 13 Mar. 1978

No Time for Sergeants (dramatization of novel by M. Hyman), 1955
  Herron, I. H., *The Small Town in American Drama*, pp. 450-51

H. N. LEVITT

Beasts, 1978
  After Dark, 11:116, May 1978

BENN W. LEVY

Springtime for Henry, 1931
  After Dark, 12:20, Dec. 1979

MELVIN LEVY

Gold Eagle Guy, 1934
  Himelstein, M. Y., *Drama Was a Weapon*, pp. 164-66
  Smiley, S., *The Drama of Attack*, pp. 50, 181-84

SINCLAIR LEWIS and LLOYD LEWIS

The Jayhawker, 1934
  Herron, I. H., *The Small Town in American Drama*, pp. 268-69

SINCLAIR LEWIS and JOHN C. MOFFITT

It Can't Happen Here (dramatization of Lewis's novel), 1936
  Herron, I. H., *The Small Town in American Drama*, pp. 267-68, 269-71
  Himelstein, M. Y., *Drama Was a Weapon*, pp. 98-100
  Nannes, C. H., *Politics in the American Drama*, pp. 139-41

PAUL STEVEN LIM

Flesh, Flash, & Frank Harris, 1980

After Dark, 13:58, July 1980

Woeman, 1978
  After Dark, 11:96, Dec. 1978

HOWARD LINDSAY and RUSSEL CROUSE

General

Gould, J., "Some Clever Collaborators," pp. 140-50 in Gould's *Modern American
  Playwrights*

The Great Sebastians, 1956
  Nannes, C. H., *Politics in the American Drama*, pp. 177-82

The Prescott Proposals, 1953
  Nannes, C. H., *Politics in the American Drama*, pp. 193-96

State of the Union, 1945
  Nannes, C. H., *Politics in the American Drama*, pp. 1-4, 8-14

ROMULUS LINNEY

The Captivity of Pixie Shedman, 1981
  After Dark, 13:82, May 1981
  New York, 14:64-65, 16 Feb. 1981
  New Yorker, 56:60, 16 Feb. 1981

Childe Byron, 1977
  After Dark, 14:72, June 1981
  Drama, 142:34, 1981
  Nation, 232:347-48, 21 Mar. 1981
  New Yorker, 57:74+, 9 Mar. 1981
  Time, 117:74, 9 Mar. 1981

Holy Ghosts, 1976
  Georgia Review, 35:598-99, Fall 1981

DAVID DEMAREST LLOYD and SYDNEY ROSENFELD

The Senator, 1890
  Nannes, C. H., *Politics in the American Drama*, pp. 1-8

INGERSOLL LOCKWOOD

Washington: A Heroic Drama of the Revolution, 1875
  Shillingsburg, M. J., "The West Point Treason in American Drama, 1798-1891,"
  Educational Theatre Journal, 30:73-89, 1978

FRANK LOESSER

General

Gottfried, M., *A Theater Divided*, pp. 181-82

The Most Happy Fella (musical version of S. Howard's play *They Knew What They Wanted*), 1956
Herron, I. H., *The Small Town in American Drama*, pp. 477-78
After Dark, 12:24-25, Dec. 1979
America, 141:281, 10 Nov. 1979
High Fidelity, 30:MA16-17, Feb. 1980
High Fidelity, 30:MA36-38, Feb. 1980
New York, 12:86, 29 Oct. 1979
New Yorker, 55:142+, 22 Oct. 1979
Newsweek, 94:130, 22 Oct. 1979
Plays and Players, 27:39, Dec. 1979
Time, 114:98, 22 Oct. 1979

SEE ALSO
ABE BURROWS, JO SWERLING, and FRANK LOESSER

FREDERICK LOEWE
SEE
ALAN JAY LERNER and FREDERICK LOEWE

CORNELIUS AMBROSIUS LOGAN

The Vermont Wool-Dealer, 1840
Herron, I. H., *The Small Town in American Drama*, p. 63

Yankee Land, 1834
Herron, I. H., *The Small Town in American Drama*, pp. 61-63

JOSHUA LOGAN
SEE
THOMAS HEGGEN and JOSHUA LOGAN

HENRY WADSWORTH LONGFELLOW

Giles Corey of the Salem Farms, 1868
Herron, I. H., *The Small Town in American Drama*, pp. 18-20

John Endicott (first drafted as *The Old Colony* and redrafted as *Wenlock Christison*), 1868
Herron, I. H., *The Small Town in American Drama*, pp. 16-18

ANITA LOOS

General

Bruccoli, M. J., "Anita Loos," pp. 125-40 in *Conversations with Writers, II*, ed.

Bruccoli, C. E. F. Clark, Jr., R. Layman, M. M. Duggan, G. G. Fedricci, and C. L. White

ANITA LOOS and JOHN EMERSON

The Fall of Eve, 1925
  Life (New York), 86:18, 17 Sept. 1925
  New Republic, 44:95-96, 16 Sept. 1925

The Whole Town's Talking, 1923
  Dramatist, 14:1168-69, July 1923
  Metropolitan Magazine, 58:38-39+, Dec. 1923
  Nation, 117:304, 19 Sept. 1923
  Theatre Magazine, 38:66, Oct. 1923

JAMES LORD and GENEVIEVE SERREAU

Heartaches of a Pussycat (dramatization of a short story by H. de Balzac and inspired by the drawings of Grandville in his book *Scenes from the Private and Public Life of Animals*), 1980
  After Dark, 13:62, May 1980
  New Yorker, 56:92, 31 Mar. 1980

W. W. LORD

André, 1856
  Shillingsburg, M. J., "The West Point Treason in American Drama, 1798-1891," *Educational Theatre Journal*, 30:73-89, 1978

ROBERT LOWELL

General

Cohn, R., *Dialogue in American Drama*, pp. 280-92
Fein, R. J., *Robert Lowell*

Endecott and the Red Cross (dramatization of N. Hawthorne's story with that title and of his *The Maypole at Merry Mount*), 1964
  Drinnon, R., "The Maypole of Merry Mount: Thomas Morton & the Puritan Patriarchs," *Massachusetts Review*, 21:382-410, Summer 1980
  Holton, M., "Maule's Curse and My-Lai: Robert Lowell's *Endecott*," pp. 175-86 in *Proceedings of a Symposium on American Literature*, ed. M. Sienicka

The Old Glory (three plays: *Endecott and the Red Cross*, which see; *My Kinsman, Major Molineux*, a dramatization of N. Hawthorne's story; and *Benito Cereno*, a dramatization of H. Helville's novella), 1964
  Gottfried, M., *A Theater Divided*, pp. 71-72

CLARE BOOTHE LUCE
SEE
CLARE BOOTHE

WILLIAM LUCE

The Belle of Amherst (based on the life and writings of E. Dickinson), 1976
   Bordinat, P., "The One-Person Play: A Form of Contemporary Dramatic Biography," *Midwest Quarterly*, 21:231-40, 1980
   Meyer, H. N., "A Second Look at *The Belle of Amherst*," *Midwest Quarterly*,
   21:365-70, 1980

CHARLES LUDLAM

General

Leverett, J., "Old Forms Enter the New American Theater: Shepard, Foreman, Kirby,
   and Ludlam," pp. 107-22 in *Melodrama*, guest ed. D. C. Gerould

Conquest of the Universe; or, When Queens Collide, 1967
   After Dark, 12:26, Dec. 1979

The Enchanted Pig, 1979
   After Dark, 12:31, July 1979

Reverse Psychology, 1980
   Nation, 231:354-56, 11 Oct. 1980

DES McANUFF

The Death of Von Richthofen as Witnessed from Earth, 1982
   New York, 15:42, 9 Aug. 1982
   New Yorker, 58:81, 23 Aug. 1982
   Newsweek, 100:68, 9 Aug. 1982
   Plays and Players, 349:37, Oct. 1982
   Time, 120:74, 9 Aug. 1982

CHARLES MacARTHUR

Johnny on a Spot, 1942
   After Dark, 13:65, May 1980
   New York, 13:66+, 17 Mar. 1980
   New Yorker, 56:93-94, 10 Mar. 1980

SEE ALSO
BEN HECHT and CHARLES MacARTHUR

VAUGHN McBRIDE

The New Girl, 1982
   Time, 119:78, 12 Apr. 1982

RALPH ALAN McCANSE

Waters Over Linn Creek Town, 1951
Herron, I. H., *The Small Town in American Drama*, p. 483

MICHAEL McCLURE

General

Dasgupta, G., "Michael McClure," pp. 143-57 in Dasgupta and B. G. Marranca's *American Playwrights*

Josephine the Mouse Singer (adaptation of a story by F. Kafka), 1978
After Dark, 11:86, Mar. 1979

CARSON McCULLERS

General

Friedman, M. J., " 'The Mortgaged Heart': The Workshop of Carson McCullers," *Revue des Langues Vivantes*, [US Bicentennial Issue], pp. 143-55, 1978
McDowell, M., *Carson McCullers*
Phillips, L., "The Novelist as Playwright: Baldwin, McCullers, and Bellow," pp. 145-62 in *Modern American Drama*, ed. W. E. Taylor

The Member of the Wedding (dramatization of her novel), 1950
Herron, I. H., *The Small Town in American Drama*, pp. 398-401
Kusuhara, T., "New Indications in Conventionalism in Popular Plays," pp. 147-55 in *American Literature in the 1950's* (American Literature Society of Japan 1976 Annual Report)

GEORGE BARR McCUTCHEON

General

Lazarus, A. L., "George Barr McCutcheon: Youth and Drama," *Biography*, 4, iii:208-26, Summer 1981
Lazarus, A. L. and V. H. Jones, *Beyond Graustark*

GALT MacDERMOT
SEE
GEROME RAGNI, JAMES RADO, and GALT MacDERMOT

DENNIS McINTYRE

Modigliani, 1978
After Dark, 12:20, Jan. 1980
Nation, 229:604, 8 Dec. 1979
New York, 11:82, 12 June 1978
New York, 12:90+, 26 Nov. 1979
New Yorker, 55:115-16, 26 Nov. 1979
Plays and Players, 27:38, Feb. 1980
Time, 114:129, 26 Nov. 1979

PERCY MacKAYE

General

Meserve, W. J., *An Outline History of American Drama*, pp. 195, 246-47

The Scarecrow, 1909
  Herron, I. H., *The Small Town in American Drama*, pp. 28-30

STEELE MacKAYE

Hazel Kirke, 1880
  Meserve, W. J., *An Outline History of American Drama*, pp. 137-39

GRACE McKEANEY

General

Theatre News, 11, viii:4, May 1979

NEIL McKENZIE

Guests of the Nation (dramatization of a short story by F. O'Connor), 1980
  After Dark, 13:57, July 1980
  New Yorker, 56:92-93, 31 Mar. 1980

EUGENE McKINNEY

A Different Drummer, 1964
  Herron, I. H., *The Small Town in American Drama*, pp. 402-03

SEE ALSO
PAUL BAKER and EUGENE McKINNEY

JOHN McKINNEY
SEE
ROBERT KALFIN, STEVE BROWN, JOHN McKINNEY,
and WILLIAM BOLCOM

ARCHIBALD MacLEISH

General

Cohn, R., *Dialogue in American Drama*, pp. 250-63
Meserve, W. J., *An Outline History of American Drama*, pp. 253-54
Time, 119:78, 3 May 1982

The Fall of the City, 1937
  Jarrell, R., "*The Fall of the City*," pp. 101-11 in Jarrell's *Kipling, Auden & Co.*

J.B., 1958
  Broussard, L., *American Drama*, pp. 121-27

Fuwa, H., "Human Survival and *J.B.*," pp. 191-98 in *American Literature in the 1950's* (American Literature Society of Japan 1976 Annual Report)

Houghton, N., *The Exploding Stage*, pp. 118-19

Kotama, M. and M. Sata, "Secular Humanism," pp. 183-90 in *American Literature in the 1950's* (American Literature Society of Japan 1976 Annual Report)

Panic, 1935
Himelstein, M. Y., *Drama Was a Weapon*, pp. 194-95
Smiley, S., *The Drama of Attack*, pp. 54-55, 184-87

Scratch (dramatization of *The Devil and Daniel Webster* by S. V. Benét), 1971
Sarma, S. K., "Liberty and Union: Archibald MacLeish's *Scratch*," *Indian Journal of American Studies*, 8, ii:44-50, 1978

This Music Crept by Me Upon the Waters, 1953
Gerstenberger, D., "Three Verse Playwrights and the American Fifties," pp. 117-28 in *Modern American Drama*, ed. W. E. Taylor

JAMES McLURE

Laundry and Bourbon (see also *1959 Pink Thunderbird*), 1980
Texas Monthly, 8:196, 199, May 1980
Texas Monthly, 10:150, July 1982

Lone Star (see also *1959 Pink Thunderbird*), 1979
After Dark, 12:60-61, Aug. 1979
America, 141:16, 7 July 1979
New Republic, 181:24, 7 July 1979
New Yorker, 55:90, 18 June 1979
Texas Monthly, 7:200+, Oct. 1979
Time, 113:73, 5 Mar. 1979

1959 Pink Thunderbird (two one-acts: *Lone Star* and *Laundry and Bourbon*, which see), 1980
Texas Monthly, 8:196, 199, May 1980

Pvt. Wars, 1979
After Dark, 12:60, Aug. 1979
America, 141:16, 7 July 1979
New Republic, 181:24, 7 July 1979
New Yorker, 55:90, 18 June 1979
Texas Monthly, 7:200, Oct. 1979
Time, 113:73, 5 Mar. 1979

FRANK McMAHON

Borstal Boy (based on the memoirs of B. Behan), 1967
America, 139:90, 12 Aug. 1978

TERRENCE McNALLY

Bad Habits (two one-acts: *Ravenswood* and *Dunelawn*), 1971
    Educational Theatre Journal, 30:123, 1978

Botticelli, 1968
    After Dark, 12:64, Aug. 1979

It's Only a Play, 1982
    New York, 15:152, 6 Dec. 1982

GAIL KRIEGEL MALLIN

Holy Places, 1979
    New Yorker, 55:102, 17 Dec. 1979

PETER MALONEY

Lost and Found (presented with J. Kass's *Young Marrieds at Play* as *Handle with Care*), 1982
    Drama-Logue, 13, xxxvii:5, 16-22 Sept. 1982

KAREN MALPEDE

Making Peace: A Fantasy, 1979
    Theatre Journal, 32:268-69, 1980

ALBERT MALTZ

General

Salzman, J., *Albert Maltz*

Black Pit, 1935
    Greenfield, T. A., *Work and the Work Ethic in American Drama 1920-1970*, pp. 71-72
    Himelstein, M. Y., *Drama Was a Weapon*, pp. 63-65
    Smiley, S., *The Drama of Attack*, pp. 192-97, *passim*

The Morrison Case, 1952
    Wertheim, A., "The McCarthy Era and the American Theatre," *Theatre Journal*, 34:211-22, 1982

Private Hicks, 1936
    Himelstein, M. Y., *Drama Was a Weapon*, p. 43

ALBERT MALTZ and GEORGE SKLAR

Peace on Earth, 1933
    Himelstein, M. Y., *Drama Was a Weapon*, pp. 57-58, *passim*
    Smiley, S., *The Drama of Attack*, pp. 52, 116-20

Zero Hour, 1941
   Himelstein, M. Y., *Drama Was a Weapon*, pp. 47-48

DAVID MAMET

General

Ditsky, J., " 'He Lets You See the Thought There': The Theater of David Mamet,"
   Kansas Quarterly, 12, iv: 25-34, 1980
Gale, S. H., "David Mamet: The Plays, 1972-1980," pp. 207-23 in *Essays on Con-
   temporary American Drama*, ed. H. Bock and A. Wertheim
Mamet, D., "First Principles," *Theater*, 12:50-52, Summer/Fall 1981
Mamet, D., "Learn to Love the Theatre," *Horizon*, 21:96, Oct. 1978
Mamet, D., "Playwrights on Resident Theaters: What Is to Be Done?," *Theater*,
   10:82, Summer 1979
Miner, M. D., "Grotesque Drama in the '70s," *Kansas Quarterly*, 12, iv:99-109,
   1980
Storey, R., "The Making of David Mamet," *Hollins Critic*, 16, iv:1-11, 1979
Vallely, J., "David Mamet Makes a Play for Hollywood," *Rolling Stone*, pp. 44+,
   3 Apr. 1980

American Buffalo, 1975
   Barbera, J. V., "Ethical Perversity in America: Some Observations on David
      Mamet's *American Buffalo*," *Modern Drama*, 24, iii:270-75, Sept. 1981
   After Dark, 14:18, Aug./Sept. 1981
   Drama, 130:53, Autumn 1978
   Los Angeles, 23:218+, Mar. 1978
   Nation, 231:521-22, 15 Nov. 1980
   Nation, 233:353-54, 10 Oct. 1981
   New Leader, 64:21-22, 29 June 1981
   New West, 2:SC-30, 13 Mar. 1978
   New York, 14:66, 15 June 1981
   New Yorker, 57:127, 15 June 1981
   Plays and Players, 25:31, Aug. 1978
   Theatre Journal, 33:402-04, 1981

Dark Pony, 1977
   Educational Theatre Journal, 30:417-18, 1978
   New Yorker, 55:81, 29 Oct. 1979

Duck Variations, 1972
   Gale, S. H., "David Mamet's *The* [sic] *Duck Variations*," *Cue*, 59, i:17-18,
      Fall-Winter 1980
   Miner, M. D., "Grotesque Drama in the '70s," *Kansas Quarterly*, 12, iv:99-
      109, 1980
   Los Angeles, 24:251, June 1979
   Plays and Players, 25:30-31, Feb. 1978

Edmond, 1982
   After Dark, 15:14, Dec. 1982/Jan. 1983
   New Republic, 187:24, 12 July 1982

New York, 15:60, 8 Nov. 1982
New Yorker, 58:160, 8 Nov. 1982
Newsweek, 100:82, 8 Nov. 1982
Time, 120:82, 8 Nov. 1982

A Life in the Theatre, 1977
  "*A Life in the Theatre*: Mamet's Comedy Produced for Television," *Theatre News*, 11, ix:18-19, Summer 1979
  After Dark, 10:81-82, Jan. 1978
  After Dark, 12:22, Feb. 1980
  After Dark, 12:26, Apr. 1980
  Hudson Review, 31:154-55, Spring 1978
  Los Angeles, 25:219 + , Mar. 1980
  Mandate, 3:9 + , Jan. 1978
  New West, 5:SC-17, 25 Feb. 1980
  Plays and Players, 26:25 + , Aug. 1979

Lone Canoe; or, the Explorer, 1979
  Theatre Journal, 32:256-57, 1980

Reunion, 1976

  Educational Theatre Journal, 30:418, 1978
  Nation, 229:572, 1 Dec. 1979
  New York, 12:87, 5 Nov. 1979
  New Yorker, 55:81, 29 Oct. 1979

The Sanctity of Marriage, 1979
  New Yorker, 55:81, 29 Oct. 1979

A Sermon, 1981
  New York, 14:71, 9 Nov. 1981

Sexual Perversity in Chicago, 1974
  Los Angeles, 24:251, June 1979
  Plays and Players, 25:30-31, Feb. 1978

Shoeshine, 1979
  New Yorker, 55:72, 24 Dec. 1979

The Water Engine, 1977
  Eder, R., "David Mamet's New Realism," *New York Times Magazine*, pp. 40 + , 12 Mar. 1978
  America, 138:286, 8 Apr. 1978
  Commonweal, 105:244 + , 14 Apr. 1978
  Harper's, 256:86-87, May 1978
  Los Angeles, 25:210 + , Jan. 1980
  Nation, 226:92, 28 Jan. 1978
  New York, 11:60, 30 Jan. 1978
  New Yorker, 53:69-70, 26 Jan. 1978
  Saturday Review, 5:41, 4 Mar. 1978

Time, 111:84, 20 Mar. 1978

The Woods, 1977
   After Dark, 12:31, July 1979
   Nation, 228:581-82, 19 May 1979
   New York, 12:75, 14 May 1979
   New York, 15:93-94, 31 May 1982
   New Yorker, 55:130-31, 7 May 1979

CYNTHIA MANDELBURG
SEE
MICHAEL SUTTON and CYNTHIA MANDELBURG

BILL MANHOFF

The Owl and the Pussycat, 1964
   Gottfried, M., *A Theater Divided*, pp. 76-77

EMILY MANN

Still Life, 1981
   California, 7:116+, May 1982
   New York, 14:52+, 2 Mar. 1981
   New Yorker, 57:62, 2 Mar. 1981

JOR MARCY and JACOB A. WEISER

First American Dictator, 1939
   Nannes, C. H., *Politics in the American Drama*, pp. 199-200

WALTER MARKS and PETER MARKS

The Butler Did It, 1981
   New York, 14:66-67, 15 June 1981

GARRY MARSHALL
SEE
JERRY BELSON and GARRY MARSHALL

JANE MARTIN
(pseudonym)

Handler, 1982
   Time, 119:78, 12 Apr. 1982

Talking With (eleven monologues, including *Handler* and *Twirler*, both of which see),
   1982
   New Republic, 187:26, 1 Nov. 1982
   New York, 15:88, 18 Oct. 1982

New Yorker, 58:160, 18 Oct. 1982
Newsweek, 100:101, 25 Oct. 1982
Theatre Journal, 34, iv:543-44, Dec. 1982

Twirler, 1981
Time, 117:74, 6 Apr. 1981
Time, 119:78, 12 Apr. 1982

MARTY MARTIN

A Clown of God, 1980
Texas Monthly, 9:149, Feb. 1981

Farewell Performance, 1980
Texas Monthly, 9:149, Feb. 1981

Gertrude Stein Gertrude Stein Gertrude Stein, 1979
After Dark, 12:18, Feb. 1980
Art News, 79:7, Sept. 1980
Georgia Review, 24:497-508, Fall 1980
Horizon, 23:38-41, Nov. 1980
New York, 12:67, 6 Aug. 1979
Plays and Players, 27:36-38, Jan. 1980
Time, 114:93, 17 Sept. 1979

JUDI ANN MASON

Daughters of the Mock, 1979
Encore, 8:36-37, 5 Feb. 1979

WILLIAM MASTROSIMONE

Extremities, 1981
New Republic, 188:28, 14 Feb. 1983
Newsweek, 101:65, 24 Jan. 1983
Time, 117:73-74, 6 Apr. 1981
Time, 121:78, 3 Jan. 1983

The Woolgatherer, 1980
New York, 13:49-50, 23 June 1980
New Yorker, 56:100-01, 8 Sept. 1980

CORNELIUS MATHEWS

Witchcraft, 1846
Herron, I. H., *The Small Town in American Drama*, pp. 14-16, 91-92

JOHN MAXWELL AND TOM DUPREE

Oh, Mr. Faulkner, Do You Write?, 1981
Southern Living, 16:191-92, Nov. 1981

EDWIN JUSTUS MAYER

Children of Darkness, 1930
   After Dark, 12:26, Jan. 1980

MARK MEDOFF

Children of a Lesser God, 1979
   Garvey, L., "Medoff's *Children*," *Writer's Digest*, 61:20+, Sept. 1981
   Hall, S. M. "Ex-faculty Bad Boy Mark Medoff Takes a Tony Home to New
      Mexico," *People*, 15:78+, 12 Jan. 1981
   Vos, N., "The Witness of Silence: The Testimony of *Children of a Lesser God*
      and *The Caretaker*," *Cresset*, 44, iv:17-19, Feb. 1981
   After Dark, 12:25+, Jan. 1980
   After Dark, 13:57, June 1980
   Commonweal, 107:595-96, 24 Oct. 1980
   Drama, 143:40, Spring 1982
   Georgia Review, 35:605-06, Fall 1981
   Los Angeles, 24:386+, Dec. 1979
   Nation, 230:508-09, 26 Apr. 1980
   New Republic, 182:23-24, 7 June 1980
   New West, 4:SC-43, 3 Dec. 1979
   New York, 13:85-86, 14 Apr. 1980
   New Yorker, 56:101, 14 Apr. 1980
   Newsweek, 95:105, 14 Apr. 1980
   Texas Monthly, 9:176-77, Aug. 1981
   Time, 115:112, 14 Apr. 1980
   Time, 116:62, 7 July 1980

Firekeeper, 1978
   Texas Monthly, 6:136, July 1978
   Theatre Journal, 32:256, 1980

THOMAS MEEHAN, RICHARD RODGERS, MARTIN CHARNIN, and RAYMOND JESSEL

I Remember Mama (musical version of J. Van Druten's dramatization of K. Forbe's
   Mama's Bank Account), 1979
   After Dark, 12:61-62, Aug. 1979
   New Leader, 62:23-24, 18 June 1979
   New York, 12:74, 18 June 1979
   New Yorker, 55:79, 11 June 1979
   Newsweek, 93:75, 11 June 1979
   Plays and Players, 26:38-39, Aug. 1979
   Time, 113:62, 11 June 1979

JOHN MEIXNER

Women and Men, 1979
   Texas Monthly, 7:164-65, Apr. 1979

LEONARD MELFI

General

Marranca, B. G., "Leonard Melfi," pp. 219-26 in Marranca and G. Dasgupta's *American Playwrights*

Birdbath, 1965
  New Yorker, 58:128, 22 Mar. 1982

STEVE METCALFE

Strange Snow, 1982
  New Yorker, 57:111, 15 Feb. 1982

Vikings, 1980
  New Yorker, 56:135, 24 Nov. 1980

PATRICK MEYERS

Feedlot, 1977
  After Dark, 10:82-83, Jan. 1978

Glorious Morning, 1978
  After Dark, 11:85, Jan. 1979
  New York, 11:152 + , 13 Nov. 1978
  New Yorker, 43:153-54, 6 Nov. 1978

K2, 1982
  Theatre Crafts, 16:16-17 + , Oct. 1982

SIDNEY MICHAELS

Tricks of the Trade, 1977
  Los Angeles, 25:297, Nov. 1980
  New York Theatre Review, 1:42, Nov. 1977

EDNA ST. VINCENT MILLAY

General

Meserve, W. J., *An Outline History of American Drama*, pp. 249-50

ALAN MILLER

The Fox (dramatization of D. H. Lawrence's novella), 1982
  New York, 15:64, 30 Aug. 1982

ARTHUR MILLER

General

Asahina, R., "The Quintessence of Millerism," *Theater*, 10:99-101, Fall 1978

Bock, H., "Die Rolle der Frau in Arthur Millers frühen Dramen: Untersuchungen zu seinem Konzept gesellschaftlicher Wirklichkeit," pp. 307-22 in *Literarische Ansichten der Wirklichkeit*, ed. H.-H. Freitag and P. Hühn

Boruch, M., "Miller and Things," *Literary Review*, 24, iv:548-61, Summer 1981

Broussard, L., *American Drama*, pp. 116-21

Carson, N., *Arthur Miller*

Cohn, R., *Dialogue in American Drama*, pp. 68-96

Donahue, F., "Arthur Miller: Las dos moralidades," *Cuadernos Americanos*, 226:157-58, 1979

Ferres, J. H., *Arthur Miller*

Ganz, A. F., "Arthur Miller: Eden and After," pp. 122-44 in Ganz's *Realms of the Self*

Gianakaris, C. J., "Theatre of the Mind in Miller, Osborne and Shaffer," *Renascence*, 30:33-42, 1977

Gollub, C.-A., "Interview with Arthur Miller," *Michigan Quarterly Review*, 16:121-41, 1977

Gottfried, M., *A Theater Divided*, pp. 242-48

Gould, J., "Arthur Miller," pp. 247-63 in Gould's *Modern American Playwrights*

Günişik, S., "Arthur Miller, in Oyunlarında Sorumluluk Konusu," *Bati Edebiatlari Arastirma Dergisi*, 4:95-105, 1980 (responsibility in Miller's plays)

Hays, P. L., "Arthur Miller and Tennessee Williams," *Essays in Literature*, 4:239-49, 1977

Kanamuru, T., "McCarthyism and Arthur Miller," pp. 140-46 in *American Literature in the 1950's* (American Literature Society of Japan 1976 Annual Report)

Köhler, K., "Bewusstseinsanalyse und Gesellschaftskrise im Dramenwerk Arthur Millers," *Zeitschrift für Anglistik und Amerikanistik*, 22:18-40, 1974

Martin, R. A., *Arthur Miller*

Martin, R. A., "Introduction," pp. xv-xxxix in *The Theater Essays of Arthur Miller*, ed. Martin

Martin, R. A. and R. D. Meyer, "Arthur Miller on Plays and Playwriting: Interview," *Modern Drama*, 19:375-84, Dec. 1976

Martine, J. J., " 'All in a Boiling Soup': An Interview with Arthur Miller," pp. 177-88 in *Critical Essays on Arthur Miller*, ed. Martine

Meserve, W. J., *An Outline History of American Drama*, pp. 332-35

Miller, A., "The American Writer: The American Theatre," *Michigan Quarterly Review*, 21:4-20, Winter 1982 (also pp. 254-70 in *The Writer's Craft*, ed. R. A. Martin)

Miller, A., "Introduction to the Collected Plays," pp. 113-70 in *The Theater Essays of Arthur Miller*, ed. R. A. Martin

Moss, L., *Arthur Miller*, rev. ed.

Överland, O., "The Action and Its Significance: Arthur Miller's Struggle with Dramatic Form," *Modern Drama*, 18:1-14, 1975

Rajakrishnan, V., "After Commitment: An Interview with Arthur Miller," *Theatre Journal*, 32:196-204, 1980

Razum, H., "Schuld und Verantwortung im Werk Arthur Millers," pp. 310-20 in *Theater und Drama in Amerika*, ed. E. Lohner and R. Haas

Rudman, M., "In Conversation with Arthur Miller," *Plays and Players*, 27:20-21, Oct. 1979

Sata, M., "American Realism and Arthur Miller's Struggle," pp. 174-90 in *The Traditional and the Anti-Traditional*, ed. K. Ohashi

Scanlan, T., "Family and Society in Arthur Miller," pp. 126-55 in Scanlon's *Family, Drama, and American Dreams*

Schwarz, A., "After the Fall," pp. 161-82 in Schwarz's *From Büchner to Beckett*

Schwarz, A., "Society and Human Passion as a Tragic Motive," pp. 100-60 in Schwarz's *From Büchner to Beckett*

Stambusky, A. A., "Arthur Miller: Aristotelian Canons in the Twentieth Century Drama," pp. 91-115 in *Modern American Drama*, ed. W. E. Taylor

Styan, J. L., "Realism in America: Williams and Miller," pp. 137-48 in Vol. I of Styan's *Modern Drama in Theory and Practice*

Vajda, M., "Arthur Miller—Moralist as Playwright," *New Hungarian Quarterly*, 16:171-80, 1975

Vajda, M., "Playwriting in America Today: A Telephone Interview with Arthur Miller," *New Hungarian Quarterly*, 77:123-24, 1980

Wertheim, A., "Arthur Miller: *After the Fall* and After," pp. 19-32 in *Essays on Contemporary American Drama*, ed. H. Bock and Wertheim

White, K. S., "Scientists' Dilemmas: Prophetic Metaphors in Twentieth Century Drama," pp. 533-36 in *Proceedings of the 7th Congress of the International Comparative Literature Association, I*, ed. M. V. Dimić and J. Ferraté

After the Fall, 1964

>Burhans, Jr., C. S., "Eden and the Idiot Child: Arthur Miller's *After the Fall*," *Ball State University Forum*, 20, ii:3-16, 1979

>Engle, J. D., "The Metaphor of Law in *After the Fall*," *Notes on Contemporary Literature*, 9, iii:11-12, 1979

>Gianakaris, C. J., "Theatre of the Mind in Miller, Osborne and Shaffer," *Renascence*, 30, i:33-42, 1977

>Gottfried, M., *A Theater Divided*, pp. 149-52

>Lengeler, R., "Arthur Miller: *After the Fall*," pp. 12-28 in *Das amerikanische Drama der Gegenwart*, ed. H. Grabes

>Miller, A., "Foreward to *After the Fall*," pp. 255-57 in *The Theater Essays of Arthur Miller*, ed. R. A. Martin

All My Sons, 1947

>Greenfield, T. A., *Work and the Work Ethic in American Drama 1920-1970*, pp. 115-18, *passim*

>Herron, I. H., *The Small Town in American Drama*, pp. 466-67

>Houghton, N., *The Exploding Stage*, pp. 60-61

>Vos, N., *The Great Pendulum of Becoming*, p. 50

>*Drama*, 137:55, July 1980

>*Drama*, 143:26, Spring 1982

>*Drama*, 144:29-30, Summer 1982

The American Clock (adaptation of *Hard Times* by S. Terkel), 1979

>Moss, R. F., "Arthur Miller Reaches for Former Glory," *Saturday Review*, 7:22-23, Sept. 1980

>*After Dark*, 13:22, Feb. 1981

>*Nation*, 231:652, 13 Dec. 1980

>*New Leader*, 63:15-16, 29 Dec. 1980

>*New York*, 13:92+, 8 Dec. 1980

>*New Yorker*, 56:127-28, 8 Dec. 1980

>*Newsweek*, 96:84, 1 Dec. 1980

Saturday Review, 8:79, Jan. 1981
Time, 115:65, 9 June 1980

The Creation of the World and Other Business, 1972

Högel, R., "*The Creation of the World and Other Business*: Arthur Millers Spekulationen über die Ursprünge des Bösen," *Literatur in Wissenschaft und Unterricht*, 12:37-48, 1979

Richardson, J., "Arthur Miller's Eden," *Commentary*, 55:83-85, 1973

The Crucible (earlier version copyrighted under the title *Those Familiar Spirits*), 1953

Bonnet, J.-M., "Non et renom dans *The Crucible*," *Etudes Anglaises*, 30:179-83, 1977

Bonnet, J.-M., "Society vs. the Individual in Arthur Miller's *The Crucible*," *English Studies*, 63:32-36, Feb. 1982

Calarco, N. J., "Productions as Criticism: Miller's *The Crucible*," *Educational Theatre Journal*, 29:354-61, 1977

Ditsky, J., "Stone, Fire and Light: Approaches to *The Crucible*," *North Dakota Quarterly*, 46, ii:65-72, 1978

Foulkes, P. A., "Arthur Miller's *The Crucible*: Contexts of Understanding and Misunderstanding," pp. 295-309 in *Theater und Drama in Amerika*, ed. E. Lohner and R. Haas

Herron, I. H., *The Small Town in American Drama*, pp. 30-35

Houghton, N., *The Exploding Stage*, pp. 64-66

Liston, W. T., "John Proctor's Playing in *The Crucible*," *Midwest Quarterly*, 20:394-403, 1979

McGill, Jr., W. J., "The Crucible of History: Arthur Miller's John Proctor," *New England Quarterly*, 54, ii:258-64, June 1981

Martin, R. A., "Arthur Miller's *The Crucible*: Background and Sources," *Modern Drama*, 20:279-92, 1977

Miller, A., "Brewed in *The Crucible*," pp. 171-74 in *The Theater Essays of Arthur Miller*, ed. R. A. Martin

Miller, A., "It Could Happen Here—and Did," pp. 294-300 in *The Theater Essays of Arthur Miller*, ed. R. A. Martin

Miller, A., "Journey to *The Crucible*," pp. 27-30 in *The Theater Essays of Arthur Miller*, ed. R. A. Martin

Nannes, C. H., *Politics in the American Drama*, pp. 182-85

Schwarz, A., "The Experience of History as Fateful," pp. 61-69 in Schwarz's *From Büchner to Beckett*

Strout, C., "Analogical History: *The Crucible*," pp. 139-56 in Strout's *The Veracious Imagination*

Wertheim, A., "The McCarthy Era and the American Theatre," *Theatre Journal*, 34:211-22, 1982

Drama, 140:25-26, 1981

Death of a Salesman, 1949

Angélico da Costa, L., "The Role of Language in *Death of a Salesman*," *Estudos Anglo-Americanos*, 2:21-31, 1978

Berlin, N., "Doom-session: *The Master Builder, The Visit, Death of a Salesman*," pp. 125-51 in Berlin's *The Secret Cause*

Bordewyck, G., "Saul Bellow's *Death of a Salesman*," *Saul Bellow Journal*, 1, i:18-21, Fall 1981

Ferguson, A. R., "The Tragedy of the American Dream in *Death of a Salesman*," *Thought*, 53:83-98, 1978

Gardner, R. H., "Tragedy of the Lowest Man," pp. 122-34 in Gardner's *The Splintered Stage*

Gomwalk, P. V., "The Tragic Element in Arthur Miller's *Death of a Salesman*," *Kuka*, 1980-1981:34-40

Greenfield, T. A., *Work and the Work Ethic in American Drama 1920-1970*, pp. 101-15, *passim*

Hadommy, L., "Be-Tokh Rosho shel Willy Loman," *Bama*, 81-82:3-4, 1979

Harshbarger, K., *The Burning Jungle*

Hoeveler, D. L., "*Death of a Salesman* as Psychomachia," *Journal of American Culture*, 1:632-37, 1978

Houghton, N., *The Exploding Stage*, pp. 63-64

Innes, C., "The Salesman on the Stage: A Study in the Social Influence of Drama," *English Studies in Canada*, 3:336-50, 1977

Ito, A., "The Contrast between the City and the Country in *Death of a Salesman*," *Essays in Foreign Languages and Literatures*, 25:89-116, 1979 (in Jap.; Eng. sum. p. 223)

Jacquot, J. and C. Mounier, "*Mort d'un commis voyageur* d'Arthur Miller et ses réalisations à Broadway et au Théâtre de la Commune d'Aubervilliers," pp. 11-62 in *Les Voies de la création théâtrale, IV*, ed. D. Bablet and Jacquot

Manocchio, T. and W. Petitt, "The Loman Family," pp. 129-68 in their *Families under Stress*

Meserve, W. J., ed., *Studies in "Death of a Salesman"*

Miller, A., "*The Salesman* Has a Birthday," pp. 12-15 in *The Theater Essays of Arthur Miller*, ed. R. A. Martin

Shalvi, A., "*Motto shel Sokhen*: Hirhurim be-Shulei Hatsagat ha-Kameri," *Bama*, 81-82:10-13, 1979

Sharma, P. P., "Search for Self-Identity in *Death of a Salesman*, "*Literary Criterion*, 11, ii:74-79, 1974

Shaw, P. W., "The Ironic Characterization of Bernard in *Death of a Salesman*," *Notes on Contemporary Literature*, 11, iii:12, May 1981

Shelton, F. W., "Sports and the Competitive Ethic: *Death of a Salesman* and *That Championship Season*," *Ball State University Forum*, 20, ii:17-21, 1979

Vos, N., *The Great Pendulum of Becoming*, pp. 50-51

Walden, D., "Miller's Roots and His Moral Dilemma: Or, Continuity from Brooklyn to *Salesman*," pp. 189-96 in *Critical Essays on Miller*, ed. J. J. Martine

Waterstradt, J. A., "Making the World a Home: The Family Portrait in Drama," *Brigham Young University Studies*, 19:501-21, 1979

Wilson, R. N., "Arthur Miller: The Salesman and Society," pp. 56-71 in Wilson's *The Writer as Social Seer*

Drama, 135:38-40, Jan. 1980

Plays and Players, 27:17-18, Dec. 1979

An Enemy of the People (adaptation of play by Ibsen), 1950

Haugen, E., "Ibsen as Fellow Traveler: Arthur Miller's Adaptation of *An Enemy of the People*," *Scandinavian Studies*, 52:343-53, 1979

Theatre Journal, 32, iii:397-98, Oct. 1980

Fame, 1970

" 'Fame': Serious Playwright Turns to Comedy—And Ponders Why Such Switches Meet Public Resistance," *TV Guide*, 26:12+, 25 Nov. 1978

Incident at Vichy, 1964
John, S. B., "The Mirror of the Stage: Vichy France and Foreign Drama," pp. 200-13 in *Literature and Society*, ed. C. A. Burns

The Price, 1968
Chaikin, M., "The Ending of Arthur Miller's *The Price*," *Studies in the Humanities*, 8, ii:40-44, Mar. 1981
Higgins, D., "Arthur Miller's *The Price*: The Wisdom of Solomon," pp. 85-94 in *Itinerary 3*, ed. F. Baldanza
Vos, N., *The Great Pendulum of Becoming*, p. 68
After Dark, 12:81, July 1979
After Dark, 12:20-21, Oct. 1979
New York, 12:94-95, 9 July 1979
New Yorker, 55:96, 30 Apr. 1979
Time, 114:65, 2 July 1979

The Reason Why (see *Fame*), 1970

2 by A.M. (two one-acts: *Elegy for a Lady* and *Some Kind of Love Story*), 1982
New York, 15:77-79, 22 Nov. 1982
Newsweek, 100:117, 15 Nov. 1982

A View from the Bridge, 1955 (revised 1956)
Houghton, N., *The Exploding Stage*, p. 65
Miller, A., "Introduction to *A View from the Bridge*," pp. 218-22 in *The Theater Essays of Arthur Miller*, ed. R. A. Martin
Miller, A., "What Makes a Play Endure?," pp. 258-63 in *The Theater Essays of Arthur Miller*, ed. R. A. Martin
New Yorker, 58:92-93, 14 Feb. 1983
Time, 121:87, 14 Feb. 1983

JASON MILLER

That Championship Season, 1972
Shelton, F. W., "Sports and the Competitive Ethic: *Death of a Salesman* and *That Championship Season*," *Ball State University Forum*, 20, ii:17-21, 1979
Vos, N., *The Great Pendulum of Becoming*, pp. 88-89
Educational Theatre Journal, 29:119, 1979

JOAQUIN MILLER
(Cincinnatus Heine Miller)

General

Herron, I. H., *The Small Town in American Drama*, pp. 113-14, 122-24

SUSAN MILLER

Nasty Rumors and Final Remarks, 1979
    After Dark, 12:31, July 1979

RONALD MILNER

General

Miller, J.-M. A., "Images of Black Women in Plays by Black Playwrights," *College Language Association Journal*, 20:494-507, 1977

Jazz Set, 1979
    Theater, 11:73-79, Fall/Winter 1979

CHANAN-JACOB MINIKES

Tsvishn indianer, 1895
    Slobin, M., "From Vilna to Vaudeville: Minikes and *Among the Indians* (1895),"
    The Drama Review, 24(3[87]):17-26, Sept. 1980

JOHN MINSHULL

General

Meserve, W. J., *An Emerging Entertainment*, pp. 216-20

Rural Felicity with the Humour of Patrick and Marriage of Shelty, 1801
    Herron, I. H., *The Small Town in American Drama*, pp. 87-88

CHARLES DEE MITCHELL

Good Night, Mr. Sherlock Holmes, 1979
    Texas Monthly, 8:130, Feb. 1980

SEE ALSO
JOYCE STROUD and CHARLES DEE MITCHELL

LANGDON MITCHELL

The New York Idea, 1906
    Meserve, W. J., *An Outline History of American Drama*, p. 160

HERBERT MITGANG

Mister Lincoln, 1980
    After Dark, 13:64, May 1980
    New Yorker, 56:94, 10 Mar. 1980
    Newsweek, 95:58, 28 Jan. 1980
    People, 13:34, 18 Feb. 1980

JOHN C. MOFFITT
SEE
SINCLAIR LEWIS and JOHN C. MOFFITT

MICHAEL DORN MOODY

The Shortchanged Review, 1976
  New West, 4:SC-47, 8 Oct. 1979

WILLIAM VAUGHN MOODY

General

Meserve, W. J., *An Outline History of American Drama*, pp. 194-95, 197-98

The Great Divide (produced earlier in same year as *A Sabine Woman*), 1906
  Herron, I. H., *The Small Town in American Drama*, pp. 153-54
  Körner, C., "William Vaughn Moody: *The Great Divide*," pp. 219-34 in *Theater und Drama in Amerika*, ed. E. Lohner and R. Haas*

MICHAEL MORIARTY

Dexter Creed, 1981
  New York, 14:95, 19 Oct. 1981

CAROL ANN MORIZOT

Child of Scorn, 1978
  Texas Monthly, 6:177, Sept. 1978

ALDYTH MORRIS

Damien, 1976
  Theatre Journal, 34, iv:541-42, Dec. 1982

SIDNEY MORRIS

This Isn't Love!, 1982
  After Dark, 15:13-14, Dec. 1982/Jan. 1983

ROBERT A. MORSE

Booth, 1982
  New York, 15:52, 21 June 1982
  New Yorker, 58:94, 21 June 1982

TAD MOSEL

All the Way Home (dramatization of J. Agee's *A Death in the Family*), 1960
  Herron, I. H., *The Small Town in American Drama*, pp. 403-04

ANNA CORA MOWATT
SEE
ANNA CORA MOWATT RITCHIE

LAVONNE MUELLER

Crimes and Dreams, 1980
  New Yorker, 56:77, 26 May 1980

ROBERT MUNFORD

The Candidates; or, The Humours of a Virginia Election, 1770
  Herron, I. H., *The Small Town in American Drama*, pp. 66-69

The Patriots, 1776
  Diot, R., "Comique et rhétorique dans *The Patriots*, [une] comédie en cinq actes
    de Robert Munford (1777)," pp. 19-28 in *Séminaires 1978*, ed. J. Béranger
    and J. Cazemajou
  Meserve, W. J., *An Emerging Entertainment*, pp. 85-89

NEIL MUNRO

ECU, 1980
  After Dark, 13:67, Feb. 1981

FRANK HITCHCOCK MURDOCH

Davy Crockett, 1872
  Meserve, W. J., *An Outline History of American Drama*, pp. 131-32

JOHN MURDOCK

General

Meserve, W. J., *An Emerging Entertainment*, pp. 157-62

DALLAS MURPHY, JR.

The Terrorists, 1979
  After Dark, 12:31, July 1979

JUDITH SARGENT MURRAY

General

Meserve, W. J., *An Emerging Entertainment*, pp. 153-55

JOHN MURRELL

Farther West, 1982
  Maclean's, 95:53, 3 May 1982

Memoir, 1977
   Drama, 128:48, Spring 1978
   Plays and Players, 25:37, Mar. 1978

Waiting for the Parade, 1981
   After Dark, 13:81-82, May 1981
   New Yorker, 56:106, 108, 9 Feb. 1981

SUSAN NANUS

Survivors (dramatization of book by J. Eisner), 1981
   New York, 14:44, 16 Mar. 1981

N. RICHARD NASH

Echoes, 1980
   Los Angeles, 25:229, June 1980

N. RICHARD NASH, TOM JONES, and HARVEY SCHMIDT

110 in the Shade (musical version of Nash's *The Rainmaker*), 1963
   Herron, I. H., *The Small Town in American Drama*, pp. 482-83
   America, 109:644, 16 Nov. 1963
   New Yorker, 39:93, 2 Nov. 1963
   Newsweek, 62:63, 4 Nov. 1963
   Saturday Review, 46:32, 9 Nov. 1963
   Theatre Arts, 48:68, Jan. 1964
   Time, 82:74, 1 Nov. 1963

JOHN NASSIVERA

The Penultimate Problem of Sherlock Holmes, 1980
   After Dark, 13:62, Aug. 1980

LARRY NEAL

In an Upstate Motel, 1981
   New Yorker, 57:145, 27 Apr. 1981

JOHN NEAL

Otho, 1818
   Meserve, W. J., *An Emerging Entertainment*, pp. 272-73

KAROLYN NELKE

Casualties, 1980
   New Yorker, 56:138-39, 20 Oct. 1980

RICHARD NELSON

Conjuring an Event, 1978
    Educational Theatre Journal, 30:548-50, 1978
    New York, 11:80-81, 3 Apr. 1978
    New Yorker, 54:96-98, 27 Mar. 1978

The Killing of Yablonski, 1978
    Educational Theatre Journal, 30:548-49, 1978

Vienna Notes, 1979
    Theater, 11:73-79, Fall/Winter 1979

HOWARD NEMEROV

General

Cohn, R., *Dialogue in American Drama*, pp. 292-94

SALLY NETZEL

Attic Aphrodite, 1978
    Texas Monthly, 7:118, Jan. 1979

Jack and the Beanstalk (an adaptation), 1978
    Texas Monthly, 7:118, Jan. 1979

Standoff at Beaver and Pine, 1976
    Texas Monthly, 4:88, Aug. 1976

FREDERICK NEUMANN

Mercier and Camier (dramatization of novel by S. Beckett), 1979
    Time, 114:76, 5 Nov. 1979

BETTY NEUSTAT

The Price of Genius, 1982
    New York, 15:85, 11 Oct. 1982

DAVID NIGHBERT

Frankenstein (dramatization of M. W. Shelley's novel), 1979
    Texas Monthly, 7:170, May 1979

MORDECAI MANUEL NOAH

General

Meserve, W. J., *An Emerging Entertainment*, pp. 207-08, 253-56
Vaughn, J. A., *Early American Dramatists*, pp. 59-63

JOHN FORD NOONAN

The Club Champion's Widow, 1978
    After Dark, 11:112, May 1978
    Nation, 226:188, 18 Feb. 1978

A Coupla White Chicks Sitting Around Talking, 1979
    After Dark, 13:55, July 1980
    New York, 13:58-59, 19 May 1980
    Time, 115:68, 2 June 1980

Some Men Need Help, 1982
    After Dark, 15:14, Dec. 1982/Jan. 1983
    Newsweek, 100:82, 8 Nov. 1982
    Time, 120:82, 8 Nov. 1982

MARSHA NORMAN

Getting Out, 1977
    After Dark, 11:85, Jan. 1979
    After Dark, 12:73, Nov. 1979
    Commonweal, 106:559-60, 12 Oct. 1979
    Georgia Review, 34:497-508, Fall 1980
    Hudson Review, 32:81-85, Spring 1979
    Los Angeles, 23:246, Apr. 1978
    Ms, 6:26-28, June 1978
    Nation, 227:557, 18 Nov. 1978
    New Republic, 181:25, 7 July 1979
    New West, 3:SC-29, 13 Mar. 1978
    New York, 11:152, 13 Nov. 1978
    New York, 12:98, 28 May 1979
    New Yorker, 54:152-53, 6 Nov. 1978
    Newsweek, 93:103, 28 May 1979
    Plays and Players, 26:36-37, July 1979
    Time, 113:80, 28 May 1979

The Laundromat, 1979
    New Yorker, 55:72-73, 24 Dec. 1979

'Night, Mother, 1982
    Newsweek, 101:41-42, 3 Jan. 1983
    Time, 121:85, 7 Feb. 1983

ELLIOTT NUGENT and JAMES THURBER

General

Gould, J., "Some Clever Collaborators," pp. 151-54 in Gould's *Modern American Playwrights*

The Male Animal, 1939

Herron, I. H., *The Small Town in American Drama*, pp. 453-55
Wertheim, A., "The McCarthy Era and the American Theatre," *Theatre Journal*,
34:211-22, 1982

LIAM O'BRIEN

The Remarkable Mr. Pennypacker, 1953
Herron, I. H., *The Small Town in American Drama*, pp. 449-50
America, 90:426, 23 Jan. 1954
Catholic World, 178:388-89, Feb. 1954
Commonweal, 59:450, 5 Feb. 1954
Nation, 178:98, 30 Jan. 1954
New Yorker, 29:62-64, 9 Jan. 1954
Newsweek, 43:72, 11 Jan. 1954
Saturday Review, 37:61, 23 Jan. 1954
Theatre Arts, 38:20, Mar. 1954
Time, 63:67, 11 Jan. 1954

MICHAEL O'CONNOR
SEE
BILL IRWIN, DOUG SKINNER, and MICHAEL O'CONNOR

CLIFFORD ODETS

General

Bigsby, C. W. E., *A Critical Introduction to Twentieth-Century American Drama*,
Vol. I, pp. 163-88
Brenman-Gibson, M., *Clifford Odets*
Brenman-Gibson, M., "The Creation of Plays: With a Specimen Analysis," pp. 178-
230 in *Psychoanalysis, Creativity, and Literature*, ed. A. Roland
Cantor, H., *Clifford Odets*
Gould, J., "Clifford Odets," pp. 186-201 in Gould's *Modern American Playwrights*
Kotama, M. and M. Sata, "Secular Humanism," pp. 183-90 in *American Literature
in the 1950's* (American Literature Society of Japan 1976 Annual Report)
Mendelsohn, M. J., *Clifford Odets*
Mersand, J., *The American Drama Since 1930*, pp. 61-90
Meserve, W. J., *An Outline History of American Drama*, pp. 261-62, 344
Scanlan, T., *Family, Drama, and American Dreams*, pp. 184-89, *passim*
Shuman, R. B., "Clifford Odets: From Influence to Affluence," pp. 39-46 in *Modern
American Drama*, ed. W. E. Taylor
Wagner, A., "Clifford Odets: Interview," *Educational Theatre Journal*, 28:495-500,
Dec. 1976

Awake and Sing!, 1935
Dozier, R. J., "The Making of *Awake and Sing!*," *Markham Review*, 6:61-65,
1977
Himelstein, M. Y., *Drama Was a Weapon*, pp. 166-69
Lal, M., "The American Protest Theatre," *Humanities Review*, 2, ii:16-21, 1980
Robinson, L., "A Note on Language and Structure in Odets' *Awake and Sing!*,"
Kyushu American Literature, 18:40-44, 1977

Smiley, S., *The Drama of Attack*, pp. 49-50, 172-75
New Yorker, 55:93, 28 May 1979

The Country Girl, 1950
Drama-Logue, 13, xxxvii:5, 16-22 Sept. 1982

Golden Boy, 1937
Himelstein, M. Y., *Drama Was a Weapon*, pp. 174-76
Smiley, S., *The Drama of Attack*, pp. 105-08

Night Music, 1940
Himselstein, M. Y., *Drama Was a Weapon*, p. 178

Paradise Lost, 1935
Dozier, R. J., "Recovering Odets' *Paradise Lost*," *Essays in Literature*, 5:209-21, 1978
Himelstein, M. Y., *Drama Was a Weapon*, pp. 169-71
Smiley, S., *The Drama of Attack*, pp. 167-72

Rocket to the Moon, 1938
Plays and Players, 349:30-31, Oct. 1982
Plays and Players, 351:33, Dec. 1982

Till the Day I Die, 1935
Nannes, C. H., *Politics in the American Drama*, p. 149
Smiley, S., *The Drama of Attack*, pp. 187-88

Waiting for Lefty, 1935
Bigsby, C. W. E., *A Critical Introduction to Twentieth-Century American Drama*, Vol. I, pp. 200-02
Dozier, R. J., "Odets and 'Little Lefty,' " *American Literature*, 48:597-98, 1977
Greenfield, T. A., *Work and the Work Ethic in American Drama 1920-1970*, pp. 69-70, *passim*
Himelstein, M. Y., *Drama Was a Weapon*, pp. 37-42
Lal, M., "The American Protest Theatre," *Humanities Review*, 2, ii:16-21, 1980
Smiley S., *The Drama of Attack*, pp. 130-32, *passim*

FRANK O'HARA

A Day in the Life of the Czar, 1980
New York, 13:58 +, 10 Nov. 1980

JOHN OLIVE

Minnesota Moon, 1979
After Dark, 11:85, Apr. 1979
New Yorker, 54:47, 12 Feb. 1979

Standing on My Knees, 1981

Chicago, 31:49, Jan. 1982
New York, 15:59, 8 Nov. 1982
New Yorker, 58:160, 8 Nov. 1982

KEVIN O'MORRISON

Ladyhouse Blues, 1976
  After Dark, 12:22 +, Jan. 1980
  Nation, 229:476, 10 Nov. 1979
  New West, 5:103, 16 June 1980
  New York, 12:86-87, 29 Oct. 1979
  New Yorker, 55:81-82, 29 Oct. 1979
  Saturday Review, 7:42-44, 5 Jan. 1980
  Time, 114:102, 29 Oct. 1979

MICHAEL ONDAATJE

The Collected Works of Billy the Kid, 1975
  Los Angeles, 27:270, Sept. 1982

JOHN O'NEAL

Don't Start Me Talkin' or I'll Tell Everything I Know, 1982
  New Yorker, 58:176 +, 22 Nov. 1982

GEORGE O'NEIL

American Dream, 1933
  Vos, N., *The Great Pendulum of Becoming*, pp. 45-47
  New Outlook, 166:47, Apr. 1933
  Stage, 10:9, 14-15, Mar. 1933
  Theatre Arts Monthly, 17:34-41, May 1933
  Time, 21:29, 6 Mar. 1933
  Vanity Fair, 40:31, May 1933

EUGENE O'NEILL

General

Adler, T. P., "The Mirror as Stage Prop in Modern Drama," *Comparative Drama*, 14:355-73, 1980-81
Ahrends, G., *Traumwelt und Wirklichkeit im Spätwerk Eugene O'Neills*
Avram, R. ben, "Eugene O'Neill in the 'Divided Stream,' " pp. 38-47 in *Naturalisme américain*, ed. J. Cazemajou and J.-C. Barat
Baužytė, G., "Eschilas ir Judžino o'Nylo dramaturgija," *Literatūra*, 20, iii:36-39, 1978 (Aeschylus and O'Neill)
Bergman, I., "A Meeting with O'Neill," pp. 293-95 in *Eugene O'Neill*, ed. V. Floyd
Berlin, N., *Eugene O'Neill*
Berlin, N., "Ghosts of the Past: O'Neill and *Hamlet*," *Massachusetts Review*, 20:312-23, 1979

Bermel, A., "Poetry and Mysticism in O'Neill," pp. 245-51 in *Eugene O'Neill*, ed. V. Floyd

Bigsby, C. W. E., *A Critical Introduction to Twentieth-Century American Drama*, Vol. I, pp. 36-119

Blanke, G. H., "Die Dramenschlüsse bei O'Neill," *Das amerikanische Drama von den Anfangen bis zur Gegenwart*, 5:155-67, 1972

Broussard, L., *American Drama*, pp. 9-39

Brugger, I., "Verwendung und Bedeutung der Maske bei O'Neill," *Das amerikanische Drama von den Anfangen bis zur Gegenwart*, 5:137-54, 1972

Bryer, J. R., ed. *"The Theatre We Worked For"*

Carpenter, F. I., "The Enduring O'Neill: The Early Plays," *Eugene O'Neill Newsletter*, 1,i:1-3, 1977

Carpenter, F. I., *Eugene O'Neill*, rev. ed.

Castro, G., "Les Femmes dans le théâtre d'O'Neill: Essai d'interprétation féministe," pp. 131-58 in *Séminaires 1976*, ed. J. Beranger and J. Cazemajou

Chabrowe, L., *Ritual and Pathos*

Chioles, J., "Aeschylus and O'Neill: A Phenomenological View," *Comparative Drama*, 14:159-87, 1980

Chothia, J., *Forging a Language*

Cohn, R., *Dialogue in American Drama*, pp. 8-67

Ćosić, I., "Judžin O'Nil: Velikan svoje epohe," *Scena*, 16, i-ii:147-67, 1980 (Giant of His Era)

Cronin, H., *Eugene O'Neill, Irish and American*

Egri, P., "European Origins and American Originality: The Case of Drama," *Zeitschrift für Anglistik und Amerikanistik*, 29, iii:197-206, 1981

Egri, P., "O'Neill Productions in Hungary: A Chronological Record," *Eugene O'Neill Newsletter*, 2, ii:14, 1978

Egri, P., "The Short Story in the Drama: Chekhov and O'Neill," *Acta Litteraria Academiae Scientiarum Hungaricae*, 20:3-28, 1978

Egri, P., "The Use of the Short Story in O'Neill's and Chekhov's One-Act Plays," pp. 115-44 in *Eugene O'Neill*, ed. V. Floyd

Filipowicz-Findlay, H., "O'Neill's Plays in Poland," *Eugene O'Neill Newsletter*, 3, i:9-11, 1979

Fink, E. O., "Audience Aids for Non-Literary Allusions? Observations on the Transposition of Essential Technicalities in the Sea Plays of Eugene O'Neill," pp. 69-81 in *The Languages of Theatre*, ed. O. Zuber

Floyd, V., ed., *Eugene O'Neill*

Floyd, V., ed., *Eugene O'Neill at Work*

Fluckiger, S. L., "The Idea of Puritanism in the Plays of Eugene O'Neill," *Renascence*, 30:152-62, 1978

Frenz, H., "Eugene O'Neill and China," *Tamkang Review*, 10:5-16, 1979

Frenz, H., "Eugene O'Neill and Georg Kaiser," pp. 172-85 in *Eugene O'Neill*, ed. V. Floyd

Gardner, R. H., *The Splintered Stage*, pp. 103-04

Gatta, Jr., J. "The American Subject: Moral History as Tragedy in the Plays of Eugene O'Neill," *Essays in Literature*, 6:227-39, 1979

Going, W. T., "Eugene O'Neill, American," *Papers on Language and Literature*, 12, iv:384-401, 1976

Goldman, A., "The Culture of the Provincetown Players," *Journal of American Studies*, 12:291-310, Dec. 1978

Gorsky, S. R and L. T. Milic, "The Primacy of Data in Stylistic Analysis: A Review Essay," *Modernist Studies*, 2, iii:51-57, 1977

Gould, J., "Eugene O'Neill," pp. 50-77 in Gould's *Modern American Playwrights*

Grabes, H., "Das amerikanische Drama nach O'Neill," pp. 28-48 in *Die amerikanische Literatur der Gegenwart*, ed. H. Bungert

Granger, B. I., "Illusion and Reality in Eugene O'Neill," *Das amerikanische Drama von den Anfängen bis zur Gegenwart*, 5:129-36, 1972

Green, C., "Wolfe, O'Neill, and the Mask of Illusion," *Papers on Language and Literature*, 14:87-90, 1978

Haas, R., "Eugene O'Neill," *Das amerikanische Drama von den Anfängen bis zur Gegenwart*, 5:98-117, 1972

Haas, R., "Zugänge zum englischen und amerikanischen Drama," pp. 190-226 in Haas's *Theorie und Praxis der Interpretation*

Halio, J. L., "Eugene O'Neill: The Long Quest," pp. 13-27 in *Modern American Drama*, ed. W. E. Taylor

Herron, I. H., "O'Neill's Lost Townsmen," pp. 273-337 in Herron's *The Small Town in American Drama*

Highsmith, J. M., "The Cornell Letters: Eugene O'Neill on His Craftsmanship to George Jean Nathan," *Modern Drama*, 15:68-89, 1972

Hinden, M., " 'Splendid Twaddle': O'Neill and Richard Middleton," *Eugene O'Neill Newsletter*, 2, iii:13-16, 1979

Hinden, M., "When Playwrights Talk to God: Peter Shaffer and the Legacy of O'Neill," *Comparative Drama*, 16:49-63, Spring 1982

Jackson, E. M., "Esther M. Jackson on O'Neill the Humanist," *Eugene O'Neill Newsletter*, 1, ii:1-4, 1977

Jackson, E. M., "O'Neill the Humanist," pp. 252-56 in *Eugene O'Neill*, ed. V. Floyd

Jařab, J., "The Lasting Challenge of Eugene O'Neill: A Czechoslovak View," pp. 84-100 in *Eugene O'Neill*, ed. V. Floyd

"John Howard Lawson on Eugene O'Neill," *Eugene O'Neill Newsletter*, 3, ii:12-14, 1979

Kaes, A., "Expressionismus und der frühe O'Neill," *Studien zur Deutschen Literatur*, 43:74-87, 1975

Kennedy, J. D., "*Pierre*'s Progeny: O'Neill and the Melville Revival," *English Studies in Canada*, 3:103-17, 1977

Koreneva, M., "Eugene O'Neill and the Traditions of American Drama," pp. 143-59 in *20th Century American Literature*

Koreneva, M., "One Hundred Percent American Tragedy: A Soviet View," pp. 145-71 in *Eugene O'Neill*, ed. V. Floyd

Langford, R. E., "Eugene O'Neill: The Mask of Illusion," pp. 65-75 in *Essays in Modern American Literature*, ed. Langford et al.

Leech, C., "O'Neill in England—From *Anna Christie* to *Long Days' Journey into Night*: 1923-1958," pp. 68-72 in *Eugene O'Neill*, ed. V. Floyd

Meserve, W. J., *An Outline History of American Drama*, pp. 220-32, 284-85, 338-40

Miller, J. Y., "The Other O'Neill," pp. 455-73 in *The Twenties*, ed. W. G. French

Moleski, J. J., "Eugene O'Neill and the Cruelty of Theater," *Comparative Drama*, 15, iv:327-42, Winter 1981-1982

Morrison, K., "Conrad and O'Neill as Playwrights of the Sea," *Eugene O'Neill Newsletter*, 2, i:3-5, 1978

Nethercot, A. H., "The Psychoanalyzing of Eugene O'Neill: P.P.S.," *Modern Drama*, 16:35-48, 1973

Nicoll, A., "Eugene O'Neill," pp. 750-61 in Nicoll's *World Drama*, rev. and enl. ed.

Ó hAodha, M., "O'Neill and the Anatomy of the Stage Irishman," *Eugene O'Neill Newsletter*, 1,ii:13-14, 1977

Olsson, T., "O'Neill and the Royal Dramatic," pp. 34-60 in *Eugene O'Neill*, ed. V. Floyd

Packard, Jr., F. C., "Eugene O'Neill, Dramatic Innovator," *Eugene O'Neill Newsletter*, 3, ii:9-12, 1979 (rpt. from *Chrysalis*, 5,vii-viii, 1952)

Prasad, H. M., "Nuances of Soliloquy in the Theatre of Eugene O'Neill," *Commonwealth Quarterly*, 5, xvii:48-59, 1980

Quinby, G. H., "O'Neill in Iran," *Eugene O'Neill Newsletter*, 1, ii:10-12, 1977

Raleigh, J. H., "The Last Confession: O'Neill and the Catholic Confessional," pp. 212-28 in *Eugene O'Neill*, ed. V. Floyd

Raleigh, J. H., D. Falk, V. Floyd, E. M. Jackson, and F. Wilkins, "The Enduring O'Neill: Which Plays Will Survive?," *Eugene O'Neill Newsletter*, Jan. 1977, 2-15

Rich, J. D., "Exile without Remedy: The Late Plays of Eugene O'Neill," pp. 257-76 in *Eugene O'Neill*, ed. V. Floyd

Robinson, J. A., *Eugene O'Neill and Oriental Thought*

Robinson, J. A., "O'Neill and Albee," *West Virginia University Philological Papers*, 25:38-45, 1979

Robinson, J. A., "O'Neill's Symbolic Sounds," *Modern Language Studies*, 9, ii:36-45, 1979

Rollyson, Jr., C., "O'Neill's Mysticism: From His Historical Trilogy to *Long Day's Journey into Night*," *Studies in Mystical Literature*, 1, iii:218-36, Spring 1981

Ryan, P. M., "Stockholm Revives Eugene O'Neill," *Scandinavian Review*, 65, i:18-23, 1977

Scanlon, T., "Eugene O'Neill and the Drama of Family Dilemma," pp. 83-125 in Scanlon's *Family, Drama, and American Dreams*

Scheller, B., "O'Neill und die Rezeption spätbürgerlich-Kritischer Dramatik," *Zeitschrift für Anglistik und Americanistik*, 23, iv:314-21, 1975

Schwarz, A., "Society and Human Passion as Tragic Motive," pp. 100-60 in Schwarz's *From Büchner to Beckett*

Shaughnessy, E. L., "The Iceman Melteth: O'Neill's Return to Cultural Origin," *Eugene O'Neill Newsletter*, 3, ii:3-6, 1979

Sheaffer, L., "Saxe Commins and the O'Neills," *Eugene O'Neill Newsletter*, 2, ii:7-8, 1978

Sienicka, M., "O'Neill in Poland," pp. 101-14 in *Eugene O'Neill*, ed. V. Floyd

Styan, J. L., "Expressionism in America: O'Neill," pp. 97-111, Vol. III, of Styan's *Modern Drama in Theory and Practice*

Styan, J. L., "Realism in America: Early Variations," pp. 122-36, Vol. I, of Styan's *Modern Drama in Theory and Practice*

Tiusanen, T., "O'Neill's Significance: A Scandinavian and European View," pp. 61-67 in *Eugene O'Neill*, ed. V. Floyd

Törnqvist, E., "O'Neill's Work Method," *Studia Neophilologica*, 49:43-58, 1977

Törnqvist, E., "Strindberg and O'Neill," pp. 277-91 in *Structures of Influence*, ed. M. J. Blackwell

Voelker, P. D., "Eugene O'Neill and George Pierce Baker: A Reconsideration," *American Literature*, 49:206-20, 1977

Voelker, P. D., "Eugene O'Neill's Aesthetic of the Drama," *Modern Drama*, 21:87-99, 1978

Voelker, P. D., "O'Neill and George Pierce Baker," *Eugene O'Neill Newsletter*, 1, ii:4-6, 1977

Wasserstrom, W., "Notes on Electricity: Henry Adams and Eugene O'Neill," *Psychocultural Review*, 1:161-78, 1977

White, K. S., "Scientists' Dilemmas: Prophetic Metaphors in Twentieth Century Drama," pp. 533-36 in *Proceedings of the 7th Congress of the International Comparative Literature Association, I*, ed. M. V. Dimić and J. Ferraté

Wilkins, F., "The Pressure of Puritanism in Eugene O'Neill's New England Plays," pp. 237-44 in *Eugene O'Neill*, ed. V. Floyd

Wittenberg, J. B., "Faulkner and Eugene O'Neill," *Mississippi Quarterly*, 33:327-41, 1980

Ah, Wilderness!, 1933
> Lucow, B., "O'Neill's Use of Realism in *Ah, Wilderness!*," *Notes on Modern American Literature*, 1:Item 10, 1977
>
> Van Laan, T. F., "Singing in the Wilderness: The Dark Vision of Eugene O'Neill's Only Mature Comedy," *Modern Drama*, 22:9-18, 1979
>
> *Educational Theatre Journal*, 30:422-24, 1978

All God's Chillun Got Wings, 1924
> Hinden, M., "The Transitional Nature of *All God's Chillun Got Wings*," *Eugene O'Neill Newsletter*, 4, i-ii:3-5, 1980
>
> Robinson, J. A., "Christianity and *All God's Chillun Got Wings*," *Eugene O'Neill Newsletter*, 2, i:1-3, 1978
>
> Weixlmann, J., "Staged Segregation: Baldwin's *Blues for Mister Charlie* and O'Neill's *All God's Chillun Got Wings*," *Black American Literature Forum*, 11:35-36, 1977

The Ancient Mariner (see *The Rime of the Ancient Mariner*)

Anna Christie, 1921
> *Plays and Players*, 27:30-31, Dec. 1979

Beyond the Horizon, 1920
> Houghton, N., *The Exploding Stage*, pp. 47-48
>
> Prasad, H. M., "The Tragic Mode: A Study in Eugene O'Neill's *Beyond the Horizon, The Emperor Jones* and *The Hairy Ape*," *Osmania Journal of English Studies*, 15:21-30, 1979
>
> Scheick, W. J., "The Ending of O'Neill's *Beyond the Horizon*," *Modern Drama*, 20:293-98, 1977

Bound East for Cardiff, 1916
> Voelker, P. D., "The Uncertain Origins of Eugene O'Neill's *Bound East for Cardiff*," *Studies in Bibliography*, 32:273-81, 1979

Days without End, 1933
> Myers, A. B., " 'Hysteria Night in the Sophomore Dormitory': Eugene O'Neill's *Days without End*," *Columbia Library Columns*, 28, ii:3-13, 1979

Desire under the Elms, 1924

Asselineau, R., "O'Neill's Transcendental Phase," pp. 115-23 in Asselineau's *The Transcendentalist Constant in American Literature*

Berlin, N., "Passion: *Hippolytus, Phaedra, Desire under the Elms*," pp. 33-63 in Berlin's *The Secret Cause*

Blesch, Jr., E. J., "Lots of Desire, No Elms: A Consideration of Eugene O'Neill's *Desire under the Elms* on Film," *Nassau Review*, 4, ii:14-22, 1981

Bowles, P., "Another Biblical Parallel in *Desire under the Elms*," *Eugene O'Neill Newsletter*, 2, iii:10-12, 1979

Hinden, M., "Desire and Forgiveness: O'Neill's Diptych," *Comparative Drama*, 14:240-50, 1980

Hinden, M., "*Desire under the Elms*: O'Neill and the American Romance," *Forum*, 15, i:44-51, 1977

Lemanis, M., "*Desire under the Elms* and Tragic Form: A Study of Misalliance," *South Dakota Review*, 16, iii:46-55, 1978

Nolan, P. J., "*Desire under the Elms*: Characters by Jung," *Eugene O'Neill Newsletter*, 5, ii:5-10, Summer-Fall 1981

Taylor, W. E., "*Six Characters in Search of an Author* and *Desire under the Elms*: What O'Neill Did Not Learn from Europe," pp. 29-37 in *Modern American Drama*, ed. Taylor

Voelker, P. D., "Lust under Some Elms: *Desire* at the Guthrie," *Eugene O'Neill Newsletter*, 4, iii:9-12, 1980

Vos, N., *The Great Pendulum of Becoming*, pp. 29, 48-49

Dynamo, 1929

Tuck, S., " 'Electricity Is God Now': D. H. Lawrence and O'Neill," *Eugene O'Neill Newsletter*, 5, ii:10-15, Summer-Fall, 1981

The Emperor Jones, 1920

Gálik, M., "Chao—The King of Hell and *The Emperor Jones*: Two Plays by Hung Shen and O'Neill," *Asian and African Studies*, 12:123-31, 1976

Hinden, M., "*The Emperor Jones*: O'Neill, Nietzsche, and the American Past," *Eugene O'Neill Newsletter*, 3, iii:2-4, 1980

Kellman, A. J., "*The Emperor Jones* and *The Hairy Ape*: A Beginning and an End," *Eugene O'Neill Newsletter*, 2, i:9-10, 1978

Nolan, P. J., "*The Emperor Jones*: A Jungian View of the Origin of Fear in the Black Race," *Eugene O'Neill Newsletter*, 4, i-ii:6-9, 1980

Prasad, H. M., "The Tragic Mode: A Study in Eugene O'Neill's *Beyond the Horizon, The Emperor Jones* and *The Hairy Ape*," *Osmania Journal of English Studies*, 15:21-30, 1979

Sittler, L., "*The Emperor Jones*—ein individuationsprozess im sinne C. G. Jungs?," *Amerikastudien*, 23:118-30, 1978

Viswanathan, R., "The Ship Scene in *The Emperor Jones*," *Eugene O'Neill Newsletter*, 4, iii:3-5, 1980

Fog, 1917

Wolter, J., "O'Neill's 'Open Boat,' " *Literatur in Wissenschaft und Unterricht*, 11, iv:222-29, 1978

The Great God Brown, 1926

Ben-Zvi, L., "*Exiles, The Great God Brown*, and the Specter of Nietzsche," *Modern Drama*, 24, iii:251-69, Sept. 1981

Green, C., "Wolfe, O'Neill, and the Mask of Illusion," *Papers on Language and Literature*, 14, i:87-90, 1978

The Hairy Ape. 1922

Bowles, P., "*The Hairy Ape* as Existential Allegory," *Eugene O'Neill Newsletter*, 3, i:2-3, 1979

Floyd, V., "The Search for Self in *The Hairy Ape*: An Exercise in Futility?," *Eugene O'Neill Newsletter*, 1, iii:4-7, 1978

Frenz, H., "Three European Productions of *The Hairy Ape*," *Eugene O'Neill Newsletter*, 1, iii:10-12, 1978

Greenfield, T. A., *Work and the Work Ethic in American Drama 1920-1970*, pp. 81-82

Hinden, M., "Ironic Use of Myth in *The Hairy Ape*," *Eugene O'Neill Newsletter*, 1, iii:2-4, 1978

Hughes, A. D., "Biblical Allusions in *The Hairy Ape*," *Eugene O'Neill Newsletter*, 1, i:7-9, 1978

Juhl, P., "Eugene O'Neills *The Hairy Ape*: Bemerkungen zu Sinn und Struktur des Dramas," pp. 235-53 in *Theater und Drama in Amerika*, ed. E. Lohner and R. Haas

Jurich, J., "Jack London and *The Hairy Ape*," *Eugene O'Neill Newsletter*, 3, iii:6-8, 1980

Kaes, A., "Charakterisierung bei O'Neill und Kaiser," *Studien zur Deutschen Literatur*, 43:102-17, 1975

Kellman, A. J., "*The Emperor Jones* and *The Hairy Ape*: A Beginning and an End," *Eugene O'Neill Newsletter*, 2, i:9-10, 1978

McIlvaine, R., "Crane's *Maggie*: A Source for *The Hairy Ape*?," *Eugene O'Neill Newsletter*, 2, iii:8-10, 1979

Prasad, H. M., "The Tragic Mode: A Study in Eugene O'Neill's *Beyond the Horizon, The Emperor Jones* and *The Hairy Ape*," *Osmania Journal of English Studies*, 15:21-30, 1979

Rutenberg, M. E., "Bob Smith Ain't So Dumb: Directing *The Hairy Ape*," *Eugene O'Neill Newsletter*, 3, iii:11-15, 1980

Saqqaf, A. Y., "The Nature of Conflict in *The Hairy Ape*," *Journal of English*, 1:77-84, 1975

Vos, N., *The Great Pendulum of Becoming*, pp. 31-33

Vyzga, B. J., "Designing O'Neill's *The Hairy Ape*," *Eugene O'Neill Newsletter*, 3, iii:15-17, 1980

Hughie, 1958

Bilman, C., "Language as Theme in Eugene O'Neill's *Hughie*," *Notes on Modern American Literature*, 3:Item 25, 1979

Butler, R., "Artifice and Art: Words in *The Iceman Cometh* and *Hughie*," *Eugene O'Neill Newsletter*, 5, i:3-6, Spring 1981

Carpenter, F. I., "*Hughie: By Way of Obit*," *Eugene O'Neill Newsletter*, 2, ii:1-3, 1978

Mayberry, R., "Sterile Wedding: The Comic Structure of O'Neill's *Hughie*," *Massachusetts Studies in English*, 7, iii:10-19, 1980

Shaughnessy, E. L., "Question and Answer in *Hughie*," *Eugene O'Neill Newsletter*, 2, ii:3-7, 1978

Drama, 136:42, Apr. 1980

Plays and Players, 27:22-23, Feb. 1980

The Iceman Cometh, 1946
    Alexander, D. M., "Hugo of *The Iceman Cometh*: Realism and O'Neill," *American Quarterly*, 5:357-66, Winter 1953
    Barbera, J. V., "Pipe Dreams, Games and Delusions," *Southern Review*, 13, ii:120-28, July 1980
    Butler, R., "Artifice and Art: Words in *The Iceman Cometh* and *Hughie*," *Eugene O'Neill Newsletter*, 5, i:3-6, Spring 1981
    Ditsky, J. M., "O'Neill's Evangel of Peace: *The Iceman Cometh*," pp. 93-110 in Ditsky's *The Onstage Christ*
    Egri, P., "Eugene O'Neill: *The Iceman Cometh*," *Hungarian Studies in English*, 11:95-105, 1977
    Egri, P., "*The Iceman Cometh*: European Origins and American Originality," *Eugene O'Neill Newsletter*, 5, iii:5-10, Winter 1981 (revision of *Annales Univ. Scientiarum Budapestinensis de Rolando Eötvös Nominatae*, 11:83-107, 1980)
    Frazer, W., " 'Revolution' in *The Iceman Cometh*," *Modern Drama*, 22:1-8, 1979
    Heilman, R. B., *Tragedy and Melodrama*, pp. 49-55
    Houghton, N., *The Exploding Stage*, pp. 50-52
    Innes, C., "The Salesman on the Stage: A Study in the Social Influence of Drama," *English Studies in Canada*, 3:336-50, 1977
    Mounier, C., "Le Marchand de glace est passé d'Eugene O'Neill et la mise en scène de Gabrial Garran au Théâtre de la Commune d'Aubervilliers," pp. 62-102 in *Les Voies de la création théâtrale, IV*, ed. D. Bablet and J. Jacquot
    Suyama, S., "Eugene O'Neill *Iceman Kitaru*: Moo Hitori no Sisyphe to Kankyaku no Shisei," pp. 297-312 in *Bungaku to America*, Vol. III
    Watson, J. G., "The Theater in *The Iceman Cometh*: Some Modernist Implications," *Arizona Quarterly*, 34:230-38, 1978
    Welch, D. M., "Hickey as Satanic Force in *The Iceman Cometh*," *Arizona Quarterly*, 34:219-29, 1978
    Wiles, T. J., "Tammyite, Progressive, and Anarchist: Political Communities in *The Iceman Cometh*," *CLIO*, 9:179-96, 1980
    Vos, N., *The Great Pendulum of Becoming*, pp. 82-83, 86-87
    Drama, 136:35-36, 41-43, Apr. 1980
    Plays and Players, 27:23, Mar. 1980

Long Day's Journey into Night, 1956
    Barlow, J. E., "*Long Day's Journey into Night*: From Early Notes to Finished Play," *Modern Drama*, 22:19-28, 1979
    Brown, A., "Staging O'Neill's 'Simple Play,' " pp. 288-89 in *Eugene O'Neill*, ed. V. Floyd
    Egri, P., "The Reinterpretation of the Chekhovian Mosaic Design in O'Neill's *Long Day's Journey into Night*," *Acta Litteraria Academiae Scientiarum Hungaricae*, 22, i-ii:29-71, 1980
    Eldridge, F., "Reflections on *Long Day's Journey into Night*: First Curtain Call for Mary Tyrone," pp. 286-87 in *Eugene O'Neill*, ed. V. Floyd
    Fitzgerald, G., "Another Neurotic Electra: A New Look at Mary Tyrone," pp. 290-92 in *Eugene O'Neill*, ed. V. Floyd
    Houghton, N., *The Exploding Stage*, pp. 52-54

Manocchio, T. and W. Petitt, "The Tyrone Family," pp. 102-28 in their *Family under Stress*

McDonald, D., "The Phenomenology of the Glance in *Long Day's Journey into Night*," *Theatre Journal*, 31:343-56, 1979

Ooi, V.C.H., "Transcending Culture: A Cantonese Translation [by Ts'ao Yü] and Production of O'Neill's *Long Day's Journey into Night*," pp. 51-68 in *The Languages of Theatre*, ed. O. Zuber

Raphael, J. E., "On Directing *Long Day's Journey into Night*," *Eugene O'Neill Newsletter*, 5, i:7-10, Spring 1981

Reilly, K. P., "Pitching the Mansion and Pumping the Morphine: Eugene O'Neill's *Long Day's Journey into Night*," *Gypsy Scholar*, 5:22-33, 1978

Schvey, H. I., " 'The Past Is the Present, Isn't It?' Eugene O'Neill's *Long Day's Journey into Night*," *Dutch Quarterly Review*, 10:84-99, 1980

Sewall, R. B., "*Long Day's Journey into Night*," pp. 161-74 in Sewall's *The Vision of Tragedy*, new ed., enl.

Tuck, S., "House of Compson, House of Tyrone: Faulkner's Influence on O'Neill," *Eugene O'Neill Newsletter*, 5, iii:10-16, Winter 1981

Vos, N., *The Great Pendulum of Becoming*, pp. 49-50, 68, 83, 84-85

Wertheim, A., "Gaspard the Miser in O'Neill's *Long Day's Journey into Night*," *American Notes and Queries*, 18:39-42, 1979

Wilson, R. N., "Eugene O'Neill: The Web of Family," pp. 72-88 in Wilson's *The Writer as Social Seer*

After Dark, 12:25, Mar. 1980

After Dark, 13:68, Jan. 1981

Cross Currents, 29:446-56, Winter 1979/1980

Educational Theatre Journal, 30:422-24, 1978

Maclean's, 93:69, 20 Oct. 1980

New Yorker, 57:62, 65, 16 Mar. 1981

Newsweek, 97:104, 20 Apr. 1981

The Long Voyage Home, 1917

Drama, 133:46-47, Summer 1979

Plays and Players, 26:24 + , May 1979

Marco Millions, 1928

Fairservis, W., "Managing the Magic of *Marco Millions*," *Eugene O'Neill Newsletter*, 2, iii:18-21, 1979

Frenz, H., "*Marco Millions*, O'Neill's Chinese Experience and Chinese Drama," *Comparative Literature Studies*, 18:362-67, Sept. 1981

Robinson, J. A., "Taoism and O'Neill's *Marco Millions*," *Comparative Drama*, 14:251-62, 1980

A Moon for the Misbegotten, 1947

Hinden, M., "Desire and Forgiveness: O'Neill's Diptych," *Comparative Drama*, 14:240-50, 1980

Raleigh, J. H., "The Irish Atavism of *A Moon for the Misbegotten*," pp. 229-36 in *Eugene O'Neill*, ed. V. Floyd

More Stately Mansions, 1962

Petite, J., "The Paradox of Power in *More Stately Mansions*," *Eugene O'Neill Newsletter*, 5, iii:2-5, Winter 1981

Mourning Becomes Electra, 1939

Feldman, R., "The Longing for Death in O'Neill's *Strange Interlude* and *Mourning Becomes Electra*," *Literature and Psychology*, 31, i:39-48, 1981

Houghton, N., *The Exploding Stage*, pp. 49-50

Kennedy, J. D., "O'Neill's Lavinia Mannon and the Dickinson Legend," *American Literature*, 49:108-13, 1977

Melchinger, S., "Die Yankee-Elektra: O'Neil und Aischylos—vergleichende Bemerkungen," pp. 254-62 in *Theater und Drama in Amerika*," ed. E. Lohner and R. Haas

Roberts, P., "Orestes in Modern Drama: *Mourning Becomes Electra*," pp. 170-82 in Roberts's *The Psychology of Tragic Drama*

Romano, J., " 'Mourning Becomes Electra': Eugene O'Neill's Dramatic Trilogy Was Rooted in Classical Tragedy—And His Own Tormented Life," *TV Guide*, 26:23 +, 2 Dec. 1978

The Rime of the Ancient Mariner (also known as *The Ancient Mariner*; dramatization of poem by S. T. Coleridge), 1924

Cunningham, F. R., "*The Ancient Mariner* and the Genesis of O'Neill's Romanticism," *Eugene O'Neill Newsletter*, 3, i:6-9, 1979

Strange Interlude, 1928

Feldman, R., "The Longing for Death in O'Neill's *Strange Interlude* and *Mourning Becomes Electra*," *Literature and Psychology*, 31, i:39-48, 1981

Gottfried, M., *A Theater Divided*, p. 62

Robinson, L., "John Howard Lawson's *Souls*: A Harbinger of *Strange Interlude*," *Eugene O'Neill Newsletter*, 4, iii:12-13, 1980

Thirst, 1916

Wolter, J., "O'Neill's 'Open Boat,' " *Literatur in Wissenschaft und Unterricht*, 11, iv:222-29, 1978

A Touch of the Poet, 1957

Fuchs, E., "O'Neill's *Poet*: Touched by Ibsen," *Educational Theatre Journal*, 31:513-16, 1978

Josephson, L., *A Role*

Keller, D., "Staging *A Touch of the Poet*," *Eugene O'Neill Newsletter*, 4, i-ii:10-12, 1980

After Dark, 10:80-81, Mar. 1978

Nation, 226:60-61, 21 Jan. 1978

New Leader, 61:25-26, 30 Jan. 1978

New Republic, 178:24-25, 28 Jan. 1978

New York, 11:57-58, 16 Jan. 1978

New Yorker, 53:59, 9 Jan. 1978

Newsweek, 91:71, 9 Jan. 1978

Saturday Review, 5:41, 4 Mar. 1978

Theater, 9:147-48, Spring 1978

Time, 111:68, 9 Jan. 1978

Welded, 1924

Harris, Jr., A. B., "A Tangible Confrontation: *Welded*," *Theatre News*, 13, vii:9-10, Fall 1981

Törnqvist, E., "Platonic Love in O'Neill's *Welded*," pp. 73-83 in *Eugene O'Neill*, ed. V. Floyd
New York, 14:39, 29 June 1981

JOEL OPPENHEIMER

The Great American Desert, 1961
Bertholf, R., "On *The Great American Desert* and *The Woman Poems*," *Credences*, 1(2[2]):26-35, July 1975

BARRY OPPER
SEE
MICHAEL E. DAWDY, CANDACE LAUGHLIN, and BARRY OPPER

JOHN ORLOCK

Indulgences in the Louisville Harem, 1979
Texas Monthly, 7:198, Dec. 1979

J. R. ORTON

Arnold, 1854
Shillingsburg, M. J., "The West Point Treason in American Drama, 1798-1891," *Educational Theatre Journal*, 30:73-89, 1978

PAUL OSBORN

A Bell for Adano (dramatization of novel by J. Hersey), 1944
Greenfield, T. A., *Work and the Work Ethic in American Drama 1920-1970*, pp. 91-92

Morning's at Seven, 1939
After Dark, 13:57, June 1980
Commonweal, 107:335-36, 6 June 1980
Nation, 230:540, 3 May 1980
New York, 13:78, 21 Apr. 1980
New Yorker, 56:77, 21 Apr. 1980
Newsweek, 95:112, 21 Apr. 1980
Time, 115:84, 21 Apr. 1980

BOB OST

Breeders, 1979
After Dark, 12:31, July 1979

STUART OSTROW

Stages, 1978
After Dark, 11:111, May 1978

ROCHELLE OWENS
(pseud. of Rochelle Bass)

General

Cohn, R., "Camp, Cruelty, Colloquialism," pp. 281-303 in *Comic Relief*, ed. S. B. Cohen

Cohn, R., *Dialogue in American Drama*, pp. 303-07

Marranca, B. G., "Rochelle Owens," pp. 159-82 in Marranca and G. Dasgupta's *American Playwrights*

Kontraption, 1978
    After Dark, 11:116, May 1978

OYAMO
(pseud. of Charles Gordon)

The Resurrection of Lady Lester, 1981
    New Yorker, 57:69-70, 23 Nov. 1981

NORMAN PANAMA
SEE
JEROME CHODOROV and NORMAN PANAMA

RALPH PAPE

Say Goodnight, Gracie, 1979
    Chicago, 29:163 + , Jan. 1980
    Horizon, 22:48, Oct. 1979
    New York, 12:66, 6 Aug. 1979
    New Yorker, 55:94, 96, 2 Apr. 1979
    Newsweek, 94:65, 30 July 1979

PETER PARNELL

Scooter Thomas Makes It to the Top of the World, 1977
    Educational Theatre Journal, 30:271-72, 1978

The Sorrows of Stephen (inspired by Goethe's *Sorrows of Young Werther*), 1979
    After Dark, 12:19, Feb. 1980
    America, 141:391, 15 Dec. 1979
    Nation, 229:509, 17 Nov. 1979
    New York, 12:130, 12 Nov. 1979
    New Yorker, 55:113-14, 10 Dec. 1979
    Plays and Players, 27:38-39, Dec. 1979

JOHN PATRICK

The Hasty Heart, 1945
    Los Angeles, 27:238, June 1982

ROBERT PATRICK

General

Dasgupta, G., "Robert Patrick," pp. 171-82 in Dasgupta and B. G. Marranca's *American Playwrights*

My Cup Ranneth Over, 1978
  After Dark, 11:84, Sept. 1978

T-Shirts, 1978
  After Dark, 13:62, Aug. 1980

E. J. PATTERSON

A Matter of Ignorance, 1980
  Theatre Journal, 33:123, 1981

JAMES KIRKE PAULDING

The Bucktails; or, Americans in England, 1812
  Herron, I. H., *The Small Town in American Drama*, pp. 45-46

JOHN HOWARD PAYNE

General

Meserve, W. J., *An Emerging Entertainment*, pp. 280-90
Meserve, W. J., *An Outline History of American Drama*, pp. 54-56, 99, 105-06
Vaughn, J. A., *Early American Dramatists*, pp. 70-79

JOHN HOWARD PAYNE and WASHINGTON IRVING

Charles the Second; or, The Merry Monarch, 1824
  Meserve, W. J., *An Outline History of American Drama*, pp. 84-85

JOSEPHINE PRESTON PEABODY

General

Meserve, W. J., *An Outline History of American Drama*, pp. 195-96

SYBILLE PEARSON

Sally and Marsha, 1982
  America, 146:320, 24 Apr. 1982
  New Yorker, 58:98, 8 Mar. 1982
  Plays and Players, 344:30, May 1982

LEE PENNINGTON

General

Wills, J. R., "Prevailing Shadows: The Plays of Lee Pennington," *Southern Quarterly*, 20, i:25-34, Fall 1981

ROB PENNY

Who Loves the Dancer, 1982
  New Yorker, 58:129, 22 Mar. 1982

S. J. PERELMAN

General

Time, 114:123, 29 Oct. 1979

COLERIDGE-TAYLOR PERKINSON
SEE
PAUL CARTER HARRISON and COLERIDGE-TAYLOR PERKINSON

ARNOLD PERL

Tevya and His Daughters (dramatization of tales by S. Aleichem), 1957
  Nation, 185:231, 5 Oct. 1957

The World of Sholom Aleichem (adaptation of short stories by Aleichem and others),
  1953
  Catholic World, 178:147, Nov. 1953
  Commentary, 17:389-92, Apr. 1954
  Nation, 177:277-78, 3 Oct. 1983
  New York, 15:52-54, 22 Feb. 1982
  New Yorker, 58:94, 1 Mar. 1982
  Saturday Review, 36:30, 16 May 1953
  Theatre Arts, 37:82-83, July 1953
  Time, 119:70, 22 Feb. 1982

PAUL PETERS

Mother (adaptation of play by Brecht, based on a novel by Gorki), 1935
  Himelstein, M. Y., *Drama Was a Weapon*, pp. 65-67, *passim*

PAUL PETERS and GEORGE SKLAR

Stevedore, 1934
  Himelstein, M. Y., *Drama Was a Weapon*, pp. 59-61, *passim*
  Smiley, S., *The Drama of Attack*, pp. 52-53, 129-31

LOUIS PETERSON

Crazy Horse, 1979
  Encore, 8:34, 17 Dec. 1979

LOUIS PHILLIPS

The Ballroom in St. Patrick's Cathedral, 1978
  New Yorker, 54:57, 60, 11 Dec. 1978

JOHN PIELMEIER

Agnes of God, 1980
    America, 146:382, 15 May 1982
    New Leader, 65:20, 19 Apr. 1982
    New York, 15:71-72, 12 Apr. 1982
    New Yorker, 58:125-26, 12 Apr. 1982
    Time, 115:58, 31 Mar. 1980
    Time, 119:77, 12 Apr. 1982

MARIA HENRIETTA PINCKNEY

General

Meserve, W. J., *An Emerging Entertainment*, pp. 243-44

MIGUEL PIÑERO

The Sun Always Shines for the Cool, 1975
    After Dark, 12:27, Dec. 1979
    Encore, 8:36-37, 1 Oct. 1979

JOSEPH PINTAURO

Snow Orchid, 1982
    New York, 15:84, 29 Mar. 1982

ABE POLSKY

Devour the Snow, 1979
    After Dark, 12:63-64, Aug. 1979
    After Dark, 12:20, 22, Jan. 1980
    Nation, 229:571-72, 1 Dec. 1979
    New West, 3:SC-40, 27 Mar. 1978
    New York, 12:98, 19 Nov. 1979
    New Yorker, 55:92-93, 28 May 1979
    New Yorker, 55:100-02, 19 Nov. 1979
    Time, 113:93, 21 May 1979

BERNARD POMERANCE

The Elephant Man, 1977
    Loder, K., " 'The Elephant Man': The Play: David Bowie," *Rolling Stone*, 13
      Nov. 1980, pp. 8 +
    After Dark, 11:84-85, Mar. 1979
    After Dark, 12:88-89, June 1979
    After Dark, 13:58, July 1980
    After Dark, 13:27, Dec. 1980
    America, 140:135, 24 Feb. 1979
    Christian Century, 97:14-18, 2 Jan. 1980
    Commentary, 68:62-64, July 1979

Commonweal, 106:180-81, 30 Mar. 1979
Drama, 127:72, Winter 1977-1978
Drama, 138:18-19, Oct. 1980
Georgia Review, 33:573-74, Fall 1979
Harper's, 262:66-68, May 1981
Horizon, 22:16-24, June 1979
Hudson Review, 32:403-10, Autumn 1979
Nation, 228:156, 10 Feb. 1979
New Leader, 62:23-24, 7 May 1979
New Republic, 180:24-26, 17 Feb. 1979
New Republic, 180:24-25, 12 May 1979
New West, 5:SC-24, 19 May 1980
New York, 12:120-21, 29 Jan. 1979
New York, 12:84-85, 7 May 1979
New York, 13:54-55, 13 Oct. 1980
New Yorker, 54:45-46, 29 Jan. 1979
New Yorker, 55:95, 30 Apr. 1979
Newsweek, 93:67, 5 Feb. 1979
People, 12:77 + , 10 Dec. 1979
Plays and Players, 25:36, Jan. 1978
Saturday Review, 6:60, 17 Mar. 1979
Texas Monthly, 9:175-76, Aug. 1981
Theatre Crafts, 14:24-27 + , Jan./Feb. 1980
Theatre Journal, 33:541-42, 1981
Time, 113:64, 29 Jan. 1979

Quantrill in Lawrence, 1980
Plays and Players, 27:18-19, May 1980

COLE PORTER

General

Smith, J., "Cole Porter in the American Musical Theatre," pp. 47-70 in *Drama, Dance and Music*, ed. J. Redmond

SEE ALSO
BURT SHEVELOVE
AND
BELLA SPEWACK, SAM SPEWACK, and COLE PORTER

ROBERT A. POTTER

Queen Margaret of England (devised from Shakespeare's *Henry VI*, Parts I, II, and III), 1977
Theatre News, 10, ii:8, Nov. 1977

EMERY POTTLE
SEE
GILBERT EMERY

WILLIAM PRATT

Ten Nights in a Barroom, 1858

Greenfield, T. A., *Work and the Work Ethic in American Drama 1920-1970*, pp. 29-30

JAMES PRIDEAUX

Jane Heights (dramatized amalgam of C. Bronte's *Jane Eyre* and E. Bronte's *Wuthering Heights*), 1980
After Dark, 12:26, Apr. 1980

Mixed Couples, 1980
After Dark, 13:24-26 + , Feb. 1981
After Dark, 13:28, Mar. 1981
New York, 14:44-45, 12 Jan. 1981
New Yorker, 56:90, 19 Jan. 1981

MICHAEL PROCASSION
SEE
MICHAEL CRISTOFER

DAVID RABE

General

Asahina, R., "The Basic Training of American Playwrights: Theater and the Vietnam War," *Theater*, 9, ii:30-37, 1978
Brustein, R., "The Crack in the Chimney: Reflections on Contemporary American Playwriting," *Theater*, 9, ii:21-29, 1978
Hertzbach, J. S., "The Plays of David Rabe: A World of Streamers," pp. 173-86 in *Essays on Contemporary American Drama*, ed. H. Bock and A. Wertheim
Homan, R. L., "American Playwrights in the 1970's: Rabe and Shephard," *Critical Quarterly*, 24:73-82, Spring 1982
Phillips, J. A., "Descent into the Abyss: The Plays of David Rabe," *West Virginia University Philological Papers*, 25:108-17, 1979
Werner, C., "Primal Screams and Nonsense Rhymes: David Rabe's Revolt," *Educational Theatre Journal*, 30:517-29, 1978

In the Boom Boom Room (revision of his *Boom Boom Room*), 1974
Brown, J., "*In the Boom Boom Room*," pp. 37-55 in Brown's *Feminist Drama*

The Orphan, 1973
Kellman, B., "David Rabe's *The Orphan*: A Peripatetic Work in Progress," *Theatre Quarterly*, 7:72-74 + , Spring 1977

Sticks and Bones, 1969
Adler, T. P., "'The Blind Leading the Blind': Rabe's *Sticks and Bones* and Shakespeare's *King Lear*," *Papers on Language and Literature*, 15:203-06, 1979
Bernstein, S. J., *The Strands Entwined*, pp. 15-36
Drama, 128:70, Spring 1978
Plays and Players, 25:24-25, Apr. 1978

Streamers, 1976

After Dark, 10:79, Mar. 1978
Drama, 128:69-70, Spring 1978
Educational Theatre Journal, 30:273, 1978
Los Angeles, 23:208, Feb. 1978
Plays and Players, 25:24-25, Apr. 1978

JAMES RADO
SEE NEXT ENTRY

GEROME RAGNI, JAMES RADO, and GALT MacDERMOT

Hair, 1967
 Geraths, A., "G. Ragni, J. Rado, G. MacDermot: *Hair*," pp. 65-85 in *Das amerikanische Drama der Gegenwart*, ed. H. Grabes
 New York, 12:11, 19 Mar. 1979

AYN RAND

The Night of January 16, 1936
 Commonweal, 22:528, 27 Sept. 1935
 Newsweek, 6:29, 28 Sept. 1935
 Theatre Arts Monthly, 19:823, Nov. 1935
 Time, 26:22, 30 Sept. 1935

The Unconquered, 1940
 Commonweal, 31:412, 1 Mar. 1940
 Theatre Arts, 24:236, Apr. 1940

J. RANELLI

There's a Message for You from the Man in the Moon, 1981
 Theatre Journal, 33:537, 1981

DAVID RAYFIEL

Nathan Weinstein, Mystic, Connecticut, 1966
 Gottfried, M., *A Theater Divided*, pp. 274-75

MARK REED

Let's Get Rich, 1920
 Greenfield, T. A., *Work and the Work Ethic in American Drama 1920-1970*,
 pp. 61-63

ARTHUR REEL

Heart of Darkness (dramatization of novella by J. Conrad), 1978
 New York, 11:80, 4 Sept. 1978

KENNETH REXROTH
General

Cohn, R., *Dialogue in American Drama*, pp. 263-65

JONATHAN REYNOLDS

Geniuses, 1982
  Nation, 235:154-55, 21-28 Aug. 1982
  New Republic, 187:23-24, 12 July 1982
  New York, 15:92, 31 May 1982
  New Yorker, 58:102+, 24 May 1982
  Newsweek, 100:75, 19 July 1982

Tunnel Fever; or, The Sheep Is Out, 1979
  After Dark, 12:31, July 1979

RONALD RIBMAN
General

Weales, G., "Ronald Ribman: The Artist of the Failure Clowns," pp. 75-90 in *Essays on Contemporary American Drama*, ed. H. Bock and A. Wertheim

The Burial of Esposito, 1969
  After Dark, 12:64, Aug. 1979

Cold Storage, 1977
  After Dark, 10:82+, Mar. 1978
  America, 138:124, 18 Feb. 1978
  Nation, 226:61, 21 Jan. 1978
  New York, 11:68, 23 Jan. 1978
  New Yorker, 53:68-69, 16 Jan. 1978
  Saturday Review, 5:41, 4 Mar. 1978

Harry, Noon and Night, 1965
  Gottfried, M., *A Theater Divided*, pp. 72-73

The Journey of the Fifth Horse (dramatization, in part, of story by Turgenev, *The Diary of a Superfluous Man*), 1966
  Gottfried, M., *A Theater Divided*, pp. 74-75
  Theatre Journal, 34, iv:536-38, Dec. 1982

ELMER RICE
General

Bigsby, C. W. E., *A Critical Introduction to Twentieth-Century American Drama*, Vol. I, pp. 126-31
Broussard, L., *American Drama*, pp. 39-50
Gould, J., "Elmer Rice," pp. 8-25 in Gould's *Modern American Playwrights*
Greenfield, T. A., "Elmer Rice," pp. 37-54 in Greenfield's *Work and the Work Ethic in American Drama 1920-1970*

Mersand, J., *The American Drama Since 1930*, pp. 35-45

Meserve, W. J., *An Outline History of American Drama*, pp. 237-38, 260-61, 263-65, 340-41

Palmieri, A. F. R., *Elmer Rice*

The Adding Machine, 1923
Greenfield, T. A., *Work and the Work Ethic in American Drama 1920-1970*, pp. 39-42, *passim*
Kaes, A., "Elmer Rice: *The Adding Machine*," *Studien zur Deutschen Literatur*, 43:121-34, 1975
Drama, 138:56, Oct. 1980

American Landscape, 1938
Himelstein, M. Y., *Drama Was A Weapon*, pp. 145-46

Between Two Worlds, 1934
Himelstein, M. Y., *Drama Was a Weapon*, pp. 193-94

Cue for Passion, 1958
Schulz, D., "Elmer Rice, *Cue for Passion*, Paul Baker, *Hamlet ESP*," pp. 293-306 in *Anglo-Amerikanische Shakespeare-Bearbeitungen des 20. Jahrhunderts*, ed. H. Priessnitz

Flight to the West, 1940
Nannes, C. H., *Politics in the American Drama*, pp. 168-70

Judgment Day, 1934
Himelstein, M. Y., *Drama Was a Weapon*, pp. 192-93
Smiley, S., *The Drama of Attack*, pp. 154-57, *passim*

We, the People, 1933
Himelstein, M. Y., *Drama Was a Weapon*, pp. 187-88
Smiley, S., *The Drama of Attack*, pp. 157-61, *passim*

JACK RICHARDSON
General

Gottfried, M., *A Theater Divided*, pp. 276-77

Wellwarth, G., *The Theatre of Protest and Paradox*, rev. ed., pp. 337-44

Gallows Humor, 1961
Szilassy, Z., "*Gallows Humour* [sic] or the Weeping of the Willow Tree?," *Studies in English and American*, 3:45-59, 1977

WILLIS RICHARDSON

The Chipwoman's Fortune, 1923
Bigsby, C. W. E., *A Critical Introduction to Twentieth-Century American Drama*, Vol. I, pp. 238-39
Greenfield, T. A., *Work and the Work Ethic in American Drama 1920-1970*, p. 133

DAVID RICHMOND
SEE
BOB HALL and DAVID RICHMOND

LYNN RIGGS

Green Grow the Lilacs, 1931
Herron, I. H., *The Small Town in American Drama*, pp. 174-75

Roadside; or, Borned in Texas, 1936
Herron, I. H., *The Small Town in American Drama*, pp. 173-74

DAVID RIMMER

Album, 1980
After Dark, 13:27, Dec. 1980
New Yorker, 56:147, 13 Oct. 1980

MARY ROBERTS RINEHART

General

Cohn, J., "Mary Roberts Rinehart," pp. 180-220 in *10 Women of Mystery*, ed. E. F. Bargainnier

DAVID W. RINTELS

Clarence Darrow (dramatization of *Clarence Darrow for the Defense* by I. Stone), 1974
Bordinat, P., "The One-Person Play: A Form of Contemporary Dramatic Biography," *Midwest Quarterly*, 21:231-40, 1980

ANNA CORA MOWATT RITCHIE

General

Vaughn, J. A., *Early American Dramatists*, pp. 79-88

Fashion; or, Life in New York, 1845
Meserve, W. J., *An Outline History of American Drama*, pp. 86-88

ERIKA RITTER

Automatic Pilot, 1980
Maclean's, 93:54, 14 July 1980

The Passing Scene, 1982
Maclean's, 95:62, 18 Jan. 1982

Splits, 1978
After Dark, 11:26, Feb. 1979

PETER ROBILOTTA
SEE
STEWART BIRD and PETER ROBILOTTA

RICHARD RODGERS

General

Time, 115:83, 14 Jan. 1980

SEE ALSO
GEORGE ABBOTT, RICHARD RODGERS, and LORENZ HART
AND
OSCAR HAMMERSTEIN II, BENJAMIN GLAZER,
and RICHARD RODGERS
AND
OSCAR HAMMERSTEIN II and RICHARD RODGERS
AND
GEORGE S. KAUFMAN, MOSS HART, RICHARD RODGERS,
and LORENZ HART
AND
THOMAS MEEHAN, RICHARD RODGERS, MARTIN CHARNIN,
and RAYMOND JESSEL

JOHN WILLIAM ROGERS, JR.

General

Herron, I. H., *The Small Town in American Drama*, pp. 166-68

ROBERT ROGERS

Ponteach; or, The Savages of America, 1766
    Anderson, M. J., "*Ponteach*: The First American Problem Play," *American Indian Quarterly*, 3:225-41, 1977
    Meserve, W. J., *An Emerging Entertainment*, p. 53
    Meserve, W. J., *An Outline History of American Drama*, pp. 11-12
    Morsberger, R. E., "The Tragedy of *Ponteach* and the Northwest Passage," *Old Northwest*, 4:241-57, 1978
    Vaughn, J. A., *Early American Dramatists*, pp. 10-11
    Winton, C., "The Theater and Drama," pp. 89-90 in *American Literature, 1764-1789*, ed. E. Emerson

MARY ROHDE

Lady Bug, Lady Bug, Fly Away Home, 1978
    Texas Monthly, 6:140, 142, May 1978
    Theatre Journal, 32:255, 1980

DAVID ROSE
SEE
MOSS HART and DAVID ROSE

NORMAN ROSE
SEE
GEORGE GONNEAU and NORMAN ROSE

PETER ROSE

The Circular Heavens, 1979
    Theatre Journal, 32:268, 1980

SHELDON ROSEN

Ned and Jack, 1981
    New Leader, 64:22, 29 June 1981
    New York, 14:45, 1 June 1981
    New Yorker, 57:124, 1 June 1981
    New Yorker, 57:182, 16 Nov. 1981

SYDNEY ROSENFELD
SEE
DAVID DEMAREST LLOYD and SYDNEY ROSENFELD

CLARENCE E. ROSS

Gas Light (based on P. Hamilton's play *Gaslight*), 1982
    Los Angeles, 27:276-77, Apr. 1982

JUDITH ROSS

An Almost Perfect Person, 1977
    Mandate, 3:9, Jan. 1978

SUSANNA HASWELL ROWSON

General

Meserve, W. J., *An Emerging Entertainment*, pp. 115-19

JOSÉ RUIBAL

The Man and the Fly, 1968
    New York, 15:75-76, 1 Mar. 1982
    New Yorker, 58:54, 22 Feb. 1982

DAVID RUSH

Beethoven/Karl, 1979
    New Yorker, 54:46, 29 Jan. 1979

JOHN RUSTAN and FRANK SEMERANO

The Attempted Murder of Peggy Sweetwater, 1982
  Los Angeles, 27:254 + , July 1982

The Tangled Snarl, 1982
  Los Angeles, 27:254 + , July 1982

MORRIE RYSKIND
SEE
GEORGE S. KAUFMAN and MORRIE RYSKIND
AND
GEORGE S. KAUFMAN, MORRIE RYSKIND, GEORGE GERSHWIN, and IRA GERSHWIN

BERNARD SABATH

The Boys in Autumn, 1981
  California, 6:138, Nov. 1981

LILLIAN SABINE

The Rise of Silas Lapham (dramatization of W. D. Howells's novel), 1919
  Greenfield, T. A., *Work and the Work Ethic in American Drama 1920-1970*,
    pp. 56-58
  Dramatic Mirror, 8:1901, 11 Dec. 1919
  Review, 1:648, 6 Dec. 1919
  Theatre (New York), 31:18, 20, Jan. 1920

HOWARD SACKLER

Goodbye Fidel, 1980
  New York, 13:61, 5 May 1980
  New Yorker, 56:109, 5 May 1980

Semmelweiss, 1977
  Time, 117:60, 1 June 1981

BURY ST. EDMUND
(pseud. of Lenny Kleinfeld)
SEE
STUART GORDON and BURY ST. EDMUND

WILLIAM SAROYAN

General

Bigsby, C. W. E., *A Critical Introduction to Twentieth-Century American Drama*,
  Vol. I, pp. 133-38
Gould, J., "Clifford Odets," pp. 201-03 in Gould's *Modern American Playwrights*
Meserve, W. J., *An Outline History of American Drama*, pp. 310-13, 345-46

Ralea, C., "William Saroyan: 'Nu vreau să scriu nimic fără umor şi fără lumină!,'"
    România Literară, 26 June 1980:19
Time, 117:60, 1 June 1981

The Cave Dwellers, 1957
    Texas Monthly, 7:152, July 1979

The Great American Goof, 1940
    Drama, 132:72-73, Spring 1979
    Musical Courier, 121:3, 1 Feb. 1940
    Musical Courier, 123:12, 1 Mar. 1941

Hello Out There, 1941
    Herron, I. H., *The Small Town in American Drama*, pp. 441-42

Love's Old Sweet Song, 1940
    Himelstein, M. Y., *Drama Was a Weapon*, p. 149

My Heart's in the Highlands, 1939
    Herron, I. H., *The Small Town in American Drama*, pp. 439-41

The Slaughter of the Innocents, 1952
    Wertheim, A., "The McCarthy Era and the American Theatre," *Theatre Journal*,
        34:211-22, 1982
    Theatre Arts, 36:33-56, Nov. 1952

The Time of Your Life, 1939
    Vos, N., *The Great Pendulum of Becoming*, pp. 83-84

OSCAR SAUL

Medicine Show, 1940
    Himelstein, M. Y., *Drama Was a Weapon*, pp. 210-11

OSCAR SAUL and LOUIS LANTZ

The Revolt of the Beavers, 1937
    Himelstein, M. Y., *Drama Was a Weapon*, pp. 102-03, *passim*

LEMUEL SAWYER

General

Meserve, W. J., *An Emerging Entertainment*, pp. 267-68

JOHN SAYLES

New Hope for the Dead, 1981
    After Dark, 14:16-17, Oct. 1981

Turnbuckle, 1981

After Dark, 14:16-17, Oct. 1981

DORE SCHARY

Sunrise at Campobello, 1958
  Nannes, C. H., *Politics in the American Drama*, pp. 122-33

RICHARD SCHECHNER

General

Innes, C., "Secular Religions, Communion, Myths: Disciples: Europe and America,"
  pp. 177-87 in Innes's *Holy Theatre*

The Balcony (adaptation of J. Genêt's play), 1979
  Schechner, R., "Genêt's *The Balcony*: A 1981 Perspective on a 1979/80 Pro-
    duction," *Modern Drama*, 25:82-104, Mar. 1982
  New Yorker, 55:116, 26 Nov. 1979

Richard's Lear (an amalgam of Shakespeare's *Richard III* and *King Lear*), 1981
  Zarilli, P., "Richard Schechner's *Richard's Lear*," *The Drama Review*, 25:92-
    97, Winter 1981

JAMES SCHEVILL

General

Cohn, R., *Dialogue in American Drama*, pp. 276-80

MURRAY SCHISGAL

Luv, 1963
  Gottfried, M., *A Theater Divided*, pp. 217-18

Twice Around the Park (two one-acts: *A Need for Brussels Sprouts* and *A Need for
  Less Expertise*), 1982
  Nation, 236:600 + , 4 Dec. 1982
  New Leader, 65:22, 27 Dec. 1982
  New Republic, 187:29, 13 Dec. 1982
  New York, 15:105, 15 Nov. 1982
  New Yorker, 58:174, 15 Nov. 1982
  Newsweek, 100:117, 15 Nov. 1982

HARVEY SCHMIDT
SEE
TOM JONES and HARVEY SCHMIDT
AND
N. RICHARD NASH, TOM JONES, and HARVEY SCHMIDT

BARBARA SCHNEIDER

Details Without a Map, 1980
  Texas Monthly, 9:226, 228, Dec. 1981

HOWARD SCHUMAN

Censored Scenes from King Kong, 1977
　　New Yorker, 56:87-88, 17 Mar. 1980
　　Plays and Players, 25:35, Jan. 1978

STEPHEN SCHWARTZ
SEE
JOHN-MICHAEL TEBELAK and STEPHEN SCHWARTZ

JOE SEARS
SEE
JASTON WILLIAMS and JOE SEARS

JOHN WILLIAM SEE

The Lady Cries Murder, 1981
　　Los Angeles, 27:227 + , Jan. 1982

FRANK SEMERANO
SEE
JOHN RUSTAN and FRANK SEMERANO

ANDREI SERBAN

General

Kauffmann, S., "Trilogy," pp. 108-11 in Kauffmann's *Persons of the Drama*

Electra (adaptation of play by Sophocles), 1974
　　Nation, 220:59-60, 18 Jan. 1975
　　New Republic, 171:42 + , 23 Nov. 1974

Medea (adaptation of play by Euripides), 1972
　　Nation, 214:411, 27 Mar. 1972
　　Nation, 220:59-60, 18 Jan. 1975
　　New Republic, 166:24, 24 June 1972
　　New Republic, 171:42 + , 23 Nov. 1974
　　New Yorker, 47:69, 12 Feb. 1972
　　Saturday Review, 55:12-13, 11 Mar. 1972

The Trojan Women (adaptation of play by Euripides), 1974
　　Nation, 220:59-60, 18 Jan. 1975
　　New Republic, 171:42 + , 23 Nov. 1974
　　Saturday Review, 2:41-42, 8 Feb. 1975

ANDREI SERBAN and PATRICK BURKE

The Master and Margarita (dramatization of novel by M. Bulgakov), 1978
　　After Dark, 11:29 + , Feb. 1979
　　New York, 11:118, 11 Dec. 1978

New Yorker, 54:86, 4 Dec. 1978
Newsweek, 92:102+, 11 Dec. 1978

RAYMOND SERRA

Manny, 1979
    After Dark, 12:31, July 1979

GENEVIEVE SERREAU
SEE
JAMES LORD and GENEVIEVE SERREAU

WILLIAM SEVERSON

Bucking the Tiger, 1981
    Theatre Journal, 34:263-64, 1982

ANNE SEXTON

General

Maryan, C., "The Poet on Stage," pp. 89-95 in *Anne Sexton*, ed. J. D. McClatchy

NTOZAKE SHANGE
(Paulette Williams)

General

Blackwell, H., "An Interview with Ntozake Shange," *Black American Literature Forum*, 13:134-38, 1979
Fabre, G., "Ntozake Shange," *Revue Française d'Etudes Américaines*, 10:259-70, 1980

Boogie Woogie Landscapes, 1980
    Miller, J.-M. A., "Three Theatre Pieces by Ntozake Shange," *Theatre News*, 14, iv:8, Apr. 1982

For Colored Girls Who Have Considered Suicide/When the Rainbow Is Enuf, 1976
    Brown, J., "*For Colored Girls Who Have Considered Suicide/When the Rainbow Is Enuf*," pp. 114-32 in Brown's *Feminist Drama*
    Christ, C. P., " 'i found god in myself. . . & i love her fiercely': Ntozake Shange," pp. 97-117 in Christ's *Diving Deep and Surfacing*
    Flowers, S. H., "*Colored Girls*: Textbook for the Eighties," *Black American Literature Forum*, 15, ii:51-54, Summer 1981
    Gillespie, P. P., "American Women Dramatists, 1960-1980," pp. 197-99 in *Essays on Contemporary American Drama*, ed. H. Bock and A. Wertheim
    Peters, E., "Some Tragic Propensities of Ourselves: The Occasion of Ntozake Shange's *For Colored Girls Who Have Considered Suicide/When the Rainbow Is Enuf*," *Journal of Ethnic Studies*, 6, i:79-85, 1978
    Rushing, A. B., "*For Colored Girls*: Suicide or Struggle," *Massachusetts Review*, 22:539-50, Autumn 1981
    Educational Theatre Journal, 29:262-63, 1977

Negro History Bulletin, 41:797-800, Jan. 1978
Plays and Players, 27:16-17, 1979
Texas Monthly, 6:96, Jan. 1978
Theatre Arts, 12, vii:4, Apr. 1980

Mother Courage and Her Children (adaptation of play by Brecht), 1980
Essence, 11:21, Aug. 1980
New York, 13:80-81, 26 May 1980
New Yorker, 56:77, 26 May 1980

A Photograph: A Still Life with Shadows/A Photograph: A Study in Cruelty (revised
in 1979 as *A Photograph: Lovers in Motion*), 1977
Miller, J.-M. A., "Three Theatre Pieces by Ntozake Shange," *Theatre News*,
14, iv:8, Apr. 1982
After Dark, 10:80, Apr. 1978
New Leader, 61:29, 2 Jan. 1978
New York, 11:58, 16 Jan. 1978
New Yorker, 53:48, 2 Jan. 1978
Saturday Review, 5:42, 18 Feb. 1978

Spell #7, 1979
Miller, J.-M. A., "Three Theatre Pieces by Ntozake Shange," *Theatre News*,
14, iv:8, Apr. 1982
New York, 12:57, 30 July 1979
New Yorker, 55:73, 9 July 1979
Newsweek, 94:65, 30 July 1979

Where the Mississippi Meets the Amazon, 1977
New Yorker, 53:48-49, 2 Jan. 1978

ADELE EDLING SHANK

Sunset/Sunrise, 1980
Time, 115:58, 31 Mar. 1980

TERRENCE SHANK

The Grapes of Wrath (dramatization of novel by J. Steinbeck), 1980
After Dark, 13:63, Sept. 1980
New West, 5:SC-25, 2 June 1980

JACK SHARKEY

Saving Grace, 1982
Drama-Logue, 13, xxxvi:8, 9-15 Sept. 1982

IRWIN SHAW

Bury the Dead, 1936
Bigsby, C. W. E., *A Critical Introduction to Twentieth-Century American Drama*,
Vol. I, pp. 202-04

Himelstein, M. Y., *Drama Was a Weapon*, pp. 45-46, *passim*
Smiley, S., *The Drama of Attack*, pp. 121-22

The Gentle People, 1939
Himelstein, M. Y., *Drama Was a Weapon*, pp. 176-77
Smiley, S., *The Drama of Attack*, pp. 92-96, 111-13

Retreat to Pleasure, 1940
Himelstein, M. Y., *Drama Was a Weapon*, pp. 178-79

WALLACE SHAWN

Hotel Play, 1981
Newsweek, 98:81, 7 Sept. 1981

The Mandrake (adaptation of Machiavelli's play), 1977
After Dark, 11:114, May 1978

Marie and Bruce, 1979
After Dark, 13:66, May 1980
New Republic, 182:28-29, 5 Apr. 1980
New York, 13:85-86, 18 Feb. 1980
New Yorker, 55:64-65, 11 Feb. 1980
Newsweek, 95:117, 18 Feb. 1980
Plays and Players, 27:28-29, Oct. 1979

EDWARD SHEEHAN

Kingdoms, 1981
After Dark, 14:16, Mar. 1982
New York, 15:98-99, 28 Dec. 1981/4 Jan. 1982
New Yorker, 57:57, 28 Dec. 1981

EDWARD SHELDON

General

Ruff, L. K., *Edward Sheldon*

The Boss, 1911
Greenfield, T. A., *Work and the Work Ethic in American Drama 1920-1970*,
pp. 33-35
Meserve, W. J., *An Outline History of American Drama*, pp. 199-201

"*The Nigger*," 1909
Herron, I. H., *The Small Town in American Drama*, pp. 210-12
Nannes, C. H., *Politics in the American Drama*, pp. 42-43

SAM SHEPARD

General

Auerbach, D., *Sam Shepard, Arthur Kopit, and the Off Broadway Theater*

Brustein, R., "The Crack in the Chimney: Reflections on Contemporary American Playwriting," *Theater*, 9, ii:21-29, 1978

Cohn, R., "Camp, Cruelty, Colloquialism," pp. 281-303 in *Comic Relief*, ed. S. B. Cohen

Cohn, R., "Sam Shepard: Today's Passionate Shepard and His Loves," pp. 161-72 in *Essays on Contemporary American Drama*, ed. H. Bock and A. Wertheim

Falk, F., "The Role of Performance in Sam Shepard's Plays," *Theatre Journal*, 33, ii:182-98, May 1981

Glore, J., "The Canonization of Mojo Rootforce: Sam Shepard Live at the Pantheon," *Theater*, 12:53-65, Summer/Fall 1981

Homan, R. L., "American Playwrights in the 1970's: Rabe and Shepard," *Critical Quarterly*, 24:73-82, Spring 1982

Kerjan, L., "Sam Shepard et l'invisible espace," *Revue Française d'Etudes Américaines*, 10:271-84, 1980

Klaić, D., "Dramaturgija Sema Šēpardor," *Književnost*, xii:1986-97, 1980

Leverett, J., "Old Forms Enter the New American Theater: Shepard, Foreman, Kirby, and Ludlam," pp. 107-22 in *Melodrama*, guest ed. D. C. Gerould

Marranca, B., ed., *American Dreams*

Marranca, B. G., "Sam Shepard," pp. 81-111 in Marranca and G. Dasgupta's *American Playwrights*

Rouyer, P., "Le Naturalisme et sa descendence aujourd'hui: Sam Shepard est-il," pp. 48-111 in *Naturalisme américain*, ed. J. Cazemajou and J.-C. Barat

Shepard, S., "Time," *Theater*, 9:9, Spring 1978

Shepard, S., "Visualization, Language and the Inner Library," *The Drama Review*, 21, iv:49-58, 1977

Smith, P., "Sam Shepard: 9 Random Years (7 + 2)," *After Dark*, 12:62-63, Jan. 1980

Stasio, M., "Sam Shepard: An Outlaw Comes Home," *After Dark*, 12:58-61, Jan. 1980

Wetzsteon, R., "The Genius of Sam Shepard," *New York*, 13:20, 23, 25, 24 Nov. 1980

Wetzsteon, R., "Sam Shepard: Escape Artist," *Partisan Review*, 49, ii:253-61, 1982

Action, 1974

　　McCarthy, G., " 'Acting It Out': Sam Shepard's *Action*," *Modern Drama*, 24, i:1-12, Mar. 1981

　　New West, 5:SC-24, 19 May 1980

　　Theatre Journal, 32, iv:532-34, Dec. 1980

Angel City, 1976

　　Rosen, C., "Sam Shepard's *Angel City*: A Movie for the Stage," *Modern Drama*, 22:39-46, 1979

　　Educational Theatre Journal, 29:112-13, 1977

　　Educational Theatre Journal, 29:415-16, 1977

Buried Child, 1978

　　Paul, J. S., "The Power of Proximity: *Nevis Mountain Dew* and *Buried Child* in the Second City," *Cresset*, 43, vi:12-14, Apr. 1980

　　Stasio, M., "Sam Shepard: An Outlaw Comes Home," *After Dark*, 12:58-61, Jan. 1980

　　After Dark, 11:27, Feb. 1979

　　After Dark, 12:26, Jan. 1980

America, 139:500, 30 Dec. 1978
Drama, 138:25, Oct. 1980
Drama, 138:56-57, Oct. 1980
Georgia Review, 33:570-72, Fall 1979
Hudson Review, 32:85-88, Spring 1979
Nation, 227:621-22, 2 Dec. 1978
New York, 11:117-18, 27 Nov. 1978
New Yorker, 54:151, 6 Nov. 1978
Newsweek, 92:106, 30 Oct. 1978
Plays and Players, 26:36-37, Feb. 1979
Texas Monthly, 8:132, Feb. 1980
Time, 112:76, 18 Dec. 1978

Curse of the Starving Class, 1977
    Stasio, M., "Sam Shepard: An Outlaw Comes Home," *After Dark*, 12:58-61,
        Jan. 1980
    America, 138:286, 8 Apr. 1978
    Drama, 125:60-61, Summer 1977
    Drama, 137:65-66, July 1980
    Educational Theatre Journal, 29:409-10, 1977
    Nation, 226:348-49, 25 Mar. 1978
    New Republic, 178:24-25, 8 Apr. 1978
    New Yorker, 54:57-58, 13 Mar. 1978
    Plays and Players, 24:24-25, June 1977
    Time, 111:84-85, 20 Mar. 1978

Inacoma, 1977
    Kleb, J., "Sam Shepard's *Inacoma* at the Magic Theatre," *Theater*, 9:59-64,
        Fall 1977

Jacaranda, 1979
    Georgia Review, 33:572-73, Fall 1979

Seduced, 1978
    After Dark, 11:84, Apr. 1979
    Drama, 137:64-65, July 1980
    Nation, 228:221, 24 Feb. 1979
    New Yorker, 54:46-47, 12 Feb. 1979
    Newsweek, 91:94, 8 May 1978
    Plays and Players, 26:36-37, Apr. 1979
    Plays and Players, 27:20, June 1980

Suicide in B Flat, 1976
    After Dark, 12:93, June 1979
    After Dark, 12:27, Nov. 1979

The Tooth of Crime, 1972
    Powe, B. W., "*The Tooth of Crime*: Sam Shepard's Way with Music," *Modern
        Drama*, 24, i:13-25, Mar. 1981

True West, 1980 (revised 1982)

Kleb, W., "Sam Shepard's *True West*," *Theater*, 12, i:65-71, Fall/Winter 1980
After Dark, 13:29, Mar. 1981
Commonweal, 110:49-50, 28 Jan. 1983
Drama, 144:29, Summer 1982
Nation, 232:123-24, 31 Jan. 1981
New Republic, 184:21-23, 31 Jan. 1981
New York, 14:45-46, 12 Jan. 1981
New Yorker, 56:81-82, 12 Jan. 1981
New Yorker, 58:160, 29 Nov. 1982
Newsweek, 97:63, 5 Jan. 1981
Time, 117:92, 5 Jan. 1981

La Turista, 1966
Ganz, A. F., "Afterword," pp. 215-19 in Ganz's *Realms of the Self*

SAM SHEPARD and PATTI SMITH

Cowboy Mouth, 1971
New West, 5:SC-24, 19 May 1980
Theatre Journal, 32, iv:532-34, Dec. 1980

SEE ALSO
JOSEPH CHAIKIN and SAM SHEPARD

ARCHIE SHEPP

Junebug Graduates Tonight, 1967
Greenfield, T. A., *Work and the Work Ethic in American Drama 1920-1970*,
pp. 144-45

JAMES SHERMAN

Magic Time, 1981
New Yorker, 57:99, 21 Dec. 1981

MARTIN SHERMAN

Bent, 1979
Cameron, B., "*Bent* on Broadway," *Theater*, 11, iii:113-18, 1980
After Dark, 12:16-17, Feb. 1980
America, 142:64, 26 Jan. 1980
Commentary, 69:74-75, Mar. 1980
Drama, 133:57, Summer 1979
Georgia Review, 34:497-508, Fall 1980
Maclean's, 94:63, 30 Mar. 1981
Nation, 229:700 + , 29 Dec. 1979
New Republic, 182:24, 5 Jan. 1980
New York, 12:110-11, 17 Dec. 1979
New Yorker, 55:100, 17 Dec. 1979
Newsweek, 94:115, 17 Dec. 1979

Plays and Players, 26:23-24, June 1979
Saturday Review, 6:56+, 13 Oct. 1979
Saturday Review, 7:30+, 2 Feb. 1980
Theatre Journal, 32, iii:398-99, Oct. 1980
Time, 114:84, 17 Dec. 1979

ROBERT E. SHERWOOD

General

Bigsby, C. W. E., *A Critical Introduction to Twentieth-Century American Drama*,
    Vol. I, pp. 138-46
Embler, W., "Comedy of Manners 1927-1939," pp. 59-70 in *Modern American*
    Criticism, ed. W. E. Taylor
Gould, J. "Robert Sherwood," pp. 99-117 in Gould's *Modern American Playwrights*
Meserve, W. J., *An Outline History of American Drama*, pp. 271-72, 275-76, 344

Abe Lincoln in Illinois, 1938
    Herron, I. H., *The Small Town in American Drama*, pp. 420-23
    Himelstein, M. Y., *Drama was a Weapon*, pp. 143-44
    Nannes, C. H., *Politics in the American Drama*, pp. 154-55

Idiot's Delight, 1936
    Himelstein, M. Y., *Drama Was a Weapon*, pp. 138-39, *passim*
    Nannes, C. H., *Politics in the American Drama*, pp. 153-54

The Petrified Forest, 1935
    Broussard, L., *American Drama*, pp. 106-10
    Smiley, S., *The Drama of Attack*, p. 49

The Road to Rome, 1928
    Nannes, C. H., *Politics in the American Drama*, pp. 151-53

The Rugged Path, 1945
    Greenfield, T. A., *Work and the Work Ethic in American Drama 1920-1970*,
        pp. 93-94

There Shall Be No Night, 1940
    Himelstein, M. Y., *Drama Was a Weapon*, pp. 147-49
    Nannes, C. H., *Politics in the American Drama*, pp. 156-57

BURT SHEVELOVE

Happy New Year (musical adaptation of P. Barry's *Holiday* by adding Cole Porter
songs), 1979
    After Dark, 13:55, July 1980
    New Yorker, 56:110, 5 May 1980
    Time, 115:83, 12 May 1980

Too Much Johnson (adaptation of play by W. Gillette), 1964
    Gottfried, M., *A Theater Divided*, pp. 226-28

TED SHINE

General

Dodson, O., "Who Has Seen the Wind? Part III," *Black American Literature Forum*, 14:54-59, 1980

Contributions (three plays: *Shoes*, *Plantation*, and *Contribution*), 1970
   Encore, 7:32, 17 Apr. 1978

R. A. SHIOMI

Yellow Fever, 1982
   New Yorker, 58:86, 17 Jan. 1983

MAX SHULMAN and ROBERT PAUL SMITH

The Tender Trap, 1954
   America, 92:257, 27 Nov. 1954
   Catholic World, 180:227-28, Dec. 1954
   Commonweal, 61:166, 12 Nov. 1954
   Drama-Logue, 13, xxxvii:6, 16-22 Sept. 1982
   Nation, 179:390, 30 Oct. 1954
   New Republic, 131:23, 1 Nov. 1954
   New Yorker, 30:83, 23 Oct. 1954
   Newsweek, 44:94, 25 Oct. 1954
   Saturday Review, 37:27, 30 Oct. 1954
   Theatre Arts, 38:25, 91, Dec. 1954
   Time, 64:41, 25 Oct. 1954

PAUL SHYRE

Paris Was Yesterday (adaptation of writings by J. Flanner), 1979
   After Dark, 12:24, Apr. 1980
   New Yorker, 55:47, 31 Dec. 1979

CLAIRE SIFTON and PAUL SIFTON

1931—, 1931
   Himelstein, M. Y., *Drama Was a Weapon*, pp. 157-59
   Smiley, S., *The Drama of Attack*, pp. 51, 161-63

SHEL SILVERSTEIN

The Lady or the Tiger, 1981
   After Dark, 14:20, Aug./Sept. 1981
   New York, 14:72, 9 Nov. 1981

WILLARD SIMMS

Einstein: Man Behind the Genius, 1982
   Drama-Logue, 13, xxxvi:9, 9-15 Sept. 1982

WILLIAM GILMORE SIMMS

Benedict Arnold: The Traitor, 1863
  Shillingsburg, M. J., "The West Point Treason in American Drama, 1798-1891,"
  Educational Theatre Journal, 30:73-89, 1978

MAYO SIMON

These Men, 1980
  After Dark, 13:66, May 1980
  Nation, 230:285, 8 Mar. 1980
  New York, 13:64-65, 25 Feb. 1980
  New Yorker, 56:100, 25 Feb. 1980

NEIL SIMON

General

McGovern, E. M., *Neil Simon*
"*Playboy* Interview: Neil Simon," *Playboy*, 26:57 + , Feb. 1979
Simon, E. V., "My Life with a Very Funny Father," *Seventeen*, 38:154-57, Nov.
  1979
Walden, D., "Neil Simon: Toward Act III," *MELUS*, 7, ii:77-86, 1980

Barefoot in the Park, 1963
  Greenfield, T. A., *Work and the Work Ethic in American Drama 1920-1970*,
    pp. 149-50

Chapter Two, 1977
  After Dark, 10:21-22, Feb. 1978
  After Dark, 12:18, Oct. 1979
  Hudson Review, 31:155-56, Spring 1978
  Saturday Review, 5:45, 4 Feb. 1978

Come Blow Your Horn, 1961
  Greenfield, T. A., *Work and the Work Ethic in American Drama 1920-1970*,
    pp. 147-49

Fools, 1981
  After Dark, 14:72, June 1981
  Los Angeles, 26:409 + , Dec. 1981
  New Leader, 64:20, 4 May 1981
  New York, 14:54, 20 Apr. 1981
  New Yorker, 57:133, 20 Apr. 1981
  Time, 117:63, 20 Apr. 1981

"*I Ought To Be in Pictures*," 1980
  After Dark, 12:26, Apr. 1980
  After Dark, 13:57, June 1980
  Georgia Review, 34:497-508, Fall 1980
  Los Angeles, 25:216 + , Mar. 1980

New West, 5:127, 11 Feb. 1980
New York, 13:86, 14 Apr. 1980
New Yorker, 56:105-06, 14 Apr. 1980
Newsweek, 95:106-07, 14 Apr. 1980
Plays and Players, 27:34, June 1980
Saturday Review, 7:56, May 1980
Time, 115:112, 14 Apr. 1980

Last of the Red Hot Lovers, 1969
Drama, 133:62-63, Summer 1979
Plays and Players, 26:23-24, May 1979

The Prisoner of Second Avenue, 1970
Greenfield, T. A., *Work and the Work Ethic in American Drama 1920-1970*,
pp. 151-53

JOHNNY SIMONS and DOUGLAS BALENTINE

Nova's Shady Grove, 1977
Texas Monthly, 6:97, Feb. 1978

The Return of Tarzan! (adapted from E. R. Burroughs), 1978
Texas Monthly, 6:216, 218, Nov. 1978

Van Gogh/Gauguin, 1978
Texas Monthly, 6:216, Nov. 1978

ISAAC BASHEVIS SINGER and EVE FRIEDMAN

Teibele and Her Demon (dramatization of one of Singer's short stories), 1978
After Dark, 12:17, Mar. 1980
America, 142:64, 26 Jan. 1980
Nation, 230:29, 5 Jan. 1980
New York, 13:70-71, 31 Dec. 1979
New Yorker, 55:47, 31 Dec. 1979
Time, 114:44, 31 Dec. 1979

DOUG SKINNER
SEE
BILL IRWIN, DOUG SKINNER, and MICHAEL O'CONNOR

GEORGE SKLAR

Life and Death of an American, 1939
Himelstein, M. Y., *Drama Was a Weapon*, pp. 109-10
Smiley, S. *The Drama of Attack*, pp. 132-33

SEE ALSO
ALBERT MALTZ and GEORGE SKLAR
AND
PAUL PETERS and GEORGE SKLAR

BERNARD SLADE

A Romantic Comedy, 1979
    After Dark, 12:20, Jan. 1980
    America, 141:391, 15 Dec. 1979
    New York, 12:90, 26 Nov. 1979
    New Yorker, 55:100, 19 Nov. 1979
    Newsweek, 94:75, 26 Nov. 1979
    Plays and Players, 27:36-38, Feb. 1980
    Time, 114:115, 19 Nov. 1979

Special Occasions, 1982
    New York, 15:54, 22 Feb. 1982
    New Yorker, 57:110, 15 Feb. 1982

Tribute, 1978
    After Dark, 11:85+, Oct. 1978
    Los Angeles, 24:170+, Aug. 1979
    Maclean's, 91:80, 15 May 1978
    New Republic, 179:29, 8 July 1978
    New West, 4:SC-27+, 4 July 1979
    New York, 11:74+, 19 June 1978
    New Yorker, 54:51, 26 June 1978
    Newsweek, 91:106, 12 June 1978
    Plays and Players, 25:38-39, Aug. 1978
    Time, 111:84, 12 June 1978

PATTY GIDEON SLOANE

Night on Bare Mountain, 1979
    Texas Monthly, 8:199, May 1980

ESTHER SMITH
SEE
LILLIAN SMITH and ESTHER SMITH

GLENN ALLEN SMITH

Years in the Making, 1979
    Theatre Journal, 32:255-56, 1980

JAMES EDGAR SMITH

The Scarlet Stigma (dramatization of *The Scarlet Letter* by N. Hawthorne), 1899
    Herron, I. H., *The Small Town in American Drama*, pp. 24, 25-27

LILLIAN SMITH and ESTHER SMITH

Strange Fruit (dramatization of L. Smith's novel), 1945
    Catholic World, 162:358, Jan. 1946
    Commonweal, 43:264, 21 Dec. 1945
    Harper's Bazaar, 80:106, Jan. 1946
    Life, 19:33-35, 24 Dec. 1945
    New Republic, 113:839, 17 Dec. 1945
    New Yorker, 21:54+, 8 Dec. 1945
    Newsweek, 26:92, 10 Dec. 1945
    Opportunity, 24:24-25, Jan. 1946
    Theatre Arts, 29:674, Dec. 1945
    Theatre Arts, 30:73-75, Feb. 1946
    Time, 46:77, 10 Dec. 1945
    Vogue, 106:145, 1 Dec. 1945

PATTI SMITH
SEE
SAM SHEPARD and PATTI SMITH

RICHARD PENN SMITH

General

Meserve, W. J., *An Outline History of American Drama*, pp. 48-49, 100

ROBERT PAUL SMITH
SEE
MAX SHULMAN and ROBERT PAUL SMITH

WINCHELL SMITH and FRANK BACON

Lightnin', 1918
    Herron, I. H., *The Small Town in American Drama*, pp. 205-06

W. D. SNODGRASS

The Fuehrer Bunker, 1981
    Nation, 232:802-03, 27 June 1981
    New Leader, 64:22, 29 June 1981

STEPHEN SONDHEIM

General

Adler, T. P., "The Musical Dramas of Stephen Sondheim: Some Critical Aproaches," *Journal of Popular Culture*, 12:513-25, Winter 1978

SEE ALSO
ARTHUR LAURENTS, LEONARD BERNSTEIN, and STEPHEN SONDHEIM
AND
ARTHUR LAURENTS, JULE STYNE, and STEPHEN SONDHEIM
AND
GEORGE FURTH and STEPHEN SONDHEIM
AND
HUGH WHEELER, LEONARD BERNSTEIN, RICHARD WILBUR,
JOHN LATOUCHE, and STEPHEN SONDHEIM

FRANK SOUTH

2 by South (two plays: *Precious Blood* and *Rattlesnake in a Cooler*), 1981
 Los Angeles, 26:352+, Aug. 1982
 New Leader, 64:20, 16 Nov. 1981
 New York, 14:71-72, 2 Nov. 1981
 New Yorker, 57:158, 160, 26 Oct. 1981
 Newsweek, 98:72, 26 Oct. 1981
 Theatre Journal, 34:252-53, 1982

BELLA SPEWACK and SAM SPEWACK

General

Gould, J., "Some Clever Collaborators," pp. 135-40 in Gould's *Modern American Playwrights*

Clear All Wires!, 1932
 Himelstein, M. Y., *Drama Was a Weapon*, pp. 186-87

BELLA SPEWACK, SAM SPEWACK, and COLE PORTER

Leave It to Me! (musical based on the Spewacks' *Clear all Wires!*), 1938
 Himelstein, M. Y., *Drama Was a Weapon*, pp. 207-08

BARRIE STAVIS and LEONA STAVIS

The Sun and I, 1937
 Himelstein, M. Y., *Drama Was a Weapon*, p. 101

WILLIS STEELL
SEE
CLYDE FITCH and WILLIS STEELL

GERTRUDE STEIN

General

Cohn, R., *Dialogue in American Drama*, pp. 201-07

GERTRUDE STEIN and VIRGIL THOMSON

Four Saints in Three Acts, 1934

Harris, D., "The Original *Four Saints in Three Acts*," *The Drama Review*,
26:101-30, Spring 1982

JOSEPH STEIN, JERRY BOCK, and SHELDON HARNICK

Fiddler on the Roof (musical version of stories by S. Aleichem), 1964
Gottfried, M., *A Theater Divided*, pp. 200-02
After Dark, 14:16, Oct. 1981
Dance Magazine, 54:36-38 +, Oct. 1980
Dance Magazine, 55:110, Sept. 1981

JOHN STEINBECK

General

John, S. B., "The Mirror of the Stage: Vichy France and Foreign Drama," pp. 200-
13 in *Literature and Society*, ed. C. A. Burns
Kiernan, T., *The Intricate Music*

Burning Bright (dramatization of his novel), 1950
Beatty, S., "Steinbeck's Play-Women: A Study of the Female Presence in *Of
Mice and Men, Burning Bright, The Moon is Down*, and *Viva Zapata!*," pp.
7-16 in *Steinbeck's Women*, ed. T. Hayashi

The Moon Is Down (dramatization of his novel), 1942
Beatty, S., "Steinbeck's Play-Women: A Study of the Female Presence in *Of
Mice and Men, Burning Bright, The Moon Is Down*, and *Viva Zapata!*," pp.
7-16 in *Steinbeck's Women*, ed. T. Hayashi
Greenfield, T. A., *Work and the Work Ethic in American Drama 1920-1970*,
pp. 88-90

Of Mice and Men (dramatization of his novel), 1937
Beatty, S., "Steinbeck's Play-Women: A Study of the Female Presence in *Of
Mice and Men, Burning Bright, The Moon Is Down*, and *Viva Zapata!*," pp.
7-16 in *Steinbeck's Women*, ed. T. Hayashi
Educational Theatre Journal, 30:123, 1978
Saturday Review, 6:57, 20 Jan. 1979

GEORGE ALEXANDER STEVENS

Lecture on Heads, 1764
Kahan, G., "The American Career of George Alexander Stevens' *Lecture on
Heads*," *Theatre Survey*, 18, ii:60-71, 1977

WALLACE STEVENS

General

Cohn, R., *Dialogue in American Drama*, pp. 227-28

Three Travelers Watch at Sunrise, 1916
Meserve, W. J., *An Outline History of American Drama*, p. 249

MICHAEL STEWART, MARK BRAMBLE, and JERRY HERMAN

The Grand Tour (musical version of S. N. Behrman's play *Jacobowsky and the Colonel*, based on a play by F. Werfel), 1979
    Nation, 228:156, 10 Feb. 1979
    New Leader, 62:21-22, 29 Jan. 1979
    New York, 12:119, 29 Jan. 1979
    New Yorker, 54:88, 22 Jan. 1979
    Plays and Players, 26:32, Mar. 1979
    Time, 113:84, 22 Jan. 1979

MICHAEL STEWART, MARK BRAMBLE, DOUG KATSAROS, and RICHARD ENGQUIST

Elizabeth and Essex (musical version of M. Anderson's play *Elizabeth the Queen*), 1978
    After Dark, 13:66, May 1980
    New York,13:67, 24 Mar. 1980
    New Yorker, 56:94, 10 Mar. 1980
    Plays and Players, 27:14-15, May 1980

MICHAEL STEWART and CY COLEMAN

I Love My Wife (musical based on a play by L. Rego), 1977
    After Dark, 11:83-84, Jan. 1979
    After Dark, 13:67, May 1980
    Drama, 127:56, Winter 1977/1978
    Hudson Review, 31:148, Spring 1978
    Los Angeles, 25:278+, May 1980
    Plays and Players, 25:28-29, Spring 1978

MICHAEL STEWART and JERRY HERMAN

Hello, Dolly! (musical version of T. Wilder's play *The Matchmaker*), 1964
    Gottfried, M., *A Theater Divided*, pp. 199-200
    Herron, I. H., *The Small Town in American Drama*, p. 482
    Drama, 135:43-44, Jan. 1980
    New York, 11:89-90, 20 Mar. 1978
    Plays and Players, 27:25+, Nov. 1979

MILAN STITT

The Runner Stumbles, 1976
    Stitt, M., *The Runner Stumbles* (includes an "Afterword")
    Horizon, 22:30-35, Oct. 1979

JOHN AUGUSTUS STONE

Metamora; or, The Last of the Wampanoags, 1829
    Meserve, W. J., *An Outline History of American Drama*, pp. 78-79

ALLAN STRATTON

Nurse Jane Goes to Hawaii, 1980
    After Dark, 13:67, Feb. 1981

Rexy!, 1981
    Maclean's, 94:60, 16 Mar. 1981

JOYCE STROUD and CHARLES DEE MITCHELL

Dracula, Lord of the Undead (adaptation of B. Stoker's novel), 1978
    Texas Monthly, 6:211, Oct. 1978

JULE STYNE
SEE
ARTHUR LAURENTS, JULE STYNE, and STEPHEN SONDHEIM

KAREN SUNDE

The Running of the Deer, 1978
    After Dark, 11:116, May 1978

MICHAEL SUTTON and CYNTHIA MANDELBURG

The Looking-glass, 1982
    New York, 15:49-50, 28 June 1982

JEFFREY SWEET

Porch, 1978
    After Dark, 11:80, Feb. 1979
    After Dark, 13:63, Nov. 1980

Stops Along the Way, 1981
    After Dark, 13:80, May 1981
    New Yorker, 57:66, 16 Mar. 1981

JO SWERLING
SEE
ABE BURROWS, JO SWERLING, and FRANK LOESSER

ROBIN SWICORD

Last Days at the Dixie Girl Café, 1979
    After Dark, 12:64, Aug. 1979
    New York, 12:73, 4 June 1979
    New Yorker, 55:93, 28 May 1979
    Plays and Players, 26:40-41, Aug. 1979

TED TALLY

Coming Attractions, 1980
  After Dark, 13:68, Mar. 1981
  New York, 13:59-60, 15 Dec. 1980
  New Yorker, 56:80, 82, 15 Dec. 1980
  Saturday Review, 8:80-81, Mar. 1981
  Time, 116:86, 15 Dec. 1980

Hooters, 1978
  New York, 15:59-60, 8 Nov. 1982
  New Yorker, 58:135-36, 1 Nov. 1982

Terra Nova, 1977
  "Playwrights on Resident Theatres: Going the Distance with *Terra Nova*," *The-ater*, 10, iii:83-84, Summer 1979
  Drama, 133:15-16, Summer 1979
  Educational Theatre Journal, 30:419, 1978
  Los Angeles, 24:255, Mar. 1979
  New West, 4:SC-32, 26 Feb. 1979

IRVING TALMADGE

The Path of Flowers (adaptation of play by V. Katayev), 1936
  Himelstein, M. Y., *Drama Was a Weapon*, pp. 97-98

JOSEPH TANGI

Man in the Deadpan, 1979
  After Dark, 12:20, Feb. 1980

BOOTH TARKINGTON

General

Herron, I. H., *The Small Town in American Drama*, pp. 200-02, 238-39, 245-47

RONALD TAVEL

General

Marranca, B. G., "Ronald Tavel," pp. 193-207 in Marranca and G. Dasgupta's *American Playwrights*

The Ovens of Anita Orangejuice: A History of Modern Florida, 1977
  After Dark, 11:114, May 1978

The Understudy, 1981
  Theatre Journal, 34:258-59, 1982

RENÉE TAYLOR and JOSEPH BOLOGNA

It Had to Be You, 1981

After Dark, 14:64, July 1981
New York, 14:96-97, 25 May 1981
New Yorker, 57:143, 18 May 1981

SAMUEL TAYLOR

The Happy Time (dramatization of novel by R. Fontaine), 1950
Texas Monthly, 7:136, Feb. 1979

TOM TAYLOR

Woody Guthrie, 1975
Los Angeles, 26:242, Mar. 1981
Texas Monthly, 6:98, Feb. 1978

JOHN-MICHAEL TEBELAK and STEPHEN SCHWARTZ

Godspell (based on the Gospel of Matthew), 1971
Christian Century, 99:46, 20 Jan. 1982
Drama, 142:36, 1981
People, 14:101-02, 15 Dec. 1980

HOWARD TEICHMANN

Smart Aleck, 1979
New Yorker, 55:113-14, 3 Dec. 1979

MEGAN TERRY

General

Asahina, R., "The Basic Training of American Playwrights: Theater and the Vietnam War," *Theater,* 9,ii:30-37, 1978
Cohn, R., "Camp, Cruelty, Colloquialism," pp. 281-303 in *Comic Relief,* ed. S. B. Cohen
Jacquot, J., "The Open Theatre: *The Serpent:* Création par l'Open Theatre Ensemble en collaboration avec Jean-Claude van Itallie, sous la direction de Joseph Chaikin," pp. 271-308 in *Les Voies de la création théâtrale,* I, ed. Jacquot
Marranca, B. G., "Megan Terry," pp. 183-92 in Marranca and G. Dasgupta's *American Playwrights*
Terry, M., "Two Pages a Day," *The Drama Review,* 21, iv:59-64, 1977

Hothouse, 1974
After Dark, 12:20, Feb. 1980

Viet Rock, 1966
Conlin, K., "The Lady Doth Protest: Women Fuse Politics, Protest, and Playwriting," *Theatre Southwest,* 6, iii:13-17, Oct. 1980

STEVE TESICH

General

Kuller, D., "Playwright Steve Tesich," *Rocky Mountain Magazine,* 2:74+, Mar. 1980

Division Street, 1980
    After Dark, 13:63, Aug. 1980
    After Dark, 13:24, Dec. 1980
    Commonweal, 107:662-63, 21 Nov. 1980
    Georgia Review, 35:602-03, Fall 1981
    Horizon, 23:32, Dec. 1980
    Los Angeles, 25:246+, July 1980
    New York, 13:102+, 20 Oct. 1980
    New Yorker, 56:137, 20 Oct. 1980
    Theatre Journal, 33:116-17, 1981

Old Bones, 1980
    After Dark, 13:67, May 1980

Passing Game, 1977
    After Dark, 10:26, Feb. 1978
    Encore, 7:34, 16 Jan. 1978
    Nation, 225:668, 17 Dec. 1977

Touching Bottom (three plays: *The Road, A Life,* and *Baptismal*), 1978
    After Dark, 11:87, Mar. 1979

ROBERT THOM

Children of the Ladybug, 1957
    Poetry, 89:378-82, Mar. 1957
    Saturday Review, 40:46, 19 Jan. 1957

Compulsion (dramatization of novel by M. Levin), 1957
    America, 98:404, 4 Jan. 1958
    Catholic World, 186:307, Jan. 1958
    Commonweal, 67:514, 14 Feb. 1958
    Nation, 185:374-75, 16 Nov. 1957
    New Republic, 137:21-22, 25 Nov. 1957
    New Yorker, 33:83, 2 Nov. 1957
    Newsweek, 50:98, 4 Nov. 1957
    Saturday Review, 40:27, 9 Nov. 1957
    Theatre Arts, 42:18, Jan. 1958
    Time, 70:93, 4 Nov. 1957

AUGUSTUS THOMAS

General

Gottlieb, L. C., "The Antibusiness Theme in Late Nineteenth Century American Drama," *Quarterly Journal of Speech,* 64:415-26, 1978

Alabama, 1891
    Herron, I. H., *The Small Town in American Drama*, pp. 209-10

Arizona, 1899
    Herron, I. H., *The Small Town in American Drama*, pp. 140-43

Colorado, 1901
    Herron, I. H., *The Small Town in American Drama*, pp. 143-44

The Copperhead, 1918
    Herron, I. H., *The Small Town in American Drama*, pp. 147-49

In Mizzoura, 1893
    Herron, I. H., *The Small Town in American Drama*, pp. 144-47

Rio Grande, 1916
    Herron, I. H., *The Small Town in American Drama*, pp. 143-44

DENMAN THOMPSON

The Old Homestead, 1886
    Herron, I. H., *The Small Town in American Drama*, pp. 77-78, 178-79
    Meserve, W. J., *An Outline History of American Drama*, pp. 128-29

ERNEST THOMPSON

General

Nist, E., "Patience Is Golden," *Writer's Digest*, 62:20 + , July 1982

On Golden Pond, 1978
    After Dark, 11:97, Dec. 1978
    After Dark, 12:22-23, May 1979
    After Dark, 13:66, May 1980
    Commonweal, 106:403-04, 6 July 1979
    Encore, 7:28, 16 Oct. 1978
    Georgia Review, 33:574-75, Fall 1979
    Nation, 227:357-58, 7 Oct. 1978
    New York, 12:75, 19 Mar. 1979
    New Yorker, 54:67, 25 Sept. 1978
    New Yorker, 55:107-08, 12 Mar. 1979
    Newsweek, 93:103, 12 Mar. 1979
    Plays and Players, 26:35-36, June 1979
    Theatre Journal, 33:541, 1981
    Time, 113:83, 12 Mar. 1979

The West Side Waltz, 1981
    After Dark, 14:17-18, Mar. 1982
    Los Angeles, 26:240 + , Mar. 1981
    New Leader, 65:20, 11 Jan. 1982
    New York, 14:87, 30 Nov. 1981

New Yorker, 57:95, 30 Nov. 1981
Newsweek, 98:110, 30 Nov. 1981
Time, 118:90, 30 Nov. 1981

GARLAND LEE THOMPSON

Incarnations of Reverend Goode Blaque Dresse, 1978
Encore, 7:31, 22 May 1978

JUDITH THOMPSON

The Crackwalker, 1981
Maclean's, 95:63, 15 Feb. 1982

WILLIAM TAPPAN THOMPSON

General

Shippey, H. P., "William Tappan Thompson as Playwright," pp. 51-80 in *Gyascutus*, ed. J. L. W. West III

Major Jones' Courtship; or, Adventures of a Christmas Eve, by Major Jones, 1850
Herron, I. H., *The Small Town in American Drama*, pp. 73-75

VIRGIL THOMSON
SEE
GERTRUDE STEIN and VIRGIL THOMSON

JAMES THURBER
SEE
ELLIOTT NUGENT and JAMES THURBER

TED TILLER

Count Dracula (based on B. Stoker's novel), 1978
After Dark, 11:116, May 1978

TOM TOPOR

Nuts, 1980
After Dark, 13:55-56, July 1980
California, 6:138, Nov. 1981
Los Angeles, 26:304, Oct. 1981
New Yorker, 56:69, 12 May 1980

DAN TOTHEROH

General

Herron, I. H., *The Small Town in American Drama*, pp. 170-72

DAVID TRAINER

Chevalière, 1981
   Theatre Journal, 34:266-67, 1982

SOPHIE TREADWELL

Hope for a Harvest, 1941
   Greenfield, T. A., *Work and the Work Ethic in American Drama 1920-1970*,
   pp. 60-61
   Himelstein, M. Y., *Drama Was a Weapon*, pp. 151-52

Machinal, 1928
   Greenfield, T. A., *Work and the Work Ethic in American Drama 1920-1970*,
   pp. 58-59
   Parent, J., "Arthur Hopkins' Production of Sophie Treadwell's *Machinal*," *The
   Drama Review*, 26:87-100, Spring 1982

MICHEL TREMBLAY

General

Parker, B., "Is There a Canadian Drama?," pp. 152-87 in *The Canadian Imagination*,
   ed. D. Staines
Ripley, J., "From Alienation to Transcendence: The Quest for Selfhood in Michel
   Tremblay's Plays," *Canadian Literature*, 85:44-59, Summer 1980

Bonjour, Là, Bonjour, 1978
   After Dark, 12:63, Aug. 1979
   After Dark, 13:68, Jan. 1981
   New Yorker, 56:156, 158, 27 Oct. 1980
   Theatre Journal, 32, iii:392-93, Oct. 1980

Damnee Manon, Sacree Sandra, 1980
   After Dark, 12:25, Mar. 1980

Hosanna, 1974
   After Dark, 12:20, Mar. 1980

The Impromptu of Outremont, 1980
   After Dark, 13:63, Aug. 1980

JOSÉ TRIANA

General

Dauster, F. N., "The Game of Chance: The Theater of José Triana," pp. 167-89 in
   Dramatists in Revolt, ed. L. F. Lyday and G. W. Woodyard

The Night of the Assassins, 1965
   Murch, A. C., "Genêt—Triana—Kopit: Ritual as 'Danse macabre,'" *Modern
   Drama*, 15:369-82, 1973

ELIZABETH TROTTER

Alice Adams (dramatization of novel by B. Tarkington), 1921
Herron, I. H., *The Small Town in American Drama*, pp. 245-47

DENNIS TROUTE

War Stories, 1979
Texas Monthly, 7:204+, Oct. 1979

GEORGE TROW

Elizabeth Dead, 1980
After Dark, 13:66, Feb. 1981
Newsweek, 96:106-07, 15 Dec. 1980

The Tennis Game, 1978
After Dark, 11:85, Jan. 1979

NEIL TUCKER

Oil!, 1980
After Dark, 13:59, June 1980

MARTIN F. TUPPER

Washington, 1876
Shillingsburg, M. J., "The West Point Treason in American Drama, 1798-1891,"
Educational Theatre Journal, 30:73-89, 1978

JOHN D. TURNBULL

General

Meserve, W. J., *An Emerging Entertainment*, pp. 205-07

MARK TWAIN
SEE
BRET HARTE and MARK TWAIN

ROYALL TYLER

General

Carson, A. L. and H. L. Carson, *Royall Tyler*
Meserve, W. J., *An Emerging Entertainment*, pp. 95-102
Meserve, W. J., *An Outline History of American Drama*, pp. 20-23

The Contrast, 1787
Herron, I. H., *The Small Town in American Drama*, pp. 39-42
Siebert, Jr., D. T., "Royall Tyler's 'Bold Example': *The Contrast* and the English
Comedy of Manners," *Early American Literature*, 13:3-11, 1978

Winton, C., "The Theater and Drama," pp. 102-03 in *American Literature, 1764-1789*, ed. E. Emerson

Vaughn, J. A., *Early American Dramatists*, pp. 24-37

PETER UDELL
SEE
KETTI FRINGS, GARRY GELD, and PETER UDELL

YALE UDOFF

The Example, 1979
  After Dark, 12:20, Feb. 1980

LUIS VALDEZ

General

Bagdy, B., "El Teatro Campesino: Interviews with Luis Valdez," *The Drama Review*, 11:70-80, Summer 1967

Brown, E. G., "The Teatro Campesino's Vietnam Trilogy," *Minority Voices*, 4, i:29-38, Spring 1980

Bruce-Novoa, J., "El Teatro Campesino de Luis Valdez," *Texto Crítico*, 10:65-75, 1978

Cárdenas de Dwyer, C., "The Development of Chicano Drama and Luis Valdez' *Actos*," pp. 160-66 in *Modern Chicano Writers*, ed. J. Sommers and T. Ybarra-Frausto

Herms, D., "Luis Valdez, Chicano Dramatist: An Introduction and an Interview," pp. 257-78 in *Essays on Contemporary American Drama*, ed. H. Bock and A. Wertheim

Bernabé, 1970
  Bassnett-McGuire, S., "El Teatro Campesino: From Actos to Mitos," *Theatre Quarterly*, 9:18-21, Summer 1979
  Bravo-Elizondo, P., "Symbolic Motifs in Two Chicano Dramas," pp. 47-54 in *Identity and Awareness in the Minority Experience*, ed. G. E. Carter and B. L. Mouser

Zoot Suit, 1978
  Brokaw, J. W., "Mexican-American Drama," p. 253 in *Essays on Contemporary American Drama*, ed. H. Bock and A. Wertheim
  Cizmar, P., "Luis Valdez: Has He Bought into a Three-piece Zoot Suit," *Mother Jones*, 4:46+ , June 1979
  Davis, R. G. and B. Diamond, "*Zoot Suit* on the Road," *Theatre Quarterly*, 9:21-25, Summer 1979
  Grandjeat, Y.-C., "Le Théâtre chicano en marge de *Zoot Suit*: Dixiéme Festival Tenaz," *Revue Française d'Etudes Américaines*, 10:249-54, 1980
  Huerta, J. A., "Luis Valdez's *Zoot Suit*: A New Direction for Chicano Theater?," *Latin American Theatre Review*, 13, ii, supp.:69-76, 1980
  Orth, M., "*Zoot Suit*: Luis Valdez Breakes the Rules, Again," *Rolling Stone*, 26 Nov. 1981, pp. 25+
  Orth, M. and W. Murray, " 'Zoot Suit': The Triumph of El Pachuco," *New West*, 3:47, 11 Sept. 1978

"Racism on the Great White Way: The Casting of *Zoot Suit*," *Encore*, 8:25, 7 May 1979

Shibley, G. E., "Sleepy Lagoon: The True Story," *New West*, 4:88, 15 Jan. 1979

After Dark, 12:87, June 1979

America, 140:336, 21 Apr. 1979

Dance Magazine, 56:100 + , Jan. 1982

Drama, 133:13, Summer 1979

Encore, 8:30-35, 7 May 1979

Los Angeles, 23:323, Nov. 1978

Nation, 227:88 + , 22 July 1978

Nation, 228:358, 7 Apr. 1979

Nation, 228:444 + , 21 Apr. 1979

New Republic, 180:24, 21 Apr. 1979

New York, 12:93, 9 Apr. 1979

New Yorker, 55:94, 2 Apr. 1979

Newsweek, 92:85, 4 Sept. 1979

Newsweek, 93:85-86, 26 May 1979

Plays and Players, 26:16-17, Mar. 1979

Saturday Review, 6:59, 26 May 1979

Theater, 10:123-28, Spring 1979

Theatre Journal, 31:263-64, 1979

Time, 113:78, 9 Apr. 1979

RUSSELL VANDENBROUCKE and JAMES R. WINKER

The Canterbury Tales (adaptation from Chaucer), 1982

Drama-Logue, 13, xxxvii:4, 16-22 Sept. 1982

DAVID VANDO and MARK BARKAN

Bugles at Dawn (musical adaptation of S. Crane's novel *The Red Badge of Courage*), 1982

After Dark, 15:11-12, Dec. 1982/Jan. 1983

JOHN VAN DRUTEN

Bell, Book and Candle, 1950

Wertheim, A., "The McCarthy Era and the American Theatre," *Theatre Journal*, 34:211-22, 1982

I Remember Mama (dramatization of *Mama's Bank Account* by K. Forbes), 1944

New York, 12:60-61, 14 May 1979

JEAN-CLAUDE van ITALLIE

General

Cohn, R., "Camp, Cruelty, Colloquialism," pp. 281-303 in *Comic Relief*, ed. S. B. Cohen

Dasgupta, G., "Jean-Claude van Itallie," pp. 65-79 in Dasgupta and B. G. Marranca's *American Playwrights*

Bag Lady, 1979
    After Dark, 12:21, Mar. 1980
    Georgia Review, 34:497-508, Fall 1980

JEAN-CLAUDE van ITALLIE and JOSEPH CHAIKIN

The Serpent: A Ceremony (based on Genesis), 1968
    Jacquot, J., "The Open Theatre: *The Serpent*: Création par l'Open Theatre Ensemble en collaboration avec Jean-Claude van Itallie, sous la direction de Joseph Chaikin," pp. 271-308 in *Les Voies de la création théâtrale*, I, ed. Jacquot
    Wieselhuber, F., "Jean-Claude van Itallie: *The Serpent*," pp. 133-48 in *Das amerikanische Drama der Gegenwart*, ed. H. Grabes

MELVIN VAN PEEBLES

Waltz of the Stork, 1982
    Rein, R., "Broadway's Baadasssss: Melvin Van Peebles Won't Fold His Play and Just Go Away," *People*, 17:57-58 + , 15 Feb. 1982
    New York, 15:70-71, 18 Jan. 1982

RON VAWTER
SEE
SPALDING GRAY, ELIZABETH LeCOMPTE, LIBBY HOWES, JIM CLAYBURGH, and RON VAWTER

GORE VIDAL

General

Gould, J., "Edward Albee and the Current Scene," pp. 286-87 in Gould's *Modern American Playwrights*

The Best Man, 1960
    Vidal, G., "Political Melodramas," pp. 259-64 in Vidal's *Matters of Fact and of Fiction* (originally appeared in the 4 May 1973 *New Statesman*)

MOREY VINION

The Rugged Path, 1945
    Nannes, C. H., *Politics in the American Drama*, pp. 157-59

LULA VOLLMER

Sentinels, 1931
    Commonweal, 15:301, 13 Jan. 1932
    Outlook, 160:22, 6 Jan. 1932

The Shame Woman, 1923

Nation, 117:587-88, 21 Nov. 1923
Theatre Magazine, 38:68, Dec. 1923

Sun-Up, 1923
   Current Opinion, 75:701-06+, Dec. 1923
   Drama, 17:116, Jan. 1927
   Theatre Magazine, 38:16, July 1923
   Theatre Magazine, 38:26+, Oct. 1923

Troyka, 1930
   Life (New York), 95:18, 18 Apr. 1930
   Outlook, 154:631, 16 Apr. 1930
   Theatre Magazine, 51:70+, May 1930

KURT VONNEGUT, JR.

Happy Birthday, Wanda June (first produced in 1960 as *Penelope*), 1970
   Plays and Players, 25:32, Oct. 1977

KEVIN WADE

Key Exchange, 1981
   After Dark, 14:14, Oct. 1981
   America, 145:163, 26 Sept. 1981
   Hudson Review, 34:562-68, Winter 1981/1982
   Los Angeles, 26:410+, Dec. 1981
   New Republic, 185:27-28, 14 Oct. 1981
   New York, 14:47, 22 June 1981
   New Yorker, 57:87, 22 June 1981
   Saturday Review, 8:47, Sept. 1981
   Time, 118:72, 3 Aug. 1981

DEREK WALCOTT

General

Hamner, R. D., "Derek Walcott's Theater of Assimilation," *West Virginia University Philological Papers*, 25:86-93, 1979
Hamner, R. D., "Mythological Aspects of Derek Walcott's Drama," *Ariel*, 8, iii:35-58, 1977

The Dream on Monkey Mountain, 1970
   Brown, L. W., "The Revolutionary Dream of Walcott's Makak," pp. 58-62 in *Critics on Caribbean Literature*, ed. E. Baugh

Remembrance, 1978
   New Yorker, 55:105-06, 21 May 1979

Ti-Jean and His Brothers, 1958
   Ashaolu, A. O., "Allegory in *Ti-Jean and His Brothers*," *World Literature Written in English*, 16:203-11, 1977

GEORGE F. WALKER

General

O'Hara, J., "The Odd Man Out in Canadian Theatre," *Maclean's*, 95:16, 19-20, 8 Mar. 1982

Zastrozzi, 1979
America, 146:135, 20 Feb. 1982
New Republic, 186:26-27, 10 Feb. 1982
New York, 15:57-58, 1 Feb. 1982
New Yorker, 57:116-17, 1 Feb. 1982
Plays and Players, 343:36, Apr. 1982

JOSEPH A. WALKER

The River Niger, 1972
Fontenot, C. J., "Mythic Patterns in *River Niger* and *Ceremonies in Dark Old Men*," MELUS, 7, i:41-49, 1980

IRA WALLACH

Absence of a Cello, 1964
America, 111:497, 24 Oct. 1964
Commonweal, 81:100-01, 16 Oct. 1964
Saturday Review, 47:30, 24 Oct. 1964
Time, 84:82, 2 Oct. 1964

EUGENE WALTER

The Undertow, 1907
Nannes, C. H., *Politics in the American Drama*, pp. 51-55

JEFF WANSHEL

Holeville, 1980
After Dark, 12:21, Mar. 1980

A Metamorphosis in Miniature (dramatization of F. Kafka's story "The Metamorphosis"), 1982
Nation, 234:250-51, 27 Feb. 1982

DOUGLAS TURNER WARD

General

Dodson, O., "Who Has Seen the Wind? Part III," *Black American Literature Forum*, 14:54-59, 1980

Happy Ending, 1965
Greenfield, T. A., *Work and the Work Ethic in American Drama 1920-1970*, pp. 141-43

Redeemer, 1979
    Theatre Journal, 31:413-14, 1979

THEODORE WARD

Big White Fog, 1940
    Theatre Arts, 25:853-54, Dec. 1940

Our Lan', 1947
    Greenfield, T. A., *Work and the Work Ethic in American Drama 1920-1970*,
        pp. 133-34
    Catholic World, 166:172, Nov. 1947
    Commonweal, 46:622, 10 Oct. 1947
    Forum, 108:372, Dec. 1947
    Nation, 165:426, 18 Oct. 1947
    New Yorker, 23:49, 4 Oct. 1947
    Newsweek, 30:74, 6 Oct. 1947
    Saturday Review of Literature, 30:24, 18 Oct. 1947
    School and Society, 66:325-26, 25 Oct. 1947
    Theatre Arts, 31:57, June 1947
    Time, 50:67, 6 Oct. 1947

ANDY WARHOL

Andy Warhol's Last Love, 1978
    Carroll, N., "Organic Analysis," *The Drama Review*, 22, iii: 33-44, Sept. 1978
    Schechner, R., "Anthropological Analysis," *The Drama Review*, 22, iii:23-32,
        Sept. 1978
    Shank, A. E. and T. Shank, "Squat Theatre's *Andy Warhol's Last Love*," *The
        Drama Review*, 22, iii:11-22, Sept. 1978
    Squat Theatre, "Answers," *The Drama Review*, 22, iii:3-10, 1978

MERCY OTIS WARREN

General

Meserve, W. J., *An Emerging Entertainment*, pp. 65-75
Merserve, W. J., *An Outline History of American Drama*, pp. 14-17
Vaughn, J. A., *Early American Dramatists*, pp. 18-21
Wilson, J. H. and S. L. Bollinger, "Mercy Otis Warren: Playwright, Poet, and His-
    torian of the American Revolution (American, 1728-1814)," pp. 161-82 in *Fe-
    male Scholars*, ed. J. R. Brink
Winton, C., "The Theater and Drama," pp. 97-100 in *American Literature, 1764-
    1789*, ed. E. Emerson

ROBERT PENN WARREN and AARON FRANKEL

Willie Stark: His Rise and Fall (dramatization of Warren's novel *All the King's Men*),
    1958
    Herron, I. H., *The Small Town in American Drama*, pp. 405-06

SAMUEL J. WARSHAWSKY

A Woman of Destiny, 1936
  Nannes, C. H., *Politics in the American Drama*, p. 162

DALE WASSERMAN

One Flew Over the Cuckoo's Nest (dramatization of novel by K. Kesey), 1963
  Fifer, E., "From Tragicomedy to Melodrama: The Novel Onstage," *Lex et Scientia*, 13, i-ii:75-80, 1977
  Drama, 140:38, 1981
  Plays and Players, 27:29, June 1980

Play with Fire, 1978
  New West, 3:SC-39, 23 Oct. 1978

DALE WASSERMAN, MITCH LEIGH, and JOE DARION

Man of La Mancha (musical version of Cervantes' *Don Quixote*), 1965
  Harrison, J., "*Man of La Mancha*: Doddering Nausea or Craftsmanship?," *Journal of Popular Culture*, 12:540-44, Winter 1978
  Los Angeles, 23:246, Apr. 1978
  New West, 3:SC-29, 10 Apr. 1978

WENDY WASSERSTEIN

Isn't It Romantic, 1981
  New York, 14:36, 29 June 1981
  New Yorker, 57:87, 22 June 1981

Uncommon Women and Others, 1977
  After Dark, 10:25-26, Feb. 1978
  After Dark, 12:21, Mar. 1980

GUS WEILL

The November People, 1978
  New Yorker, 53:45, 23 Jan. 1978

KURT WEILL
SEE
MAXWELL ANDERSON and KURT WEILL
AND
PAUL GREEN and KURT WEILL
AND
MOSS HART, KURT WEILL, and IRA GERSHWIN

ARNOLD WEINSTEIN and WILLIAM BOLCOM

Dynamite Tonite, 1967
  Gottfried, M., *A Theater Divided*, p. 209

JACOB A. WEISER
SEE
JOR MARCY and JACOB A. WEISER

MICHAEL WELLER

At Home, 1981
  Drama, 140:40, 1981

Loose Ends, 1979
  Rudnick, P., "Recording Our Times," *Horizon*, 22:36-41, Dec. 1979
  Witham, B. B., "Images of America: Wilson, Weller and Horovitz," *Theatre Journal*, 34:223-32, 1982
  After Dark, 12:61, Aug. 1979
  Commentary, 68:61, Aug. 1979
  Drama, 143:40-41, Spring 1982
  Georgia Review, 33:575-76, Fall 1979
  Nation, 229:59-60, 14 July 1979
  New Leader, 62:24, 18 June 1979
  New Republic, 181: 24-25, 7 July 1979
  New York, 12:100+, 5 Mar. 1979
  New Yorker, 55:90, 92, 18 June 1979
  Newsweek, 94:81, 2 July 1979
  Plays and Players, 27:39-40, Oct. 1979
  Time, 113:65, 19 Feb. 1979

RICHARD WESLEY

General

Allen, B., "Richard Wesley: Igniting the Darkness," *Essence*, 9:30-32, Dec. 1978

The Mighty Gents (revised 1977, 1978; 1977 version known as *The Last Street Play*), 1974
  After Dark, 11:79, June 1978
  Encore, 7:29-30, 22 May 1978
  Nation, 226:549, 6 May 1978
  New York, 11:83+, 8 May 1978
  New Yorker, 54:93, 24 Apr. 1978
  Saturday Review, 5:24, 24 June 1978

JOHN WEXLEY

They Shall Not Die, 1934
  Herron, I. H., *The Small Town in American Drama*, pp. 214-16
  Himelstein, M. Y., *Drama Was a Weapon*, pp. 130-33
  Nannes, C. H., *Politics in the American Drama*, pp. 100-01
  Smiley, S., *The Drama of Attack*, pp. 147-53, *passim*

EDITH WHARTON
SEE
CLYDE FITCH and EDITH WHARTON

HUGH WHEELER, LEONARD BERNSTEIN, RICHARD WILBUR,
JOHN LATOUCHE, and STEPHEN SONDHEIM

Candide (revision of the 1956, 1968, 1971, and 1973 musical versions of Voltaire's
story), 1982
   High Fidelity, 33:MA22-MA24, Feb. 1983
   New Republic, 187:28-29, 13 Dec. 1982
   New York, 15:80, 25 Oct. 1982
   New York, 15:106, 15 Nov. 1982
   New Yorker, 58:152-53, 1 Nov. 1982
   Newsweek, 100:102, 8 Nov. 1982
   Opera, 32 festival issue: 38-39, Autumn 1981
   Opera, 33:1253-54, Dec. 1982
   Opera News, 47:37-38, 1 Jan. 1983

JOYCE A. WHITCOMB

Option, 1980
   New York, 13:72-73, 18 Aug. 1980

JOHN BLAKE WHITE

General

Meserve, W. J., *An Emerging Entertainment*, pp. 195-96, 201-03

WILLIAM M. WHITEHEAD

and if that Mockingbird don't sing. . ., 1982
   Texas Monthly, 10:194, June 1982

RON WHYTE

Funeral March for a One-Man Band, 1978
   After Dark, 11:80, July 1978

RICHARD WILBUR
SEE
HUGH WHEELER, LEONARD BERNSTEIN, RICHARD WILBUR,
JOHN LATOUCHE, and STEPHEN SONDHEIM

THORNTON WILDER

General

Bigsby, C. W. E., *A Critical Introduction to Twentieth-Century American Drama*,
   Vol. I, pp. 256-73

Broussard L., *American Drama*, pp. 92-103

Cohn, R., *Dialogue in American Drama*, pp. 211-25

Durzak, M., "Thornton Wilder, ein Lehrmeister des Dramatikers Max Frisch," pp. 157-75 in *Max Frisch*, ed. G. P. Knapp

Gardner, R. H., *The Splintered Stage*, pp. 104-06

Gontrum, P., "The Influence of Thornton Wilder on Max Frisch," *Proceedings of the Pacific Northwest Conference on Foreign Languages*, 29, i:14-17, 1978

Gould J., "Thornton Wilder," pp. 204-24 in Gould's *Modern American Playwrights*

Haas, R., "Zugänge zum englischen und amerikanischen Drama," pp. 190-226 in Haas's *Theorie und Praxis der Interpretation*

Herron, I. H., "Our Vanishing Towns: Grover's Corners, New Hampshire, and Towns Beyond," pp. 410-20 in Herron's *The Small Town in American Drama*

Meserve, W. J., *An Outline History of American Drama*, pp. 306-10, 345

Oppel, H., "Thorton Wilder in Deutschland: Wirkung und Wertung seines Werkes im deutschen Sprachraum," *Akademie der Wissenschaften und der Literatur, abhandlungen der Klasse Literatur*, 3:3-31, 1976-1977

Scanlan, T., *Family, Drama, and American Dreams*, pp. 201-13

Selig, K. L., "Thornton Wilder and the Spanish *Comedia*," *Revista Hispanica Moderna*, 38:139, 1974-1975

Stürzl, E., "Weltbild und Lebensphilosophie Thornton Wilders," *Das amerikanische Drama von den Anfängen bis zur Gegenwart*, 5:195-208, 1972

White, K. S., "Scientists' Dilemmas: Prophetic Metaphors in Twentieth Century Drama," pp. 533-36 in *Proceedings of the 7th Congress of the International Comparative Literature Association, I*, ed. M. V. Dimić and J. Ferraté

Wilder, A. N., *Thornton Wilder and His Public*

Wilder, T., "Some Thoughts on Playwriting," pp. 115-26 in Wilder's *American Characteristics, and Other Essays*, ed. D. Gallup (this essay first appeared in *The Intent of the Artist*, ed. A. Centeno, 1940)

Wilder, T., "Forward to *The Angel That Troubled the Waters and Other Plays*," pp. 95-99 in Wilder's *American Characteristics, and Other Essays*

The Long Christmas Dinner, 1966

    Vučhović, T., "Vajlderove 'vežbe prstiju': Dugi božićni ručak," *Scena*, 15, i:83-100, 1979

The Matchmaker (revision of his *The Merchant of Yonkers*), 1954

    Wilder, T., "Preface to Three Plays: *Our Town, The Skin of Our Teeth, The Matchmaker*," pp. 104-11 in Wilder's *American Charactertistics, and Other Essays*

    Drama, 130:63-65, Autumn 1978

    Drama, 131:60-61, Winter 1979

    Educational Theatre Journal, 29:557-59, 1977

    Plays and Players, 25:33, Sept. 1978

Our Town, 1939

    Sell, R., "Hawthorne and Wilder: From 'Main-Street' to Our Town," *Literatur in Wissenschaft und Unterricht*, 11:149-60, 1978

    Vos, N., *The Great Pendulum of Becoming*, pp. 64-66

    Wilder, T., "A Preface for *Our Town*," pp. 100-03 in Wilder's *American Characteristics, and Other Essays*

    Wilder, T., "Preface to Three Plays: *Our Town, The Skin of Our Teeth, The*

Matchmaker," pp. 104-11 in Wilder's *American Characteristics, and Other Essays*
After Dark, 14:16, Nov. 1981
Time, 118:74-75, 27 July 1981

The Skin of Our Teeth, 1942
    Durzak, M., "Max Frisch und Thornton Wilder: Der vierte Akt von *The Skin of Our Teeth,"* pp. 97-120 in *Frisch*, ed. M. Jurgensen
    Helmetag, C. H., "Mother Courage and Her American Cousins in *The Skin of Our Teeth,"* *Modern Language Studies*, 8, iii:65-69, 1978
    Schik, B., "Thornton Wilder und das 'totale Theater': *The Skin of Our Teeth,"* pp. 263-77 in *Theater und Drama in Amerika*, ed. E. Lohner and R. Haas
    Wilder, T., "Preface to Three Plays: *Our Town, The Skin of Our Teeth, The Matchmaker,"* pp. 104-11 in Wilder's *American Characteristics, and Other Essays*

G. P. WILKINS

Young New York, 1856
    Meserve, W. J.,, *An Outline History of American Drama*, pp. 88-89

JASTON WILLIAMS and JOE SEARS

Greater Tuna, 1982
    After Dark, 15:12, Dec. 1982/Jan. 1983
    New Yorker, 58:136, 1 Nov. 1982
    Texas Monthly, 10:150+, July 1982

JESSE LYNCH WILLIAMS

The Stolen Story (dramatization of his short story), 1906
    Nannes, C. H., *Politics in the American Drama*, pp. 57-58

Why Marry?, 1918
    Stephens, J. L., "*Why Marry?*: The 'New Woman' of 1918," *Theatre Journal*, 34:183-96, 1982

PAULETTE WILLIAMS
SEE
NTOZAKE SHANGE

SAMM-ART WILLIAMS

Home, 1980
    After Dark, 13:62, May 1980
    Encore, 9:36-37, Apr. 1980
    Encore, 9:43, Sept. 1980
    Essence, 10:22, Apr. 1980
    Essence, 11:17+, Aug. 1980
    New York, 13:60-61, 19 May 1980

New Yorker, 56:105, 19 May 1980
Saturday Review, 7:67-68, July 1980
Time, 115:52, 19 May 1980

The Sixteenth Round, 1980
New Yorker, 56:166, 3 Nov. 1980

TENNESSEE WILLIAMS

General

Adler, T.P., "Images of Entrapment in Tennessee Williams's Later Plays," *Notes on Modern American Literature*, 5, ii:Item 11, Spring 1981
Adler, T. P., J. H. Clark, and L. Taylor, "Tennessee Williams in the Seventies: A Checklist," *Tennessee Williams Newsletter*, 2, i:24-29, 1980
Asselineau, R., "Tennessee Williams ou la nostalgie de la pureté," *Das amerikanische Drama von den Anfängen bis zur Gegenwart*, 5:276-92, 1972
"The Big Daddy of Playwrights," *After Dark*, 14:52-53, Oct. 1981
Bennett, B. H., "Williams and European Drama: Infernalists and Forgers of Modern Myths," pp. 429-59 in *Tennessee Williams*, ed. J. L. Tharpe
Berkowitz, G. M., "Williams' 'Other Places'—A Theatrical Metaphor in the Plays," pp. 712-19 in *Tennessee Williams*, ed. J. L. Tharpe
Bock, H., "Tennessee Williams, Southern Playwright," pp. 5-18 in *Essays on Contemporary American Drama*, ed. Bock and A. Wertheim
Brooks, C. B., "Williams' Comedy," pp. 720-35 in *Tennessee Williams*, ed. J. L. Tharpe
Brown, C., "Interview with Tennessee Williams," *Partisan Review*, 45:276-305, 1978
Buchloh, P. G., "Gesellschaft, Individuum und Gemeinschaft bei Tennessee Williams," *Das amerikanische Drama von den Anfängen bis zur Gegenwart*, 5:307-40, 1972
Buchloh, P. G., "Tennessee Williams: Assoziationschiffren. Zeichen der Verweisung und Akzentuierung: Versuch einer Systematisierung," pp. 405-39 in *Studien zur englischen und amerikanischen Sprache und Literatur*, ed. Buchloh, I. Leimberg, and H. Rauter
Bukoski, A., "The Lady and Her Business of Love in Selected Southern Fictions," *Studies in the Humanities*, 5, i:14-18, 1976
Capellán, A., "Tennessee Williams, tridimensional: Dramaturgo, poeta, memorialista," *Arbor*, 401:91-98, 1979
Carpenter, C. A., "Studies of Tennessee Williams' Drama: A Selective International Bibliography: 1966-1978," *Tennessee Williams Newsletter*, 2, i:11-23, 1980
Casper, L., "Triangles of Transactions in Tennessee Williams," pp. 736-52 in *Tennessee Williams*, ed. J. L. Tharpe
Chesler, S. A., "Tennessee Williams: Reassessment and Assessment," pp. 848-80 in *Tennessee Williams*, ed. J. L. Tharpe
Choukri, M., *Tennessee Williams in Tangier*
Cluck, N. A., "Showing or Telling: Narrators in the Drama of Tennessee Williams," *American Literature*, 51:84-93, 1979
Cohn, R., *Dialogue in American Drama*, pp. 97-129
Dean, D., "Williams Revised and Revived," *Mandate*, 2:43, 54, 57, Feb. 1977

Debusscher, G., "Tennessee Williams as Hagiographer: An Aspect of Obliquity in Drama," *Revue des langues vivantes*, 40:449-56, 1974

Dervin, D. A., "The Spook in the Rainforest: The Incestuous Structure of Tennessee Williams's Plays," *Psychocultural Review*, 3:153-83, 1979

Free, W. J., "Williams in the Seventies: Directions and Discontents," pp. 815-28 in *Tennessee Williams*, ed. J. L. Tharpe

Ganz, A. F., "Tennessee Williams: A Desperate Morality," pp. 107-22 in Ganz's *Realms of the Self*

Gardner, R. H., "Streetcar to the Cemetery," pp. 111-21 in Gardner's *The Splintered Stage*

Gerigk, H.-J., "Tennessee Williams und Anton Cechov," *Zeitschrift für Slavische Philologie*, 39:157-65, 1976

Gottfried, M., *A Theater Divided*, pp. 248-57

Gould, J., "Tennessee Williams," pp. 225-46 in Gould's *Modern American Playwrights*

Green, R. B., "The Italian Immigrant Woman in American Literature," pp. 341-49 in *The Italian Immigrant Woman in North America*, ed. B. B. Carole, R. F. Harney, and L. F. Tomasi

Groene, H., "Tennessee Williams im zwiespalt der meinungen: ein forschungsbericht über die english- und deutschsprachige literatur zu Williams dramatischem werk," *Literatur in Wissenschaft und Unterricht*, 5:66-87, 1972

Guintus, J. A., "Chekhov and Williams in Perspective," *English Language Notes*, 18, iii:201-05, 1980-1981

Gunn, D. W., comp., *Tennessee Williams*

Gunn, D. W., "The Various Texts of Tennessee Williams's Plays," *Educational Theatre Journal*, 30:368-75, 1978

Hays, P. L., "Arthur Miller and Tennessee Williams," *Essays in Literature*, 4:239-49, 1977

Herron, I. H., "More Southern Exposures: 'Not About Nightingales,'" pp. 344-77 in Herron's *The Small Town in American Drama*

Hirsch, F., *A Portrait of the Artist*

Holditch, W. K., "Surviving with Grace: Tennessee Williams Today," *Southern Review*, 15:753-62, 1979

Jackson, E. M., "Music and Dance as Elements of Form in the Drama of Tennessee Williams," *Das amerikanische Drama von den Anfängen bis zur Gegenwart*, 5:265-75, 1972

Jackson, E. M., "Tennessee Williams: Poetic Consciousness in Crisis," pp. 53-72, in *Tennessee Williams*, ed. J. L. Tharpe

Jackson, J. and K. Connell, "Gigolos: The Last of the Courtly Lovers," *Journal of Popular Culture*, 15, ii:130-41, Fall 1981

Jones, R. E., "Sexual Roles in the Works of Tennessee Williams," pp. 545-57 in *Tennessee Williams*, ed. J. L. Tharpe

Kahn, S., "Through a Glass Darkly: The World of Tennessee Williams," pp. 71-89 in *Modern American Drama*, ed. W. E. Taylor

Kalson, A. E., "Tennessee Williams at the Delta Brilliant," pp. 774-94 in *Tennessee Williams*, ed. J. L. Tharpe

Kauffmann, S., "About Williams: Gloom and Hope," pp. 165-68 in Kauffmann's *Persons of the Drama*

"Keep Your Eye on: Tennessee Williams," *Harper's Bazaar*, 114:262-63, Nov. 1981

Kriebel, C., "An Afternoon in Gray with Tennessee Williams," *After Dark*, 12:38-40+, Apr. 1980

Kunkel, F. L., "Tennessee Williams: God, Sex, and Death," pp. 99-107 in Kunkel's *Passion and the Passion*

"Kuo toliau nuo kranto," *Literatūra ir Menas*, 33:5, 1979 (interview)

Larsen, J. B., "Tennessee Williams: Optimistic Symbolist," pp. 413-28 in *Tennessee Williams*, ed. J. L. Tharpe

Lassell, M., "Williams on Williams," *Yale/Theatre*, 8:78-82, Fall 1976

Leavitt, R. F., ed., *The World of Tennessee Williams*

Leem, H., "A Study on Tennessee Williams' Fugitive Kind," *Yonsei Review*, 5:167-78, 1978 (in Korean)

Londre, F. H., *Tennessee Williams*

McKenna, J. J., "Interviews with Williams," *Tennessee Williams Newsletter*, 2, ii:26-28, 1980

MacNicholas, J., "Williams' Power of the Keys," pp. 581-605 in *Tennessee Williams*, ed. J. L. Tharpe

Machts, W., "Das Menschenbild in den Dramen Tennessee Williams?," *Das amerikanische Drama von den Anfängen bis zur Gegenwart*, 5:293-306, 1972

Meserve, W. J., *An Outline History of American Drama*, pp. 335-38

Niesen, G., "The Artist Against the Reality in the Plays of Tennessee Williams," pp. 463-93 in *Tennessee Williams*, ed. J. L. Tharpe

Pease, D. E., "Reflections on Moon Lake: The Presences of the Playwright," pp. 829-47 in *Tennessee Williams*, ed. J. L. Tharpe

Prenshaw, P. W., "The Paradoxical Southern World of Tennessee Williams," pp. 5-29 in *Tennessee Williams*, ed. J. L. Tharpe

Presley, D. E., "Little Acts of Grace," pp. 571-80 in *Tennessee Williams*, ed. J. L. Tharpe

Rader, D., "The Art of Theater: Tennessee Williams," *Paris Review*, 23:145-85, Fall 1981 (interview)

Rader, D., "Tennessee Williams: A Friendship," *Paris Review*, 23:186-96, Fall 1981

Richardson, T. J., "The City of Day and the City of Night: New Orleans and the Exotic Unreality of Tennessee Williams," pp. 631-46 in *Tennessee Williams*, ed. J. L. Tharpe

Sarotte, G. M. "Homosexuality and the Theater: Tennessee Williams: Theater as Psychotherapy," pp. 107-20 in Sarotte's *Like a Brother, Like a Lover*

Scanlan, T., "Family and Psyche in Tennessee Williams," pp. 156-79 in Scanlon's *Family, Drama, and American Dreams*

Scheick, W. J., "'An Intercourse Not Well Designed': Talk and Touch in the Plays of Tennessee Williams," pp. 763-73 in *Tennessee Williams*, ed. J. L. Tharpe

Seinfelt, F. W., "Thomas Mann and Some American and British Writers," pp. 260-98 in Seinfelt's *George Moore*

Spevack, M., "Tennessee Williams: The Ideas of the Theater," *Das amerikanische Drama von den Anfängen bis zur Gegenwart*, 5:249-64, 1972

Stanton, S. S., ed., *Tennessee Williams*

Stein, H., "A Day in the Life: Tennessee Williams," *Esquire*, 91:79-80, 5 June 1979 (interview)

Styan, J. L., "Realism in America: Williams and Miller," pp. 137-48 in Vol. I of Styan's *Modern Drama in Theory and Practice*

Tischler, N. M., "The South Stage Center: Hellman and Williams," pp. 323-33 in *The American South*, ed. L. D. Rubin, Jr.,

Tokushu Tennessee Williams

Vidal, G., "Some Memories of the Glorious Bird and an Earlier Self," pp. 129-47 in Vidal's *Matters of Fact and of Fiction*

And Now the Cats with Jeweled Claws (also known as *Now the Cats with Jewelled Claws*), 1982
    Time, 119:69, 28 June 1982

Camino Real, 1953
    Broussard, L., *American Drama*, pp. 110-16

Cat on a Hot Tin Roof, 1955
    Gardner, R. H., *The Splintered Stage*, pp. 89-93
    Kalson, A. E., "A Source for *Cat on a Hot Tin Roof*," *Tennessee Williams Newsletter*, 2, ii:21-22, 1980
    Vos, N., *The Great Pendulum of Becoming*, pp. 52-53, 67
    Los Angeles, 26:341 + , Nov. 1981

Clothes for a Summer Hotel, 1980
    After Dark, 12:12, Mar. 1980
    After Dark, 12:38-39, 76, Apr. 1980
    After Dark, 13:57, June 1980
    Georgia Review, 34:497-508, Fall 1980
    Horizon, 23:66-71, Apr. 1980
    Nation, 230:477, 19 Apr. 1980
    New York, 13:82+ , 7 Apr. 1980
    New Yorker, 56:116+ , 7 Apr. 1980
    Newsweek, 95:95, 7 Apr. 1980
    Plays and Players, 27:33-34, June 1980

Creve Coeur (see also *A Lovely Sunday for Creve Coeur*), 1978
    After Dark, 11:70-71, Aug. 1978
    Educational Theatre Journal, 30:552-53, 1978
    New York, 11:60-61, 26 June 1978
    Time, 111:84, 12 June 1978

The Eccentricities of a Nightingale (revision of his *Summer and Smoke*), 1964
    New West, 4:SC-39, 12 Mar. 1979

The Frosted Glass Coffin (see *Tennessee Laughs*)

The Glass Menagerie, 1944
    Adler, T. P., "The (Un)reliability of the Narrator in *The Glass Menagerie* and *Vieux carré*," *Tennessee Williams Newsletter*, 3, i:6-9, Spring 1981
    Greenfield, T. A., *Work and the Work Ethic in American Drama 1920-1970*, pp. 101-02, 120-25, *passim*
    Houghton, N., *The Exploding Stage*, pp. 55-57
    Napieralski, E. A., "Tennessee Williams' *The Glass Menagerie*: The Dramatic Metaphor," *Southern Quarterly*, 16:1-12, 1977
    Potter, A., "*The Glass Menagerie* by Tennessee Williams," *CRUX*, 14, ii:20-26, June 1980
    Sakellaridou-Hadzispyrou, E., "The Glass Spectrum in *The Glass Menagerie*," *Epistēmonikē Epetērida Philosophikēs Scholēs Aristoleleiou Panepistēmion Thessalonikēs*, 17:345-55, 1978
    Vos, N., *The Great Pendulum of Becoming*, pp. 30-33, 51-52, 67, 86

After Dark, 13:66, Feb. 1981
Mandate, 2:43 + , Feb. 1977
Plays and Players, 27:29, Jan. 1980

Hello from Bertha, 1961
    Los Angeles, 26:249, July 1981

A House Not Meant to Stand, 1981
    Theatre Journal, 34, iv:539-41, Dec. 1982
    Time, 119:69, 28 June 1982

Kingdom of Earth (*The Seven Descents of Myrtle*), 1968
    Quinby, L., "Tennessee Williams' Hermaphroditic Symbolism in *The Rose Tat-*
    too, Orpheus Descending, The Night of the Iguana, and *Kingdom of Earth,*"
    Tennessee Williams Newsletter, 1, ii:12-14, 1979
    Plays and Players, 25:39, Apr. 1978

The Lady of Larkspur Lotion, 1947
    Los Angeles, 26:249, July 1981

Life Boat Drill, 1979
    New Yorker, 55:72, 24 Dec. 1979

A Lovely Sunday for Creve Coeur (see also *Creve Coeur*), 1979
    After Dark, 11:84 + , Apr. 1979
    America, 140:135, 24 Feb. 1979
    Commonweal, 106:146-47, 16 Mar. 1979
    Nation, 228:156-57, 10 Feb. 1979
    New Yorker, 54:99-100, 5 Feb. 1979
    Newsweek, 93:68, 5 Feb. 1979
    Plays and Players, 26:37, Apr. 1979

Moony's Kid Don't Cry, 1940
    Greenfield, T. A., *Work and the Work Ethic in American Drama 1920-1970,*
    pp. 119-20

The Night of the Iguana, 1959 (revised 1961)
    Quinby, L., "Tennessee Williams' Hermaphroditic Symbolism in *The Rose Tat-*
    too, Orpheus Descending, The Night of the Iguana, and *Kingdom of Earth,*"
    Tennessee Williams Newsletter, 1, ii:12-14, 1979
    Texas Monthly, 6:124, Apr. 1978

The Notebook of Trigorin (free adaptation of Chekhov's *The Sea Gull*), 1982
    Los Angeles, 27:266 + , Sept. 1982

Now the Cats with Jewelled Claws (see *And Now the Cats with Jeweled Claws*)

Orpheus Descending (revision of his *Battle of Angels*), 1957
    Bünsch, I., "Tennessee Williams: *Orpheus Descending,*" pp. 278-94 in *Theater*
    und Drama in Amerika, ed. E. Lohner and R. Haas
    Chesler, S. A., "*Orpheus Descending,*" *Players*, 52:10-13, 1977

Ditsky, J. M., "Williams' Sweet Singer of Sex: *Orpheus Descending*," pp. 123-35 in Ditsky's *The Onstage Christ*

Normand, J., "Le Poète, image de l'étranger: L'Orphée de Tennessee Williams," *Revue Française d'Etudes Américaines*, 9:117-25, 1980; also in *French-American Review*, 4:72-79, 1980

Quinby, L., "Tennessee Williams' Hermaphroditic Symbolism in *The Rose Tattoo, Orpheus Descending, The Night of the Iguana*, and *Kingdom of Earth*," *Tennessee Williams Newsletter*, 1, ii:12-14, 1979

A Perfect Analysis Given by a Parrot (see *Tennessee Laughs*)

The Red Devil Battery Sign, 1974 (revised 1976)

Hopkins, T., "Rewrites of a Gothic Past," *Maclean's*, 93:66+, 3 Nov. 1980

Educational Theatre Journal, 30:116-17, 1978

Maclean's, 93:70, 3 Nov. 1980

The Rose Tattoo, 1951

Quinby, L., "Tennessee Williams' Hermaphroditic Symbolism in *The Rose Tattoo, Orpheus Descending, The Night of the Iguana*, and *Kingdom of Earth*," *Tennessee Williams Newsletter*, 1, ii:12-14, 1979

Encore, 8:40-41, 4 Sept. 1979

The Seven Descents of Myrtle (see *Kindgom of Earth*)

Some Problems for Moose Lodge (see *Tennessee Laughs* and *A House Not Meant to Stand*)

Something Cloudy, Something Clear, 1981

America, 145:202, 10 Oct. 1981

Time, 118:65, 21 Sept. 1981

A Streetcar Named Desire, 1947

Asselineau, R., "The Tragic Transcendentalism of Tennessee Williams," pp. 153-62 in Asselineau's *The Transcendentalist Constant in American Literature*

Dowling, E. and N. Pride, "Three Approaches to Directing *A Streetcar Named Desire*," *Tennessee Williams Newsletter*, 2, ii:16-20, 1980

Houghton, N., *The Exploding Stage*, pp. 56-57

Hulley, K., "The Fate of the Symbolic in *A Streetcar Named Desire*," pp. 89-99 in *Drama and Symbolism*, ed. J. Redmond

Nordon, P., "Le Jeu des stéréotypes dans *Un Tramway nommé Désir*," *Etudes Anglaises*, 32:154-61, 1979

Oppel, H., "'Every Man Is a King!' Zur Funktion der lokalhistorischen Elemente in *A Streetcar Named Desire*," pp. 507-22 in *Studien zur englischen und amerikanischen Sprache und Literatur*, ed. P. G. Buchloh, I. Leimberg, and H. Rauter

Quintus, J. A., "The Loss of Dear Things: Chekhov and Williams in Perspective," *English Language Notes*, 18, iii:201-06, Mar. 1981

Renaux, S., "Tennessee Williams: Attitudes toward Love and Decay in Blanche DuBois and Mrs. Stone," *Revista Letras*, 28:81-91, 1979

Rutledge, H. C., "Vergil's Dido in Modern Literature," *Classical and Modern Literature*, 1, iv:267-73, Summer 1981

Schvey, H. I., "Madonna at the Poker Night: Pictorial Elements in Tennessee Williams' *A Streetcar Named Desire*," pp. 71-77 in *From Cooper to Philip Roth*, ed. J. Bakker and D. R. M. Wilkinson

Shunami, G., "HaShimush be-Imajim ke-Babu'a shel ha-Drama ha-Psychologit," *Bama*, 81-82:75-86, 1979

Vos, N., *The Great Pendulum of Becoming*, pp. 29-30, 66-67

Zuber, O., "Problems of Propriety and Authenticity in Translating Modern Drama," pp. 92-103 in *The Languages of Theatre*, ed. Zuber

Zuber, O., "The Translation of Non-Verbal Signs in Drama," *Pacific Quarterly*, 5, i:61-74, Jan. 1980

Educational Theatre Journal, 29:251, 1977

Suddenly Last Summer, 1958

Debusscher, G., "Oedipus in New Orleans: Autobiography and Myth in *Suddenly Last Summer*," *Revue des Langues Vivantes*, 1978, U.S. Bicentennial Issue, pp. 53-63

Houston, N. B., "Meaning by Analogy in *Suddenly Last Summer, NMAL*, 4:Item 24, 1980

Reppert, C. F., "*Suddenly Last Summer*: A Re-Evaluation of Catherine Holly in Light of Melville's 'Chola Widow,'" *Tennessee Williams Newsletter*, 1, ii:8-11, 1979

Satterfield, J., "Williams's *Suddenly Last Summer*: The Eye of the Needle," *Markham Review*, 6:27-33, 1977

Taylor, W. E., "Tennessee Williams: Academia on Broadway," pp. 90-96 in *Essays in Modern American Literature*, ed. R. E. Langford

Sweet Bird of Youth, 1956

Gunn, D. W., "The Troubled Flight of Tennessee Williams's *Sweet Bird*: From Manuscript through Published Texts," *Modern Drama*, 24, i:26-35, Mar. 1981

After Dark, 12:21, Mar. 1980

Los Angeles, 25:238 + , Feb. 1980

Tennessee Laughs (three one-acts: *A Perfect Analysis Given by a Parrot, The Frosted Glass Coffin*, and, in its world premiere, *Some Problems for Moose Lodge*), 1980

After Dark, 13:66, Feb. 1981

This Property Is Condemned, 1946

Los Angeles, 26:249, July 1981

Tiger Tail (based upon his screenplay *Baby Doll* and upon two of his one-act plays, *27 Wagons Full of Cotton* and *The Long Stay Cut Short; or, The Unsatisfactory Supper*), 1978

After Dark, 10:38-39, Apr. 1978

Theatre Journal, 32:397-98, Oct. 1980

The Two-Character Play, 1967 (revised 1969)

Mandate, 2:43 + , Feb. 1977

The Unsatisfactory Supper (see also *Tiger Tail*), 1948

Los Angeles, 26:249, July 1981

Vieux Carré, 1978

Adler, T. P., "The (Un)reliability of the Narrator in *The Glass Menagerie* and *Vieux carré*," *Tennessee Williams Newsletter*, 3, i:6-9, Spring 1981

Drama, 129:68-69, Summer 1978
Drama, 130:45, Autumn 1978
Drama, 130:52-53, Autumn 1978
Plays and Players, 25:20-21, July 1978

Will Mr. Merriwether Return from Memphis?, 1980
Prosser, W., "Loneliness, Apparitions, and the Saving Grace of the Imagination," *Tennessee Williams Newsletter*, 2, ii:13-15, 1980
Time, 115:61, 4 Feb. 1980

WILLIAM CARLOS WILLIAMS

General

Fedo, D. A., *William Carlos Williams*

Many Loves, 1959
Cohn, R., *Dialogue in American Drama*, pp. 243-49
Fedo, D. A., "The William Carlos Williams-Julian Beck Correspondence and the Production of *Many Loves*," *William Carlos Williams Newsletter*, 3, ii:12-17, 1977

LAIRD WILLIAMSON

Warrior (adaptation of Shakespeare's *Macbeth*), 1978
Theatre Journal, 31:116-17, Mar. 1979

EDMUND WILSON

This Room and This Gin and These Sandwiches, 1937
New Yorker, 54:54, 26 June 1978
Theatre Arts Monthly, 21:825, Oct. 1937

LANFORD WILSON

General

Baker, R., "Bill Hurt and Lanford Wilson: Player and Playwright Meet at the Circle," *After Dark*, 11:38-41, June 1978
Dasgupta, G., "Lanford Wilson," pp. 27-39 in Dasgupta and B. G. Marranca's *American Playwrights*
Schvey, H. I., "Images of the Past in the Plays of Lanford Wilson," pp. 225-40 in *Essays on Contemporary American Drama*, ed. H. Bock and A. Wertheim
Shewey, D., "I Hear America Talking," *Rolling Stone*, 27 July 1982, pp. 18+
Wetzsteon, R., "The Most Populist Playwright," *New York*, 15:40-41+, 8 Nov. 1982

Angels Fall, 1982
America, 147:375, 11 Dec. 1982
Commonweal, 109:690-91, 17 Dec. 1982
New Republic, 188 Sp. Issue: 26-27 (3 Jan. 1983)
New York, 15:81, 1 Nov. 1982

New York, 16:58, 7 Feb. 1983
New Yorker, 58:134-35, 1 Nov. 1982
New Yorker, 58:101, 31 Jan. 1983
Newsweek, 100:95, 1 Nov. 1982
Time, 120:78, 1 Nov. 1982

Brontosaurus, 1977
New Yorker, 54:89-90, 20 Mar. 1978
Plays and Players, 347:33-34, Aug. 1982

The Fifth of July, 1978
Witham, B. B., "Images of America: Wilson, Weller and Horovitz," *Theatre Journal*, 34:223-32, 1982
After Dark, 11:38-41, June 1978
After Dark, 11:80+, July 1978
After Dark, 11:82+, July 1978
After Dark, 13:28, Jan. 1981
Hudson Review, 34:99-104, Spring 1981
Los Angeles, 24:308+, Oct. 1979
Nation, 226:579-80, 13 May 1978
Nation, 231:588-89, 29 Nov. 1980
New Republic, 184:26, 23 May 1981
New West, 4:SC-32+, 24 Sept. 1979
New York, 11:77, 15 May 1978
New York, 13:65, 17 Nov. 1980
New Yorker, 54:90, 8 May 1978
New Yorker, 56:172-73, 17 Nov. 1980
Newsweek, 96:129, 24 Nov. 1980
Texas Monthly, 8:139, Jan. 1980
Time, 116:109, 17 Nov. 1980

The Rimers of Eldritch, 1965
Winter H., "Lanford Wilson: *The Rimers of Eldritch*," pp. 120-32 in *Das amerikanische Drama der Gegenwart*, ed. H. Grabes

A Tale Told, 1981
After Dark, 14:20, Aug./Sept. 1981
Georgia Review, 35:604-05, Fall 1981
New York, 14:46-47, June 1981
New Yorker, 57:86-87, 22 June 1981
Newsweek, 97:64, 22 June 1981
Time, 117:48, 22 June 1981

Talley's Folly, 1979
Gussow, M., "Lanford Wilson on Broadway," *Horizon*, 23:30-36, May 1980
Paul, J. S., "Who Are You? Who Are We? Two Questions Raised in Lanford Wilson's *Talley's Folly*," *Cresset*, 43, viii:25-27, Sept. 1980
After Dark, 12:30+, July 1979
After Dark, 13:62, May 1980
Commonweal, 108:182, 28 Mar. 1980

Georgia Review, 34:497-508, Fall 1980
Los Angeles, 24:308 + , Oct. 1979
Nation, 228:609, 26 May 1979
Nation, 230:316, 15 Mar. 1980
New Republic, 180:24, 9 June 1979
New Republic, 182:28, 5 Apr. 1980
New West, 4:SC-32 + , 24 Sept. 1979
New York, 12:76, 21 May 1979
New York, 13:87, 10 Mar. 1980
New Yorker, 55:84, 86, 14 May 1979
New Yorker, 56:62, 3 Mar. 1980
Newsweek, 95:53, 3 Mar. 1980
Plays and Players, 26:37-38, July 1979
Plays and Players, 347:33-34, Aug. 1982
Time, 113:113, 14 May 1979

Thymus Vulgaris, 1982
    New York, 15:56, 25 Jan. 1982

ROBERT WILSON

General

Arata, L. O., "Dreamscapes and Other Reconstructions: The Theater of Robert Wilson," *Kansas Quarterly*, 12, iv:73-80, 1980
Bishop, T., "Théâtre aux Etats-Unis," *Tel Quel*, 71-73:200-07, 1977
Brustein, R., "The Crack in the Chimney: Reflections on Contemporary Playwriting," *Theater*, 9, ii:21-29, 1978
Sears, D., "The Shifting Images of Robert Wilson," *Mandate*, 2:18-20 + , Feb. 1977
Wilson, R., "Entretien (Inédit)," *Tel Quel*, 71-73:217-25, 1977

Edison, 1979
    Grimal, C., "A propos d'*Edison*: Interview," *Revue Française d'Etudes Américaines*, 10:227-30, 1980
    Theatre Journal, 32:265-66, 1980

Einstein on the Beach, 1976
    Flakes, S., "Robert Wilson's *Einstein on the Beach*," *The Drama Review*, 20:69-82, Dec. 1976
    After Dark, 9:83, Jan. 1977
    Mandate, 2:18-20, 42, Feb. 1977

I Was Sitting on My Patio This Guy Appeared I Thought I Was Hallucinating, 1977
    Wilson, R., ". . . I Thought I Was Hallucinating," *The Drama Review*, 21, iv:75-78, 1977

The Life and Times of Joseph Stalin, 1973
    Deák, F., "Robert Wilson: *The Life and Times of Joseph Stalin*," pp. 181-88 in *The New Theatre*, ed. M. Kirby

Medea (adaptation of Euripides's play), 1981

Bly, M., "Notes on Robert Wilson's *Medea*," *Theater*, 12:65-68, Summer/Fall 1981

ROBERT WILSON AND CHRISTOPHER KNOWLES

The $ Value of Man, 1975
Lubar, C., "Notes on 'The $ Value of Man,'" *Theater*, 9, ii:90 (foll. by text and orig. cast list, 91-109), 1978

JAMES R. WINKER
SEE
RUSSELL VANDENBROUCKE and JAMES R. WINKER

OWEN WISTER and KIRK LA SHELLE

The Virginian (dramatization of Wister's novel), 1904
Herron, I. H., *The Small Town in American Drama*, pp. 149-53

JUDD WOLDIN

Pettycoat Lane, 1979
New Jersey Monthly, 3:134, Oct. 1979

THOMAS WOLFE

General

Cohn, R., *Dialogue in American Drama*, pp. 176-79

Welcome to Our City (originally titled *Niggertown*), 1923
Herron, I. H., *The Small Town in American Drama*, pp. 217-19, 390-91
Rice, J. L., "Thomas Wolfe's *Welcome to Our City*," *Thomas Wolfe Review*, 5, ii:17-30, Fall 1981

VICTOR WOLFSON

Bitter Stream (dramatization of I. Silone's novel *Fontamara*), 1936
Himelstein, M. Y., *Drama Was a Weapon*, p. 69

Excursion, 1937
Himelstein, M. Y., *Drama Was a Weapon*, pp. 202-03

GRAHAME WOODS

Vicky, 1980
Theatre Journal, 32, iii:391-92, Oct. 1980

SAMUEL WOODWORTH

General

Meserve, W. J., *An Emerging Entertainment*, pp. 236-40

The Forest Rose; or, American Farmers, 1825
  Herron, I. H., *The Small Town in American Drama*, pp. 48-50, 89-90
  Meserve, W. J., *An Outline History of American Drama*, pp. 70-71

CARL WORKMAN

Diplomacy, 1982
  Los Angeles, 27:253-54, July 1982

JAMES WORKMAN

Liberty in Louisiana, 1804
  Meserve, W. J., *An Emerging Entertainment*, pp. 189-90
  Watson, C. S., "A Denunciation on the Stage of Spanish Rule: James Workman's
  Liberty in Louisiana (1804)," *Louisiana History*, 11:245-59, Summer 1970

HERMAN WOUK

The Traitor, 1949
  Nannes, C. H., *Politics in the American Drama*, pp. 185-86
  Theatre World, 45:30, May 1949

FRANCES WRIGHT

Altorf, 1819
  Meserve, W. J., *An Emerging Entertainment*, pp. 278-80

GARLAND WRIGHT

K: Impressions of the Trial (a "dramatic response" to Kafka's novel), 1977
  After Dark, 10:24-25, Feb. 1978

RICHARD WRIGHT
SEE
PAUL GREEN AND RICHARD WRIGHT

ROBERT WRIGHT
SEE
LUTHER DAVIS, ROBERT WRIGHT, GEORGE FORREST,
and ALEXANDER BORODIN
AND
CHARLES LEDERER, LUTHER DAVIS, ROBERT WRIGHT,
GEORGE FORREST, and ALEXANDER BORODIN

OLWEN WYMARK

Find Me, 1977
  Time, 113:73, 5 Mar. 1979

Loved, 1978

Newsweek, 93:115, 7 May 1979

SHERMAN YELLEN

Strangers, 1979
  After Dark, 12:23-24, May 1979
  Nation, 228:316, 24 Mar. 1979
  New Leader, 62:22, 26 Mar. 1979
  New Yorker, 55:56, 19 Mar. 1979

MAURY YESTON
SEE
ARTHUR KOPIT and MAURY YESTON

JACK ZEMAN

Past Tense, 1977
  Educational Theatre Journal, 30:418-19, 1978
  New Yorker, 56:109-10, 5 May 1980
  Time, 115:73, 5 May 1980

PAUL ZINDEL

General

Miner, M. D., "Grotesque Drama in the '70s," *Kansas Quarterly*, 12, iv:99-109, 1980

The Effect of Gamma Rays on Man-in-the-Moon Marigolds, 1965
  Miner, M. D., "Grotesque Drama in the '70s," *Kansas Quarterly*, 12, iv:99-109, 1980
  New Yorker, 54:95-96, 27 Mar. 1978

Ladies at the Alamo, 1975
  Texas Monthly, 6:136-37, June 1978

HOWARD ZINN

Emma, 1976
  Educational Theatre Journal, 29:417, 1977

LIST OF BOOKS INDEXED

Abel, Lionel. *Metatheatre: A New View of Dramatic Form*. New York: Hill & Wang, Inc., 1963.

Ahrends, Günter. *Traumwelt und Wirklichkeit im Spätwerk Eugene O'Neills*. Heidelberg: Winter, 1978.

American Literature in the 1950's (Annual Report 1976). Tokyo: Tokyo Chapter, American Literature Society of Japan, 1977.

Asselineau, Roger. *The Transcendentalist Constant in American Literature* (The Gotham Library of the New York Univ. Press). New York: The New York Univ. Press, 1980.

Auerbach, Doris. *Sam Shepard, Arthur Kopit, and the Off Broadway Theater*. Boston: Twayne, 1982.

Avery, Laurence G., ed. *Dramatist in America: Letters of Maxwell Anderson, 1912-1958*. Chapel Hill: Univ. of North Carolina Press, 1977.

Bablet, Denis and Jean Jacquot, eds. *Les Voies de la création théâtrale*, IV (Le Choeur des Muses: Recherches sur le Théâtre). Paris: CNRS, 1975.

Bach, Gerhard. *Susan Glaspell und die Provincetown Players: Die Anfänge des modernen amerikanischen Dramas und Theaters* (EurH XIV,70). Frankfort: Lang, 1979.

Bakker, J. and D. R. M. Wilkinson, eds. *From Cooper to Philip Roth: Essays on American Literature* (*Costerus* 26). Amsterdam: Rodopi, 1980.

Baldanza, Frank, ed. *Itinerary 3: Criticism*. Bowling Green, Ohio: Bowling Green Univ. Press, 1977.

Bargainnier, Earl F., ed. *10 Women of Mystery*. Bowling Green, Ohio: Bowling Green Univ. Popular Press, 1981.

Baugh, Edward, ed. *Critics on Caribbean Literature: Readings in Literary Criticism*. New York: St. Martin's Press, Inc., 1978.

Benston, Kimberly W. *Baraka: The Renegade and the Mask*. New Haven: Yale Univ. Press, 1976.

Béranger, Jean, Jean Cazemajou, and Jean-Claude Barat, eds. *Séminaires 1976* (Annales du Centre de Recherches sur l'Amérique Anglophone 2). Talence: Centre de Recherches sur l'Amérique Anglophone, Univ. de Bordeaux III, 1977.

Béranger, Jean and Jean Cazemajou, eds. *Séminaires 1978* (Annales du Centre de Recherches sur l'Amérique Anglophone 4). Talence: Centre de Recherches sur l'Amérique Anglophone, Univ. de Bordeaux III, 1979.

Berlin, Normand. *Eugene O'Neill*. New York: Grove Press, Inc., 1982.

Berlin, Normand. *The Secret Cause: A Discussion of Tragedy*. Amherst: Univ. of Massachusetts Press, 1981.

Bernstein, Samuel J. *The Strands Entwined: A New Direction in American Drama*. Boston: Northeastern Univ. Press, 1980.

Bigsby, C. W. E. *A Critical Introduction to Twentieth-Century American Drama, I, 1900-1940*. Cambridge: Cambridge Univ. Press, 1982.

Bills, Steven H. *Lillian Hellman: An Annotated Bibliography* (GRLH 141). New York: Garland, 1979.

Blackwell, Marilyn John, ed. *Structures of Influence: A Comparative Approach to August Strindberg* (UNCSGLL 98). Chapel Hill: Univ. of North Carolina Press, 1981.

Bock, Hedwig and Albert Wertheim, eds. *Essays on Contemporary American Drama.*
    München: Max Hueber Verlag, 1981.
Bogardus, Ralph F. and Fred Hobson, eds. *Literature at the Barricades: The American
    Writer in the 1930's.* University, Ala.: Univ. of Alabama Press, 1982.
Brenman-Gibson, Margaret. *Clifford Odets: American Playwright, The Years from
    1906 to 1940.* New York: Atheneum, 1981.
Brink, J. R., ed. *Female Scholars: A Tradition of Learned Women before 1800.*
    Montreal: Eden Press Women's Publications, 1980.
Broussard, Louis. *American Drama: Contemporary Allegory from Eugene O'Neill to
    Tennessee Williams.* Norman: Univ. of Oklahoma Press, 1962.
Brown, Janet. *Feminist Drama: Definition & Critical Analysis.* Metuchen, N. J.: The
    Scarecrow Press, Inc., 1979.
Brown, Lloyd W. *Amiri Baraka* (TUSAS 383). Boston: Twayne, 1980.
Bruccoli, Matthew J., C. E. Frazer Clark, Jr., Richard Layman, Margaret M. Dugan,
    Glenda G. Fedricci, and Cara L. White, eds. *Conversations with Writers, II*
    (Conversations 3). Detroit: Gale, 1977.
Bryer, Jackson R., ed. *"The Theatre We Worked For": The Letters of Eugene O'Neill
    to Kenneth Macgowan.* New Haven: Yale Univ. Press, 1982.
Buchloh, Paul Gerhard, Inge Leimberg, and Herbert Rauter, eds. *Studien zur en-
    glischen und amerikanischen Sprache und Literatur: Festschrift für Helmut Pa-
    pajewski* (KBAA 10). Neumünster: Wacholtz, 1974.
Bungaku to America: Ohashi Kenzaburo Kyoju Kanreki Kinen Ronbunshu, Vol. III.
    Tokyo: Nanundo, 1980.
Bungert, Hans, ed. *Die amerikanische Literatur der Gegenwart: Aspekte und Ten-
    denzen.* Stuttgart: Reclam, 1977.
Burns, C. A. *Literature and Society: Studies in Nineteenth and Twentieth Century
    French Literature Presented to R. J. North.* Birmingham: Goodman for Univ.
    of Birmingham, 1980.
Cantor, Harold. *Clifford Odets: Playwright-Poet.* Metuchen, N. J.: The Scarecrow
    Press, Inc., 1978.
Caroli, Betty Boyd, Robert F. Harney, and Lydio F. Tomasi, eds. *The Italian Im-
    migrant Woman in North America* (Proceedings of the 10th Annual Conference
    of the American Italian History Association Held in Toronto, Ont. (Canada),
    Oct. 28 and 29, 1977, in Conjunction with the Canadian Italian History Asso-
    ciation). Toronto: Multicultural History Society of Ontario, 1978.
Carpenter, Andrew, ed. *Place, Personality and the Irish Writer.* New York: Barnes
    & Noble, 1977.
Carpenter, Frederic I. *Eugene O'Neill,* rev. ed. (TUSAS 66). Boston: Twayne, 1979.
Carson, Ada Lou and Herbert L. Carson. *Royall Tyler* (TUSAS 344). Boston: Twayne,
    1979.
Carson, Neil. *Arthur Miller.* New York: Grove Press, Inc., 1982.
Carter, George E. and Bruce L. Mouser, eds. *Identity and Awareness in the Minority
    Experience: Past and Present* (Selected Proceedings of the 1st & 2nd Annual
    Conference on Minority Studies, March 1973 and April 1974, Vol. I,i). La Crosse:
    Institute for Minority Studies, Univ. of Wisconsin-La Crosse, 1975.
Cazemajou, Jean and Jean-Claude Barat, eds. *Naturalisme américain* (Annales du
    Centre de Recherches sur l'Amérique Anglophone 4:2). Bordeaux-Talence: Mai-
    son des Sciences de l'Homme d'Aquitaine, 1976.
Centeno, Augusto, ed. *The Intent of the Artist.* Princeton, N. J.: Princeton Univ.
    Press, 1940.

Chabrowe, Leonard. *Ritual and Pathos—The Theater of O'Neill*. Lewisburg, Penn.: Bucknell Univ. Press, 1976.

Chothia, Jean. *Forging a Language: A Study of the Plays of Eugene O'Neill*. Cambridge: Cambridge Univ. Press, 1979.

Choukri, Mohamed. *Tennessee Williams in Tangier*, tr. Paul Bowles. Santa Barbara: Cadmus, 1979.

Christ, Carol P. *Diving Deep and Surfacing: Women Writers on Spiritual Quest*. Boston: Beacon Press, 1980.

Cohen, Sarah Blacher, ed. *Comic Relief: Humor in Contemporary American Literature*. Urbana: Univ. of Illinois Press, 1978.

Cohn, Ruby. *Dialogue in American Drama*. Bloomington: Indiana Univ. Press, 1971.

Cronin, Harry. *Eugene O'Neill, Irish and American: A Study in Cultural Context*. New York: Arno, 1977.

Davy, Kate. *Richard Foreman and the Ontological-Hysteric Theatre*. Ann Arbor, Mich.: UMI Research Press, 1981.

Davy, Kate, ed. *Richard Foreman: Plays and Manifestos*. New York: New York Univ. Press, 1976.

De La Fuente, Patricia, Donald E. Fritz, Jan Seale, and Dorey Schmidt, eds. *Edward Albee: Planned Wilderness: Interview, Essays, and Bibliography* (Living Author Ser. 3). Edinburg, Tex.: School of Humanities, Pan American Univ., 1980.

Dimić, Milan V. and Juan Ferraté, eds. *Actes du VIIe congres de l'Association Internationale de Litterature Comparee/Proceedings of the 7th Congress of the International Comparative Literature Association, I: Litteratures americaines: Dependance, independance, interdependance/Literatures of America: Dependence, Independence, Interdependence* (Lib. of CRCL 2). Stuttgart: Bieber, 1979.

Ditsky, John Michael. *The Onstage Christ: Studies in the Persistence of a Theme* (Barnes & Noble Critical Studies). New York: Barnes & Noble, 1980.

Emerson, Everett, ed. *American Literature, 1764-1789: The Revolutionary Years*. Madison: Univ. of Wisconsin Press, 1977.

Estrin, Mark W. *Lillian Hellman, Plays, Films, Memoirs: A Reference Guide*. Boston: Hall, 1980.

Falk, Doris V. *Lillian Hellman*. New York: Ungar, 1978.

Fawkes, Richard. *Dion Boucicault: A Biography*. London: Quartet Books, 1979.

Fedo, David A. *William Carlos Williams: A Poet in the American Theatre*. Ann Arbor, Mich.: UMI Research Press, 1983.

Fein, Richard J. *Robert Lowell*, 2nd ed. (TUSAS 176). Boston: Twayne, 1979.

Ferres, John H. *Arthur Miller: A Reference Guide* (Ref. Pub. in Lit.). Boston: Hall, 1979.

Floyd, Virginia, ed. *Eugene O'Neill: A World View*. New York: Frederick Ungar Publishing Co., 1979.

Floyd, Virginia, ed. *Eugene O'Neill at Work: Newly Released Ideas for Plays*. New York: Frederick Ungar Publishing Co., 1981.

Fordin, Hugh. *Getting to Know Him: A Biography of Oscar Hammerstein II*. New York: Random House, 1977.

Freitag, Hans-Heinrich and Peter Hühn, eds. *Literarische Ansichten der Wirklichkeit: Studien zur Wirklichkeitskonstitution in englischsprachiger Literatur: To Honour Johannes Kleinstuck* (AAF 12). Frankfurt: Lang, 1980.

French, Warren G., ed. *The Twenties: Fiction, Poetry, Drama*. DeLand, Fla.: Everett/Edwards, Inc., 1975.

Ganz, Arthur F. *Realms of the Self: Variations on a Theme in Modern Drama* (The

Gotham Library of the New York Univ. Press). New York: New York Univ. Press, 1980.

Gardner, R. H. *The Splintered Stage: The Decline of American Theater*. New York: The Macmillan Company, 1965; London: Collier-Macmillan Limited, 1965.

Gerould, Daniel C., guest ed. *Melodrama* (New York Literary Forum 7). New York: New York Literary Forum, 1980.

Gilbert, Julie Goldsmith. *Ferber: A Biography*. Garden City, N. Y.: Doubleday, 1978.

Goldstein, Malcolm. *George S. Kaufman: His Life, His Theater*. New York: Oxford Univ. Press, 1979.

Gottfried, Martin. *A Theater Divided: The Postwar American Stage*. Boston: Little, Brown and Company, 1967.

Gottlieb, Lois C. *Rachel Crothers* (TUSAS 322). Boston: Twayne, 1979.

Gould, Jean. *Modern American Playwrights*. New York: Dodd, Mead & Company, 1966.

Grabes, Herbert, ed. *Das amerikanische Drama der Gegenwart*. Kronberg: Athenäum, 1976.

Green, Charles Lee. *Edward Albee: An Annotated Bibliography, 1968-1977* (Studies in Mod. Lit. 6). New York: AMS, 1980.

Greenfield, Thomas Allen. *Work and the Work Ethic in American Drama 1920-1970*. Columbia: Univ. of Missouri Press, 1982.

Gunn, Drewey Wayne. *Tennessee Williams: A Bibliography* (Scarecrow Author Bibliogs. 48). Metuchen, N. J.: Scarecrow, 1980.

Haas, Rudolf. *Theorie und Praxis der Interpretation: Modellanalysen englischer und amerikanischer Texte* (Grundlagen der Anglistik & Amerikanistik 5). Berlin: Schmidt, 1977.

Harshbarger, Karl. *The Burning Jungle: An Analysis of Arthur Miller's "Death of a Salesman."* Washington, D. C.: Univ. Press of America, 1978.

Hayashi, Tetsumaro, ed. *Steinbeck's Women: Essays in Criticism* (StMS 9). Muncie, Ind.: Steinbeck Society of America, English Department, Ball State Univ., 1979.

Heilman, Robert Bechtold. *Tragedy and Melodrama: Versions of Experience*. Seattle: Univ. of Washington Press, 1968.

Herron, Ima Honaker. *The Small Town in American Drama*. Dallas: Southern Methodist Univ. Press, 1969.

Hill, Errol, ed. *The Theater of Black Americans, II: The Presenters: Companies of Players; The Participators: Audiences and Critics*. Englewood Cliffs, N. J.: Prentice-Hall, 1980.

Himelstein, Morgan Y. *Drama Was a Weapon: The Left-Wing Theatre in New York, 1929-1941*. New Brunswick, N. J.: Rutgers Univ. Press, 1963.

Hirsch, Foster. *A Portrait of the Artist: The Plays of Tennessee Williams*. Port Washington, N. Y.: Kennikat, 1978.

Hirsch, Foster. *Who's Afraid of Edward Albee?* Berkeley: Creative Arts Books Co., 1978.

Houghton, Norris. *The Exploding Stage: An Introduction to Twentieth Century Drama*. New York: Weybright and Talley, 1971.

Howe, Irving. *Celebrations and Attacks: Thirty Years of Literary and Cultural Commentary*. New York: Horizon Press, 1979.

Huntsman, Jeffrey. "Introduction," *New Native American Drama: Three Plays*, Hanay Geiogamah. Norman: Univ. of Oklahoma Press, 1980.

Inge, M. Thomas, Jean Maurice Duke, and Jackson R. Bryer, eds. *Black American Writers: Bibliographical Essays*, Vol. II. New York: St. Martin's Press, Inc., 1978.

Lederer, Katherine. *Lillian Hellman* (TUSAS 338). Boston: Twayne, 1979.

Lee, Robert A., ed. *Black Fiction: New Studies in the Afro-American Novel since 1945*. New York: Barnes & Noble, 1980.

Lohner, Edgar and Rudolf Haas, eds. *Theater und Drama in Amerika: Aspekte und Interpretationen*. Berlin: Schmidt, 1978.

Londre, Felicia Hardison. *Tennessee Williams*. New York: Ungar, 1979.

Loney, Glenn, ed. *The House of Mirth: The Play of the Novel*. Madison, N. J.: Fairleigh Dickinson Univ. Press, 1981.

Lyday, Leon F. and George W. Woodyard, eds. *Dramatists in Revolt: The New Latin American Theater* (The Texas Pan American Series). Austin: The Univ. of Texas at Austin Press, 1976.

McClatchy, J. D., ed. *Anne Sexton: The Artist and Her Critics*. Bloomington: Indiana Univ. Press, 1978.

McClure, Arthur F. *William Inge: A Bibliography* (Garland Reference Library of the Humanities Series 235). New York: Garland Publishing, 1982.

McCune, Marjorie W., Tucker Orbison, and Philip M. Withim, eds. *The Binding of Proteus: Perspectives on Myth and the Literary Process*. Lewisburg, Pa.: Bucknell Univ. Press, 1980; London: Associated Univ. Press, 1980.

McDowell, Margaret. *Carson McCullers* (TUSAS 354). Boston: Twayne, 1980.

McGovern, Edythe M. *Neil Simon: A Critical Study*. New York: Ungar, 1979. (Rev. ed. of *Not-So-Simple Neil Simon*, Van Nuys, Cal.: Perivale, 1978.)

Manocchio, Tony and William Petitt. *Families under Stress: A Psychological Interpretation*. London and Boston: Routledge & Kegan Paul, 1975.

Marranca, Bonnie, ed. *American Dreams: The Imagination of Sam Shepard*. New York: Performing Arts Journal Publications, 1981.

Marranca, Bonnie G. and Gautam Dasgupta. *American Playwrights: A Critical Survey*, Vol. I. New York: Drama Book Specialists (Publishers), 1981.

Martin, Robert A. *Arthur Miller: New Perspectives* (TCV). Englewood Cliffs, N. J.: Prentice-Hall, 1982.

Martin, Robert A., ed. *The Theatre Essays of Arthur Miller*. New York: The Viking Press, 1978.

Martin, Robert A., ed. *The Writer's Craft: Hopwood Lectures, 1965-81*. Ann Arbor: Univ. of Michigan Press, 1982.

Martine, James J., ed. *Critical Essays on Arthur Miller* (Crit. Essays on Amer. Lit.). Boston: Hall, 1979.

Mendelsohn, Michael J. *Clifford Odets: Humane Dramatist*. DeLand, Fla.: Everett/ Edwards, Inc., 1969.

Mersand, Joseph. *The American Drama Since 1930: Essays on Playwrights and Plays*. Reissued Port Washington, N. Y.: Kennikat, 1968. (New York: The Modern Chapbooks, 1941 and 1949.)

Meserve, Walter J. *An Emerging Entertainment: The Drama of the American People to 1828*. Bloomington: Indiana Univ. Press, 1977.

Meserve, Walter J. *An Outline History of American Drama*. Totowa, N. J.: Littlefield, Adams & Co., 1965.

Meserve, Walter J., ed. *Studies in "Death of a Salesman."* Columbus, Ohio: Bobbs-Merrill, 1972.

Miller, R. Baxter, ed. *Black American Literature and Humanism*. Lexington: Univ. Press of Kentucky, 1981.

Moss, Leonard. *Arthur Miller*, rev. ed. (TUSAS 115). Boston: Twayne, 1980.

Nannes, Caspar H. *Politics in the American Drama*. Washington, D. C.: The Catholic Univ. of America Press, 1960.

Nicoll, Allardyce (with contributions by Arthur Wilmurt et al.). *World Drama: From Aeschylus to Anouilh*, rev. and enl. ed. New York: Barnes & Noble, 1976.

O'Daniel, Therman B., ed. *James Baldwin: A Critical Evaluation*. Washington, D. C.: Howard Univ. Press, 1977.

Ohashi, Kenzaburo, ed. *The Traditional and the Anti-Traditional: Studies in Contemporary American Literature*. Tokyo: Tokyo Chapter, American Literature Society of Japan, 1980.

Palmiere, Anthony F. R. *Elmer Rice: A Playwright's Vision of America*. Rutherford, N. J. : Fairleigh Dickinson Univ. Press, 1980; London: Associated Univ. Press, 1980.

Perry, Gerald and Roger Shatzkin, eds. *The Modern American Novel and the Movies* (Ungar Film Lib.). New York: Ungar, 1978.

Perry, John. *James A Herne: The American Ibsen*. Chicago: Nelson-Hall, 1978.

Prenshaw, Peggy Whitman, ed. *Eudora Welty: Critical Essays*. Jackson: Univ. Press of Mississippi, 1979.

Priessnitz, Horst, ed. *Anglo-Amerikanische Shakespeare-Bearbeitungen des 20. Jahrhunderts* (Ars Interpretandi 9). Darmstadt: Wissenschaftliche, 1980.

Proceedings of the Comparative Literature Symposium, Texas Tech University, Vol. IX: Ethnic Literatures since 1776: The Many Voices of America, 2 parts, ed. Wolodymr T. Zyla and Wendell M. Aycock. Lubbock: Texas Tech Press, 1978.

Redmond, James, ed. *Drama and Symbolism* (Themes in Drama 4). New York: Cambridge Univ. Press, 1982.

Redmond, James, ed. *Drama, Dance and Music* (Themes in Drama 3). New York: Cambridge Univ. Press, 1981.

Rieger, Burghard B. *Empirical Semantics: A Collection of New Approaches in the Field* (QLing 12, 13). Bochum: Brockmeyer, 1981.

Riordan, Mary Marguerite, comp. *Lillian Hellman: A Bibliography: 1926-1978* (Scarecrow Author Bibliogs. 50). Metuchen, N.J.: Scarecrow, 1980.

Roberts, Patrick. *The Psychology of Tragic Drama* (Ideas and Forms in English Literature Series). London and Boston: Routledge & Kegan Paul, 1975.

Robinson, James A. *Eugene O'Neill and Oriental Thought: A Divided Vision*. Carbondale: Southern Illinois Univ. Press, 1982.

Roland, Alan, ed. *Psychoanalysis, Creativity, and Literature: A French-American Inquiry*. New York: Columbia Univ. Press, 1978.

Rubin, Jr., L. D., ed. *The American South: Portrait of a Culture* (So. Lit. Studies). Baton Rouge: Louisiana State Univ. Press, 1980.

Ruff, Loren K. *Edward Sheldon* (TUSAS 401). Boston: Twayne, 1982.

Salzman, Jack. *Albert Maltz* (TUSAS 311). Boston: Twayne, 1978.

Sarotte, Georges Michel. *Like a Brother, Like a Lover: Male Homosexuality in the American Novel and Theater from Herman Melville to James Baldwin*, tr. Richard Miller. New York: Doubleday & Company, Inc., 1978.

Scanlan, Tom. *Family, Drama, and American Dreams* (CAS 35). Westport, Conn.: Greenwood Press, 1978.

Schlueter, June. *Metafictional Characters in Modern Drama*. New York: Columbia Univ. Press, 1979.

Schwarz, Alfred. *From Büchner to Beckett: Dramatic Theory and the Modes of Tragic Drama*. Athens: Ohio Univ. Press, 1978.

Seinfelt, Frederick W. *George Moore: Ireland's Unconventional Realist*. Philadelphia: Dorrance, 1975.

Sewall, Richard Benson. *The Vision of Tragedy*, new ed., enl. New Haven: Yale Univ. Press, 1980.

Sienicka, Marta, ed. *Proceedings of a Symposium on American Literature* (Seria Filologia Angielska 12). Poznán: Uniw. Im. Adama Mickiewicza, 1979.

Smiley, Sam. *The Drama of Attack: Didactic Plays of the American Depression.* Columbia: Univ. of Missouri Press, 1972.

Sommers, Joseph and Tomas Ybarra-Frausto, eds. *Modern Chicano Writers: A Collection of Critical Essays* (TCV). Englewood Cliffs, N. J.: Prentice-Hall, 1979.

Staines, David, ed. *The Canadian Imagination: Dimensions of a Literary Culture.* Cambridge: Harvard Univ. Press, 1977.

Stanton, Stephen S., ed. *Tennessee Williams: A Collection of Critical Essays* (TCV). Englewood Cliffs, N. J.: Prentice-Hall, 1977.

Stitt, Milan. *The Runner Stumbles: A Play in Two Acts & Night Rainbows: An Afterword.* Clifton, N. J.: White, 1977.

Strout, Cushing. *The Veracious Imagination: Essays on American History, Literature, and Biography.* Middletown, Conn.: Wesleyan Univ. Press, 1981.

Styan, J. L. *Modern Drama in Theory and Practice*, 3 vols. New York: Cambridge Univ. Press, 1981.

Taylor, William E., ed. *Modern American Drama: Essays in Criticism.* DeLand, Fla.: Everett/Edwards, Inc., 1968.

Tharpe, Jac Lyndon, ed. *Tennessee Williams: A Tribute.* Jackson: Univ. Press of Mississippi, 1977.

Tokushu Tennessee Williams (Gendai Engeki 2). Tokyo: Eichosha, 1979.

Tripp, Wendell, ed. *New York History, Vol. 62: Proceedings of the New York State Historical Association, Vol. 79.* Cooperstown: New York State Historical Association, 1981.

20th Century American Literature: A Soviet View, tr. Ronald Vroon, pref. Yury Kovalev. Moscow: Progress, 1976.

Vaughn, Jack A. *Early American Dramatists: From the Beginnings to 1900.* New York: Ungar, 1981.

Vidal, Gore. *Matters of Fact and of Fiction: Essays 1973-1976.* New York: Random House, 1977.

Vos, Nelvin. *The Great Pendulum of Becoming: Images in Modern Drama.* Grand Rapids, Mich.: Christian Univ. Press, 1980.

Wasserman, Julian N., ed.; Joy C. Linsley and Jerome A. Kramer, assoc. eds. *Edward Albee: An Interview and Essays* (Lee Lecture Series). Houston: The Univ. of St. Thomas, 1983.

Watzlawick, Paul. *An Anthology of Human Communication.* Palo Alto, Cal.: Science and Behavior Books, 1965.

Wellwarth, George. *The Theatre of Protest and Paradox: Developments in the Avant-Garde Drama*, rev. ed. New York: New York Univ. Press, 1971.

West III, James L. W., ed. *Gyascutus: Studies in Antebellum Southern Humorous and Sporting Writing* (*Costerus* 5-6). Atlantic Highlands, N. J.: Humanities, 1978.

White, Sidney Howard. *Sidney Howard* (TUSAS 288). Boston: Twayne, 1977.

Wilder, Amos Niven. *Thornton Wilder and His Public.* Philadelphia: Fortress, 1980.

Wilder, Thornton. *American Characteristics, and Other Essays*, ed. Donald Gallup, fwd. Isabel Wilder. New York: Harper & Row, Publishers, 1979.

Wilson, Robert Neal. *The Writer as Social Seer.* Chapel Hill: Univ. of North Carolina Press, 1979.

Zuber, Ortrun, ed. *The Languages of Theatre: Problems in the Translation and Transposition of Drama.* Elmsford, N. Y.: Pergamon, 1980.

Zukofsky, Louis. *Prepositions: The Collected Critical Essays of Louis Zukofsky.* Berkeley: Univ. of California Press, 1981.

LIST OF JOURNALS INDEXED

(* = ceased publication)

AB Bookman's Weekly. Clifton, N. J.
Acta Litteraria Academiae Scientiarum Hungaricae. Budapest.
After Dark: The National Magazine of Entertainment. New York.*
Akademie der Wissenschaften und der Literatur, abhandlungen der Klasse Literatur. Wiesbaden.
America (National Catholic Weekly Review). New York.
American Imago: A Psychoanalytic Journal for Culture, Science, and the Arts. Associaton for Applied Psychoanaysis. Wayne State Univ. Press, Detroit.
American Indian Quarterly: A Journal of Anthropology, History, and Literature. Society for American Indian Studies and Research. Hearst, Tex.
American Literature: A Journal of Literary History, Criticism, and Bibliography. Duke Univ. Press, Durham, N. C.
American Mercury. Shreveport, La.
American Notes and Queries. Erasmus Press, Lexington, Ken.
American Quarterly. Univ. of Pennsylvania, Philadelphia.
Das amerikanische Drama von den Anfängen bis zur Gegenwart. Darmstadt.
Amerikastudien: Deutsche gesellschaft für amerikastudien. Stuttgart.
Annales Univ. Scientiarum Budapestinensis de Rolando Eötvös Nominatae. Budapest.
Arbor: Ciencia, Pensamiento y Cultura. Madrid
Ariel: A Review of International English Literature. Univ. of Calgary, Ont., Canada.
Arizona Quarterly. Univ. of Arizona, Tucson.
Art in America. New York.
Art News. New York.
*Arts and Decoration.**
Asian and African Studies. Haifa Univ., Israel.
Atlantic Monthly. Boston.
Baker Street Journal: An Irregular Quarterly of Sherlockiana. Fordham Univ. Press, Bronx, N. Y.
Ball State University Forum. Muncie, Ind.
Bama. Jerusalem.
Bati Edebiyatlari Arastirma Dergisi. Ankara.
Biography: An Interdisciplinary Quarterly. Univ. Press of Hawaii, Honolulu.
Black American Literature Forum. Indiana State Univ., Terre Haute.
Blue Book. Chicago.*
Book News(Letter). Minneapolis.
Bookman. New York.*
Books at Iowa. Friends of the Univ. of Iowa Libraries, Iowa City.
Brigham Young University Studies. Provo, Utah.
California (formerly *New West*). Beverly Hills.
Canadian Literature: A Quarterly of Criticism and Review. University of British Columbia, Vancouver.
Carolina Comments. Division of Archives and History. Raleigh, N. C.
Catholic World (now *New Catholic World*). Missionary Society of St. Paul the Apostle in the State of New York. New York.
CEA Critic: An Official Journal of the College English Association. Texas A & M Univ., College Station.

Centerpoint: A Journal of Interdisciplinary Studies. Univ. of New York, New York.
Chicago. Chicago.
Christian Century. Chicago.
Classical and Modern Literature: A Quarterly. Terre Haute, Ind.
CLIO: A Journal of Literature, History, and the Philosophy of History. Indianapolis.
College Language Association Journal. Morehouse College, Atlanta.
Collier's. Springfield, Ohio.*
Columbia Library Columns. Columbia Univ. Libraries. New York.
Commentary: Journal of Significant Thought and Opinion on Contemporary Issues. American Jewish Committee. New York.
Commonweal. New York.
Commonwealth Quarterly. Mysore.
Comparative Drama. Western Michigan Univ., Kalamazoo.
Comparative Literature Studies. Univ. of Illinois, Champagne.
Crawdaddy: Magazine of Rock (now *Feature*). New York.
Credences: A Journal of Twentieth Century Poetry and Poetics. State Univ. of New York at Buffalo.
Cresset. Valparaiso Univ., Valparaiso, Ind.
Critical Quarterly. Manchester Univ. Press, Manchester, England.
Crosscurrents. Saskatoon, Sask., Canada.
CRUX: A Journal on the Teaching of English. Pretoria.
Cuadernos Americanos. Mexico City.
Cue (became *Cue New York*, then *New York*).
Current History: The Monthly Magazine of World Affairs. Philadelphia.
Current Opinion. New York.*
Dada/Surrealism. Hunter College, New York.
Dance Magazine. New York.
Dismisura: Revista Bimestrale di Produzione e Crit. Culturale. Alatri, Italy.
Drama: The Quarterly Theatre Review. London.
Drama Review, The (see *The Drama Review*).
Drama-Logue. Hollywood, Cal.
Dramatic Mirror. New York.*
Dramatist. Easton, Pa.*
Dutch Quarterly Review of Anglo-American Letters. Amsterdam.
Early American Literature. Univ. of Massachusetts, Amherst.
Ebony. Chicago.
Educational Theatre Journal (see *Theatre Journal*).
Encore. London.*
English Language Notes. Univ. of Colorado, Boulder.
English Studies: A Journal of English Language and Literature. Lisse, Netherlands.
English Studies in Canada. Univ. of New Brunswick, Fredericton, N. B.
Epistēmonikē Epetērida Philosophikēs Scholēs Aristoleleiou Panepistēmion Thessalonikēs.
ESQ: A Journal of the American Renaissance. Washington State Univ. Press, Pullman.
Esquire. New York.
Essays in Foreign Languages and Literature. Hokkaido Univ.
Essays in Literature. Western Illinois Univ., Macomb.
Essence. New York.
Estudos Anglo-Americanos. São Paulo, Brazil.
Etudes Anglaises: Grand-Bretagne, Etats-Unis. Centre National de la Recherche Scientifique. Paris.

Eugene O'Neill Newsletter. Suffolk Univ., Boston.
Everybody's Magazine. New York.*
Explicator. Washington, D. C.
First World: An International Journal of Black Thought. Atlanta.
Forum. Univ. of Houston, Tex.
Freedomways: A Quarterly Review of the Freedom Movement. New York.
Genre. Univ. of Oklahoma, Norman.
Georgia Review. Univ. of Georgia, Athens.
Great Lakes Review: A Journal of Midwest Culture. Central Michigan Univ., Mt. Pleasant.
Green Book. Chicago.*
Greenfield Review: A Magazine of the Arts. Greenfield Center, N. Y.
Gypsy Scholar: A Graduate Forum for Literary Criticism. Michigan State Univ., East Lansing.
Harper's. New York.
Harper's Bazaar. New York.
Hearst's Magazine. New York.*
High Fidelity (/Musical America). New York.
Hollins Critic. Hollins College, Vir.
Horizon. New York.
Hudson Review. New York.
Humanities Review. New Delhi.
Hungarian Studies in English. L. Kossuth Univ., Debrecen.
Independent. New York.*
Indian Journal of American Studies. Osmania Univ., Hyderabad.
Iowa Review. Univ. of Iowa, Iowa City.
Italian Americana. State Univ. College at Buffalo, N. Y.
Journal of American Culture. Bowling Green State Univ., Bowling Green, Ohio.
Journal of American Studies. Cambridge Univ. Press, Cambridge, England.
Journal of English. Sana'a Univ.
Journal of Ethnic Studies. Western Washington Univ., Bellingham.
Journal of Popular Culture. Bowling Green State Univ., Bowling Green, Ohio.
Kansas Quarterly. Kansas State Univ., Manhattan.
Kentucky Folklore Record: A Regional Journal of Folklore and Folklife. Western Kentucky Univ., Bowling Green, Ken.
Knjizevnost. Belgrade.
Kuka: Journal of Creative and Critical Writing. Zaria, Nigeria.
Kyushu American Literature. Fukuoka, Japan.
Labor History. New York Univ.
Latin American Theatre Review: A Journal Devoted to the Theatre and Drama of Spanish and Portuguese America. Univ. of Kansas, Lawrence.
Lex et Scientia: International Journal of Law and Science.
Life. Time, Inc. Chicago.
Life (1883-1936). New York.*
Literary Criterion. Mysore.
Literary Digest. New York.*
Literary Onomastics Studies. State Univ. College Brockport, Brockport, N. Y.
Literary Review: An International Journal on Contemporary Writers. Fairleigh Dickinson Univ., Madison, N. J.
Literatur in Wissenschaft und Unterricht. Kiel.

Literatūra. Vilnius, Lithuania.

Literatūra ir Menas.

Literature and Psychology: A Quarterly Journal of Literary Criticism as Informed by Psychology. Fairleigh Dickinson Univ., Teaneck, N. J.

Literature/Film Quarterly. Salisbury State College, Salisbury, Md.

Los Angeles. Los Angeles.

Louisiana History. Univ. of Southwestern Louisiana, Lafayette.

Maclean's. Toronto.

Mademoiselle. New York.

Magazine of Art. New York.*

Mandate Magazine: The International Magazine of Entertainment and Eros. New York.

Markham Review. Wagner College, Staten Island, N. Y.

Maske und Kothurn: Internationale Beiträge zur Theaterwissenschaft. Vienna.

Massachusetts Review: A Quarterly of Literature, the Arts and Public Affairs. Univ. of Massachusetts, Amherst.

Massachusetts Studies in English. Univ. of Massachusetts, Amherst.

MELUS. Society for the Study of the Multi-Ethnic Literature of the United States. Univ. of Southern California, Los Angeles.

Metropolitan Magazine. New York.*

Michigan Quarterly Review. Univ. of Michigan, Ann Arbor.

Midwest Quarterly: A Journal of Contemporary Thought. Pittsburg State Univ., Pittsburg, Kan.

Minnesota Review. Bloomington, Ind.

Minority Voices: An Interdisciplinary Journal of Literature and the Arts. Pennsylvania State Univ., University Park.

Mississippi Quarterly: The Journal of Southern Culture. Mississippi State Univ., Mississippi State, Miss.

Modern Drama. Graduate Centre for Study of Drama, Univ. of Toronto.

Modern Language Studies. Univ. of Rhode Island, Kingston.

Modernist Studies: Literature and Culture, 1920-1940.

Mother Jones. San Francisco.

Motion Picture Classic.

Ms: The New Magazine for Women. New York.

Musical Courier.*

Nassau Review: The Journal of Nassau Community College Devoted to Arts, Letters, and Sciences. Garden City, N. Y.

Nation. New York.

National Review: A Journal of Fact and Opinion. New York.

Negro History Bulletin. Association for the Study of Afro-American Life and History, Inc. Washington, D. C.

New England Magazine. Boston.*

New England Quarterly: A Historical Review of New England Life and Letters. Boston.

New Hungarian Quarterly. Budapest.

New Jersey Monthly. Princeton, N. J.

New Leader: A Bi-Weekly of News and Opinion. American Labor Conference on International Affairs, Inc. New York.

New Outlook. New York.*

New Republic: A Journal of Opinion. Washington, D. C.

New West (see *California*).

New York. New York.
New York Literary Forum. New York.
New York Theatre Review: America's National Theatre Magazine. New York.*
New York Times Magazine. Microfilms, Corporation of America, Sanford, N. C.
New Yorker. New York.
Newsweek. New York.
NMAL: Notes on Modern American Literature. St. John's Univ., Jamaica, N. Y.
North Dakota Quarterly. Univ. of North Dakota, Grand Forks.
Notes on Contemporary Literature. Carrollton, Ga.
Obsidian: Black Literature in Review. Wayne State Univ., Detroit.
Okike: An African Journal of New Writing. Nsukka, Nigeria.
Old Northwest: A Journal of Regional Life and Letters. Miami Univ., Oxford, Ohio.
One Act Play Magazine.*
Opera.*
Opera News. New York.
Opportunity.*
Osmania Journal of English Studies. Osmania Univ., Hyderabad.
Outlook. New York.*
Overland.*
Pacific Quarterly Moana: An International Review of Arts and Ideas. Hamilton, New
    Zealand.
*Papers on Language and Literature: A Journal of Scholars and Critics of Language
    and Literature*. Southern Illinois Univ., Edwardsville.
Paris Review. Flushing, N. Y.
Partisan Review. Boston Univ.
Pennsylvania History. Univesity Park, Pa.
People (Weekly). Time, Inc. New York.
Phantasm. Chico, Cal.
Playboy. Chicago.
Plays and Players. London.
Players Magazine: The Magazine of American Theatre. Microfilm. Northern Illinois
    Univ., DeKalb.*
Poetry. Chicago.
Il Ponte: Reviste Mensile di Politica e Letteratura.
Proceedings of the Pacific Northwest Conference on Foreign Languages.
Prospects: An Annual Journal of American Cultural Studies.
*Psychocultural Review: Interpretations in the Psychology of Art, Literature and So-
    ciety*. Redgrave Publishing Co., Pleasantville, N. Y.*
Renascence: Essays on Values in Literature. Marquette Univ., Milwaukee.
Research Studies. Pullman, Wash.
Review. St. Louis.*
Revista Hispanica Moderna: Columbia University Hispanic Studies. New York.
Revista Letras. Paraná, Brazil.
Revista/Review Interamericana. Inter American Univ. Press, San Juan, Puerto Rico.
Revue de Littérature Comparée. Paris.
Revue des Langues Vivantes. Bruxelles.
Revue Française d'Etudes Américaines. Paris.
Ridotto: Rassegna Mensile di Teatro.
Robinson Jeffers Newsletter. Los Angeles.
Rocky Mountain Magazine. Denver, Col.

Rolling Stone. New York.

România Literară: Săptăminal de Literatură şi Artă Editat de Uniunea Scriitorilor din Republica Socialīsta România. Bucharest.

Romanica: Romance Languages Literary Publication of New York University. New York.

Saturday Review (formerly *Saturday Review of Literature*). New York.*

Saturday Review of Literature (see *Saturday Review*).

Saul Bellow Journal (formerly *Saul Bellow Newsletter*).

Scandinavian Review. American-Scandinavian Foundation. New York.

Scandinavian Studies. Society for the Advancement of Scandinavian Study. Lawrence, Kan.

Scena: Časopis za Pozorišnu Umetnost. Novi Sad, Yugoslavia.

School and Society (now *U S A Today*). Society for the Advancement of Education. New York.

Scribner's Magazine. New York.*

Seventeen. New York.

Soundings: An Interdisciplinary Journal. Vanderbilt Univ., Nashville.

South Dakota Review. Univ. of South Dakota, Vermillion.

Southern Living. Birmingham, Ala.

Southern Quarterly: A Journal of the Arts in the South. Univ. of Southern Mississippi, Hattiesburg.

Southern Review: A Literary and Critical Quarterly. Louiaiana State Univ., Baton Rouge.

Southern Review: Literary and Interdisciplinary Essays. Univ. of Adelaide, Australia.

Southwest Review. Southern Methodist Univ. Press, Dallas.

Stage. New York.*

Stallion. Derby, Conn.

Steaua. Bucharest.

Stereo Review (formerly *HiFi Stereo Review*). New York.

Studia Neophilologica: A Journal of Germanic and Romance Languages and Literature. Stockholm.

Studien zur Deutschen Literatur. Tübingen.

Studies in Bibliography: Papers of the Bibliographical Society of the University of Virginia. Charlottesville.

Studies in English and American. Budapest.

Studies in the Humanities. Indiana Univ. of Pennsylvania, Indiana, Pa.

Studies in Mystical Literature. Taiwan, Republic of China.

Sunset. Menlo Park, Cal.

Survey. New York.*

Tamkang Review: A Quarterly of Comparative Studies between Chinese and Foreign Literatures. Taipei, Taiwan, Republic of China.

Tel Quel. Paris.

Tennessee Williams Newsletter. Univ. of Michigan, Ann Arbor.

Texas Monthly. Austin.

Texto Crítico.

The Drama Review: International Journal Documenting Historical and Contemporary Trends in the Performing Arts (formerly *Tulane Drama Review*). New York.

Theater (formerly *Yale/Theatre*). Yale Univ., New Haven.

Theatre Arts. Arts Publications, Inc. Manila.

Theatre Arts (formerly *Theatre Arts Monthly*). New York.*

Theatre Arts Monthly (see *Theatre Arts*, New York).

Theatre Crafts. Emmaus, Pa.

Theatre Journal: The Journal of the University and College Theatre Association (formerly *Educational Theatre Journal*). Washington, D. C.

Theatre Magazine. New York.*

Theatre News. American Theatre Association. Washington, D. C.

Theatre Quarterly. London.

Theatre Research International. International Federation for Theatre Research. Oxford, England.

Theatre Southwest: Journal of the Southwest Theatre Conference.

Theatre Studies.

Theatre Survey: The American Journal of Theatre History. State Univ. of New York at Albany.

Theatre World.

Thomas Wolfe Review. Univ. of Akron, Ohio.

Thought: A Review of Culture and Idea. Fordham Univ. Press, Bronx, N. Y.

Time. Time, Inc. Chicago.

Tulane Drama Review (see *The Drama Review*).

TV Guide. Radnor, Pa.

Twentieth Century Literature: A Scholarly and Critical Journal. Hofstra Univ., Hempstead, N. Y.

U S Catholic. Chicago.

Vanity Fair (incorporated into *Vogue*).

Vision.

Vogue. New York.

West Virginia University Philological Papers. Morgantown.

Western Illinois Regional Studies.

William Carlos Williams Newsletter (now *William Carlos Williams Review*).

Working Woman. New York.

World Literature Written in English.

Writer's Digest. Cincinnati.

Yale/Theatre (see *Theater*).

Yankee. Dublin, N. H.

Yonsei Review. Seoul.

Zeitschrift für Anglistik and Amerikanistik. Leipzig.

Zeitschrift für Slavische Philologie. Heidelberg.

INDEX OF CRITICS

(the numbers in parentheses indicate the times a name appears on
a page if more than once)

LIST OF ADAPTED AUTHORS AND WORKS

(for unchanged titles, see Index of Titles)

INDEX OF TITLES

INDEX OF PLAYWRIGHTS

(dates noted when available)